# Christian Combat
## In Modern America

DAN MARUYAMA

Trail Media
San Diego, California, U.S.A.

All scripture quotations are from the English Standard Version unless otherwise noted.

Printed in the United States of America
**ISBN-13: 978-0692427910 (Trail Media)**
**ISBN-10: 0692427910**

*Cover design and interior art:*
**Danielle Keltner** of *Dannie Ann Photography & Designs*
*http://dannieannphotodesigns.com/*

# DEDICATION

Dedicated to my wonderful family:
Monica, Jordan, Jake, and Megan

*"This day I call the heavens and the earth as witnesses against you that I have set before you life and death, blessings and curses. Now choose life, so that you and your children may live . . . "*
Deuteronomy 30:19 (NIV)

CONTENTS

# ACKNOWLEDGMENTS

I give thanks to God for His incredible love, and for specifically giving me the motivation, encouragement, and opportunity to write this book. I thank Him also for giving me experiences to share that I hope will be helpful to the reader.

I am also thankful to all of those who helped me draft and edit this work: Monica, Megan, Jake, my wise friend Danny Dutcher, Pastor Ken Webb of Christ's Fellowship Church in Valdosta, Georgia, and the wonderful folks at Trail Media: Dana, CJ, and Victoria. Their wisdom, insight, expertise, and encouragement were invaluable.

DAN MARUYAMA

# PREFACE

We often ask God, "Why is there so much suffering in the world?" Too often I think His answer is "because My people refuse to join the good fight."

This book is about spiritual combat – our role in the fight between good and evil – and so I've drawn from many of my experiences as a career officer in the United States Air Force to help illustrate the parallels between spiritual combat and physical combat. However, I do not want to mislead the reader. Although I've been to war, I'm no snake-eating, battle-hardened combat veteran. I've flown in combat, but to my knowledge I have never been shot at. I've taken cover during mortar attacks, but I've never had a near-miss. I write this so that you know I'm probably a lot like you; I've done my duty as fitfully and as well as a fallen man can be expected to do, but I'm no war hero and I'm no one of importance.

I'm also no theologian. I'm not a pastor. I don't have any religious degrees or special credentials, and I don't read Hebrew or Greek. I'm one of those people you see in church every Sunday (if you happen to go to church every Sunday) who mostly sits in the audience and sometimes helps with ministry or teaching. I'm probably a lot like you, and I can't hold up any legitimate reason why you should read this book.

Yet with all that said, in His grace God has given me experiences that offer perspective. He has given me a modicum of writing ability, and He has given me a passion to encourage others to follow Jesus in a way that results in blessing for them and for those around them. You will find endnotes with scriptural references throughout this book. I've provided those both as a further-study reference and also as a sort of guardrail to help ensure that my words do not get out in front of God's Word. My prayer is that what I've written here will deepen your knowledge of God and that it will inspire you to get in (or remain in) the spiritual fight that is raging all around us.

DAN MARUYAMA

# CHRISTIAN COMBAT

It was the middle of a dark, moonless night when a group of Marines reported that they had "troops in contact" – they were in a firefight with the enemy in the rugged mountains of Afghanistan. A young rifleman was seriously injured and needed immediate evacuation to survive. Air Force rescue crews, known by their call sign "Pedro," received the call and immediately ran to their waiting helicopter.

Within minutes they were airborne and proceeding through the inky darkness direct to the reported position of the mortally wounded Marine. Nights like this were harrowing. Even though they were wearing night vision goggles, due to the limited moon and starlight, the low-flying Pedros could not see the terrain until they were almost upon it. The pilots carefully tracked their progress on their moving GPS map, knowing that they lacked the power or time to avoid impact if they navigated into one of the soaring ridgelines that cut through much of Afghanistan. When they finally approached the firefight, they could see tracers cutting back and forth between the Marines and their enemy, engaged below and in front of them. They would have to fly their approach to land without lighting in the pitch dark, and most likely the enemy was going to be shooting at them as soon as they were able to hear them.

The Marines had cleared a landing zone in a riverbed and marked it with dimly glowing green chemlights so that the Pedros could identify it. Dry riverbeds in Afghanistan are dustbowls, and the crew knew that they would be fully engulfed in a nearly impenetrable cloud of swirling dust as they attempted to land. At least that would make it harder for the Taliban to shoot them. The pilot started the approach at 150 feet above the ground, and by 50 feet could no longer see to land. Flying on electronic cues, he struggled to keep the helicopter aligned straight and prayed that the ground below them was reasonably flat. Landing with a sideways drift or on an uneven slope could easily result in rolling the helicopter over. The last seconds of the approach seemed like hours, but the wheels of the helicopter finally settled firmly on the riverbed and the aircraft lurched to a stop. They didn't roll over. They were "safe." At the end of the approach, the pilot realized that his stomach literally hurt as it tied itself in knots worthy of the best Eagle Scout.

Now comfortably on the ground, his stomach started to untangle itself, but as the dust cleared, he felt it wrench again as he saw that he had landed less than 20 feet from a Marine, prone on the ground with his weapon pointed away from the helicopter, defending the landing zone. It was by the sheer grace of God that the pilot had not landed on top of the young American. As troops ran under the rotor disk carrying an injured Marine on a stretcher, the Pedros heard the familiar "Pop, pop, pop" of small arms fire. The enemy could see the helicopter. One of Pedro's gunners returned fire, and the pilot could feel the booming .50 caliber machine gun rattle his helmet. As he waited for the stretcher to be secured and hoped that an AK-47 round didn't come through his window, the pilot thought to himself, "This isn't what I thought about when I signed up for the Air Force."

The helicopter and its crew would make it home that night. The Marine would live and return home to his grateful family. The mission would be a success and the brave Pedro's would have much to be proud of. But in the moment of combat, in the thick of the fight (or as soon as adrenaline would allow a stray thought) those brave airmen wondered if this was really what it was supposed to be like.

Combat is hard. It is uncomfortable, gritty, demanding,

2

painful, and often deadly. It is alternately boring, horrifying, rewarding, frustrating, and exciting. And it will be necessary for good people to engage in combat as long as there are bad people on the earth.

Christians are in combat. While we live on this earth, we are engaged, both within and without ourselves, in a fight to save souls, to let good triumph, and to crush evil.

For much of my life, I was caught in the lie that embracing Christianity was more like going to an amusement park than a theater of combat. The message I often heard was that living as a follower of Christ was more like spending time at Disney Land than at the battlefront. This message was wrong, and it has been very helpful for me to learn that it was. I've found that my misconception of life as a Christian had huge impacts. My view of Christianity as a peacetime endeavor colored my picture of God, hid truths about myself, and interfered with my ability to see the world as it really is.

Jesus said, "I am the Truth." If that's true (and I believe it is), anything that keeps me from the Truth, keeps me from knowing Jesus fully. The truth is that the Bible tells us that we Christians are combatants. What does that mean? What are the implications? How does that influence my faith, my actions, my relationship with God? These questions are important—I would say critical—and so my hope in these pages is to share with some clarity the truth of what it is like to live in God's army.

DAN MARUYAMA

# PART 1: WHY GO TO WAR?

What if the Pedros refused to go to war? What if no one was on the other end of the radio when someone called to say, "I need you to save my Marine!"? Good things only happen when good men and women decide to act.

There is a foolish notion among some otherwise intelligent folks that we should all just be "nice" and then the world would run smoothly. Although this line of thinking is attractive, it ignores the fact that evil is real. If an attractive lady goes for a walk alone in the wrong part of town late on a Saturday night, some guy is going to try to mess with her . . . no matter how "nice" she is to him. If a man opens a retail store and says, "Just pay me what you think my goods are worth" some people are going to pay way less than they should . . . regardless of how nice the shopkeeper's demeanor is.

So what it is to be done? We must all reckon with the truth that evil is real.

When Adolph Hitler came to power in the 1930's, the Christian churches in Germany initially failed to oppose him. As Hitler's true colors became more and more evident, those churches in Germany remained on the sidelines and largely silent—they did not realize that they were in a spiritual war and so they remained focused on teaching and preaching but refused to engage their culture. As the

1930's came to a close and the Nazi's full malevolence was evident, the churches did try to respond, but by that time they had been so disarmed and marginalized, they were completely powerless to oppose what would become the most horrid genocide in western European history. They didn't choose sides until it was too late to do anything.[1]

Contrast Hitler with Agnes (or Anjezë) Bojaxhiu. Confronted with the abject poverty and need she found in India, she worked tirelessly both to help those in need and to encourage others to do the same. She founded an order that ran orphanages, hospitals, and care centers to minister to countless poor and destitute people throughout India and then around the globe. Before God called her home, her selflessness had given her a voice on the international stage – a voice she used to highlight the needs of the poor to both common folk and to world leaders. Who is Agnes Bojaxhiu? You probably know her as Mother Teresa of Calcutta.

Are you going to fight on the side of Hitler or of Mother Teresa, with the liars or with the truth-sayers? We don't have a choice *not* to decide – we have chosen sides many times and will continue to do so for the remainder of our time on this earth. It is built into the fabric of God's creation that we have a choice to act for good or for evil, and we don't get to choose *whether* we will take a side. We only get to choose which side we are on.[i]

The Bible says that Satan is the "ruler of this world"[ii], and Jesus said, "Do you think I came to give peace on Earth? No, I tell you, but rather division."[iii] This world is a battleground, not a playground. Every human being on this earth lives in a battleground between good and evil.

There is a war raging around us and we are in hostile territory. Our choice is not whether to fight in this war . . . our choice is only to choose which side we will be on. When you are behind enemy lines in the middle of a war, there are only two ways to NOT be in combat.

If you are not in the fight, you're either dead, or you're one of the bad guys.

---

[1] June 20, 2014, "The German Churches and the Nazi State", United States Holocaust Museum, http://www.ushmm.org/wlc/en/article.php?ModuleId=10005206

## 1-1. THE ENEMY

**Is evil really real?**

On December 6, 1941, the United States officially considered the Japanese Empire our friend. The next morning, the Japanese attacked Pearl Harbor. Before the attack, there were many indications that the Imperial Japanese Empire was not our friend, but our nation ignored those indications. We like to believe that people like us . . . but believin' don't make it so.

On September 10, 2001, we thought that planes were only hijacked when someone wanted money, release of prisoners, or some other demands. On September 12th, we realized that planes were sometimes hijacked just because people want to make us suffer.

Just as we don't like to think a nation or people is "out to get us," we don't like to think that evil is out to get us either. It's distressing to think that someone might hate us. In war, one of the chief causes of post-traumatic stress disorder (PTSD) is when soldiers have to directly confront the hate in someone trying to kill them. It is a part of our human nature to shy away from confronting the reality of evil.

Did you know that while 90% of Americans believe in God, only about 70% believe in the devil? Everyone wants to talk about heaven, but when people start talking about hell, people get uncomfortable. Why is that?

Is Satan real? Are there demons? Is evil real? The Bible says, "Yes" to all of these questions, but you don't have to be a Bible scholar to see that evil is real.

We live in a fallen world where men hit their wives, wives cheat on their husbands, and people lie. Politicians abuse power. Men like Hitler really did (and do) exist. There was an article in the news today that said a man in North Carolina killed two coworkers and then shot himself. As I write this, statistically there is probably someone somewhere in the United States who is being raped. Monday at school, countless young boys and girls are going to be bullied. Drunk dads tell their little daughters to shut up, pastors have affairs, teachers lie to their classes. It's not pretty, but its true!

This stuff doesn't happen "just because." It happens because evil is real. In its most basic form, it's seen in the little toddler girl who hits her playmate (nobody taught her to do it!). In more horrendous form, evil is seen in the death of 20 million Russian people at the hands of Joseph Stalin .

The Bible says that Satan is real.[iv] He tempted Adam and Eve to sin, causing all mankind to fall under a curse. He tried to lure the one answer to that curse, Jesus Christ, away from his destiny as Savior, and he "prowls around like a roaring lion, seeking someone to devour."[v] That old trickster the devil is intentional, not random[vi]. He is deceptive and tricky[vii]. He is subtle and aggressive[viii]. And evil wants to hurt you and your loved ones.

Understand this clearly: Satan and his followers want to hurt the people you love the most, and they want to see you suffer.

The devil doesn't sit back and say, "I sure hope he falls into that ditch." No, he digs the ditch right in the middle of your path. He covers it and camouflages it. He knocks down the warning signs, and then he puts something you really want just on the other side.

Satan is actively working to make your spouse miserable.

Satan is actively working to see your children deceived and suffering.

Satan is actively working to fill your parents, brothers, and sisters with pain and despair.

Satan is actively working to destroy the country you hold dear.

What would you do if you were at home with your family and a deranged criminal started hacking through your front door with an axe? Would you just keep watching TV? Would you open up and offer him tea? Or would you grab your shotgun, shove it in his face, and pull the trigger?

Let me say it again: evil wants to hurt you and your loved ones. In fact, Satan actively would like to destroy you and your loved ones. What are you going to do about it?

Brothers and sisters, there is a time for war and a time for peace . . . and the time for war is NOW.

## 1-2. CALLED TO SERVICE

**Who fights in war?**
In the United States we currently have an "all volunteer" force. Citizens are not forced to go to war. Many of us choose not to fight, and that's OK because our nation is not involved in total war (at least not in a political sense). Yet we still need some folks to go to war to protect our freedoms. When our nation mobilizes for war, we put out a call for warriors because we will not succeed without an army. The airmen and Marines in the story that started this chapter recognized a call to service, answered the call of their nation, and so were available to engage in combat.

Things would be different in a total war. If our nation was directly threatened with invasion and annihilation, you can bet that everyone would be called to service.

Spiritually, we are in a total war. The enemy has invaded, and everyone you and I know are at risk. You and I are called to serve in combat. Our service is necessary to combat evil that is very real.

Do you ever wonder why an all powerful God would care at all what you do? If God can make all things good by speaking it so, why doesn't He right now? I wonder these things and frankly don't have a complete answer. But I do know that, amazingly, God has chosen mankind to be a part of His work. In spite of all of our shortcomings and all of our limitations, what you and I do has consequence. God has called us to join Him in what He is doing – He has called us into His service.

Look at the pattern of history: God used Abraham's obedience to be a blessing for "all nations."[ix] God used Jonah to cause a revival that resulted in the salvation of the entire city of Nineveh.[x] God used Joseph's excellence and obedience to save the Israelites from starvation.[xi] God used the apostles' obedience to spread Christianity throughout the world. This list goes on and on and the consequences are innumerable: saved lives, saved souls, starvation averted, wars avoided or ended, tyrants crushed, nations blessed, hospitals built, the needy clothed, and so on and on and on and on.

Conversely, when people have refused to serve, the consequence of disobedience has been severe. The people of Sodom and Gomorrah ignored God's instructions, and the entire cities were razed.[xii] In Moses' time, the Israelite men followed false gods and a plague ensued, killing 24,000 people.[xiii] People and kings turned from God, and the whole nation of Israel was conquered.<sup>xiv</sup>

This pattern continues today: when people humble themselves before God and serve Him, families thrive, churches grow, and communities are blessed. However, where people refuse to serve, people and communities suffer.

In the Old Testament, God tells us through Moses that we have to make a choice that has attendant consequences<sup>xv</sup>. In the New Testament, Christ tells us that if we are with him, we will be fruitful, and if we are apart from him, we will do nothing of worth<sup>xvi</sup>. We are called into the service of a living God. We have been recruited, and He wants us to join with Him.

This is a critical point. God has not called us to a philosophy or doctrine. God has called us to join Him in what He is doing. I grew up thinking that religion was about what I thought, but in reality, religion is about what I do. God has not called us to believe that serving Him is good – He has called us to serve Him. That realization makes all the difference in how we approach life.

Imagine a soldier who knows how to shoot a rifle but never pulls the trigger or a sailor who knows how to captain the ship but never leaves port. What good are they? Is it even right to call that person a soldier or a sailor?

So it is with you and I, fellow Christian. I have to know the truth to act on it, but knowing the truth is meaningless if I never act on it.

Christ has called us to serve the Father with him, not just to know about him. The Father and the Son have engaged the enemy, and so if we are with Them, we will do the same. But this brings up a key question: Are we cut out to be successful in combat?

## 1-3. CREATED FOR COMBAT

When I was in the military, I had a friend who was one of those guys who didn't stomach bureaucracy well. He knew what he believed when it came to what's right and what's wrong, and he wasn't afraid to tell you if he thought you were wrong. If the bureaucracy said to do something stupid, he either just didn't do it or he let you know about it. Although gifted with innate leadership ability and great competence, he frequently chose to lead in a way that frustrated superiors. He was, frankly, kind of a handful during peacetime. However, someone coined the perfect phrase to describe this man: "In case of war, break glass." He was a consummate warrior. Put him in a peacetime unit and he was as likely to make you pull your hair out as impress you, but if you took him to war, he shined like a superstar. He was made for war.

So let's say it's time for you to go to war. Are YOU made for war? "Wait," you say. "I'm a lover, not a fighter" or "I wouldn't be good in combat." If you think that, you are wrong. You are a lover AND a fighter. Some of us have an easier time being the lover and some of us have an easier time being the fighter – but we were all created to do both.

Suppose I took a tool out of my toolbox and gave it to you. You might have never seen it before and have no idea what it does, but if I gave you enough time, you could probably figure out its purpose. How would you do that? You'd look at how it was made, how it functioned, and what it appeared to be suited for.

If we look at how YOU were made, how YOU function, and what YOU are suited for, what would we conclude? What were YOU made for?

Do you ever wonder why you get angry when you witness something unfair? Why can't you just say, "Oh, whatever" when you see the bully push down the little boy? It's because you were made for a world that is fair. You were made to champion fairness.

Do you ever wonder why you like excitement? At some point excitement can shift from adventure to terror, but why is it that we like to be on the adventure side of that spectrum? Why is it that we are drawn to conflict and risk? It is because we were made for adventure. We are purpose-built to engage in adventure.

Do you ever wonder why you react without thinking when a fearful situation comes up? When something scares you, your heart rate accelerates, your hands fly up, and your body goes to high-alert. This isn't because you are weak and lack emotional control. It is because you were made by your Creator to encounter fearful situations AND PREVAIL.

If God created us for sedentary peace, why do we have strong arms and legs? If pacifism on earth was His ultimate design for us, why did He make us in such a way that we get angry when we see someone kick a puppy? If we are created only for solace, harps, and happy thoughts, why do we find it inspiring to hear how David beat the giant? Could it be that God knew what He was doing and actually prepared us for service in His army?

"But wait," you might say. "I don't like conflict. And I'm not physically strong. And I turn into a bowl of jelly when I am scared. . . How can I be made for service in God's army?" First off, I'd ask you to remember that real war is not like Hollywood movies. In the movies, a Schwarzenegger-like megawarrior (or maybe a small team of megawarriors) singlehandedly destroys countless foes in a myriad of creative (and probably gratuitously-violent) ways. In real war, the army consists of infantrymen and cooks and nurses and chaplains and truck drivers and clerks and so on. Not everyone shoots a gun or wields a knife (in real armies there are about 3 support personnel for each direct combatant), but they are all a critical part of the army and absolutely necessary for success in war. Second, I'd remind you that the parallels I am drawing between real combat and Christian combat are only parallels – our war as Christians is not so often one of physical violence, but one of spiritual combat. Spiritual combat is a battle for hearts and minds. God has equipped you with what you need to do your part in His war effort.[xvii]

I spent twenty-two years in the United States Air Force working with people who did not want to die, who did not want to suffer, and who would really prefer not to have potentially life-ending mortar rounds or missiles or bullets launched at them. But these same people are the ones who, when our nation goes to war, raise their hands and say, "Send me!" Why? It is because although we find terror in war, we also find significance and purpose. Deep down inside, we are responding to an awareness that we are made for something much more important than long-living.

The fact that God made us as warriors is the final facet in

realizing why we must engage in war:
1) Evil is real and it wants to destroy our loved ones.
2) We've been called to fight the evil in this world.
3) We were made for that fight.

Now suppose it is January, 1942. Your small US town is fully aware of what happened at Pearl Harbor the month prior and the declaration of war against Japan and Germany that followed. A man in an Army uniform comes up to you and says, "Young man, the Germans and the Japs are trying to take over the world and destroy all that we hold dear. I see you are fit and bright and of fighting age. Will you fight with us?" Or maybe a poised woman comes up in her uniform and says to you, "Young lady, our men will soon be critically injured on the frontlines in Europe. You would make a perfect field nurse. Will you fight with us?" What would your answer be?

If you said, "No, I'm afraid to fight" or "No, I believe in peace" or "No, I'm not interested," you'd be mocked and scorned. And you should be. People who don't confront evil are doing evil themselves.

Ladies and gentlemen, evil is actively trying to take over the world and destroy all that we hold dear. Through Christ, God has given us what it takes to beat evil back. Will you fight?

DAN MARUYAMA

# PART 2: BASIC TRAINING

It was 0-dark-thirty and the sun had yet to rise. I woke from a deep sleep to the distant sound of knocking and then shouting. Someone was coming down the hall of our dormitory, knocking on each door and shouting something. In a few minutes, it was our turn. THUMP! THUMP! Someone pounded on our door twice, and then it swung open. Our trainer loomed large, silhouetted in the doorway, and shouted, "GET UP! PT GEAR!" We leaped from our beds, put on our PT (physical training) uniform as fast as we could, and ran out into the hall. There we were braced against the wall and told to recite memorized quotations at the top of our lungs as we waited for everyone to assemble. Eyes straight ahead. Back straight. Heels against the wall. Chin in. Being yelled at. A few minutes later we were all lined up and running out into the pre-dawn twilight to the parade field for morning physical fitness activities. This was basic training.

As you know, new military recruits don't generally show up at the frontlines asking for a rifle and the direction of the enemy. Before they become part of the combat forces, they go through basic training to prepare them to be part of a combat unit. Regardless of what service you are in, basic training does three key things: it tears away your old civilian ways of doing things, it makes you adopt the military's way of doing things, and it teaches you basic combat skills.

Christian Combat is no different. We must gain knowledge and skills that we need to be victorious in combat. However, just as in military basic training, Christian basic training doesn't start with learning skills. It starts with destruction.

## 2-1. BECOMING LESS

We called them "training sessions." They might have been called "hazing sessions" but since no one suffered any physical harm, they weren't legally "hazing." The typical training session involved all of us new Air Force recruits standing in the hall, back to the wall, arms pinned to our sides, bodies at rigid attention, chins tucked in, and our mouths bellowing at the top of our lungs whatever topic-du-jour the trainers came up with. If we were too loud, they told you to pipe down. As soon as we piped down, they scolded us for being too soft. If we kept your arms so tight against our sides that they quivered, some trainer would get centimeters from our faces, say unkind things about our family lineage, and then tell us to quit shaking. No sooner had he turned away, than his cohort stepped in and proceeded to upbraid us for keeping our arms too loose. Everyone down for pushups! Everyone up! Down! Up! The sweat rolled down our foreheads, our voices became horse, and we genuinely had a horrid time. That is exactly what the trainers wanted.

Why? The trainers didn't truly care about our volume, our body positions, what we said, or how many pushups we could do. They were breaking us. That's standard fare in military basic training, and it is a good thing. You see, it's only in being broken that you can ditch all of the unimportant stuff, find out who you really are, and learn what really matters. It never FEELS good to be broken, but like a bone that is not set right, you have to break first in order to be set it the way you are supposed to be.

God's basic training is the same way. When we begin our service to God, we MUST be broken down. In the English language (or at least the American language), we tend to think of being "broken" as a bad thing, but it often is not. We "break" the chain of events that would have led to tragedy. We "break" our bad habits. We "break" out of captivity. When we start following God, we "break" away from our old life. In God's equation, breaking down is what allows us to be built up by Him.

This concept is all over the Bible. Job's tragedies break him out of his misconceptions about God and show Him how awesomely sovereign God really is. In Proverbs 3:34, Matthew 23:12, and James 4:10 we are told to "humble ourselves" so that God can lift us up. Jesus explicitly tells his followers to put down their stuff and follow him.[xviii] In Ephesians, Paul reminds us that "You were taught, with regard to your former way of life, to put off your old self, which is being corrupted by its deceitful desires; to be made new in the attitude of your minds."[xix] And in perhaps his clearest admonition of the concept, Jesus says in Matthew 16:24, "If anyone would come after me, he must deny himself and take up his cross and follow me."

Note the action words in the passages above. We are told to *humble* ourselves, to *deny* ourselves, to *put off* our old selves, and to *follow*. In His sovereignty, God calls us to be broken but in that same sovereignty He allows us to refuse being broken. In His love He prompts us to stop clinging to the meaningless things in this world (like our own things, our own self-righteousness, and our own agendas), but in that same love He gives us the freewill to continue clinging. So ultimately we have a choice to either accept the Holy Spirit's call to be broken or to refuse Him.

In military basic training, if a recruit refuses to be broken down, he or she is eliminated from training. That person does not have what it takes to be in the military. Military trainers know that in combat someone who holds on to their self so strongly is a liability, not an asset. The same is true for us Christians. If we won't be broken—that is to say, if we will never give up the things of this world—we will never experience God's grace. Consider that seriously for a second. If you do not acquiesce to being broken, you can NEVER serve God. It doesn't matter how many times you go to church, how many prayers you say, how many worship songs you sing, or how many charities you support.

Not broken = not in the army.

"Being broken" is not the same thing as "being polished." We all have a tendency to want to put on our Christianity as a sort of jacket over our existing clothes, but the truth is that we need to be stripped naked so that we can put on a whole new set of clothes. Jesus said, "those of you who do not give up everything you have cannot be my disciples."[xx] When we decide to follow Christ, we are not trying to become better than we were before. Rather, we are sacrificing our old selves so that we can be reborn as something new. Here again modern military basic training is a perfect parallel. A new recruit does not simply put on a military jacket and press on.

Instead, the new recruit has his hair shaved off, gets new clothes, learns new ways of speaking, lives life according to a new schedule, learns new skills, and essentially submits entirely to military order.

There is a danger that we, as Christians, will try to do the spiritual equivalent of buying an old uniform at the Army surplus store. Too often we try to just put on a new set of external accoutrements without changing who we really are. Putting an army uniform on does not make you a soldier, and putting a Christian uniform on does not make you a follower of Christ.

So practically speaking, what does it mean to be broken down as a Christian? Let me give you three things to think about:

**1) Being broken means we see ourselves as we really are: desperately messed up and hopelessly inadequate.** Have you ever told a lie? I have lots of times. Do you know what that makes you and me? We are liars. Have you ever lost your temper or wanted someone else to suffer? I have. Jesus says this makes me worthy of hell[xxi]. Have you ever looked at something or someone that was not yours and wanted them? I have. That makes me one who covets . . . and according to God's commandments that means that I deserve condemnation. I am not good. In fact, I am really bad. You are too.

To be broken you must fully accept that you are NOT good as you think you are.

**2) Being "broken" means that you realize that you need something more than you can attain on your own.** If you realize that you are not good, it naturally follows to ask the question, "How do I get better?" There are two ways to get better: to try harder or to get help. If you are broken, you know that trying harder won't cut it. I wish that I could say, "You know, I finally read the Bible and now understand what is good. Now I can be good for the rest of my life . . . ." Unfortunately, my problem is not with knowing WHAT to do, my problem is with *doing* it. At times I've tried hard and succeeded in being better, but many times I try hard and fail (or even find that I don't want to try hard). Too often I don't do what I know I ought to do. How about you? Do you ever say, "I know what I should do, but I'm not going to do it?"

I love coffee. I've tried a bunch of times to quit drinking coffee, but I have never been successful. Why? It's not because I am unable. If you pointed a gun at my head and said, "Drink that coffee and I'll shoot you," I can pretty well guarantee I would be done drinking coffee. So if I am able to quit drinking coffee but I do not, what does that tell me about myself? It tells me that I'm not willing to quit drinking coffee.

In the same way, I know I am physically able to quit making selfish decisions, but I don't. The truth is that while I have the *ability*, I don't have the *will* to always do the right thing and be unselfish. That's the way I am and the way you are. In Bible terms, we are sinners.

The broken Christian realizes that he or she doesn't have it in themselves to do the right thing all the time. We realize that we need help – the kind of help that only Jesus Christ can give!

**3) Being broken means we leave our old life behind.** The Bible tells us that when we become Christians, "the old has passed away, the new has come"[xxii] and that we are "born again"[xxiii]. When we choose to follow Christ, we don't just put on our "Jesus Loves Me" lapel pin and go about our normal business. When we choose to follow Christ, he changes our lives.

When I commanded an Air Force squadron, I had to kick out several of my young troops because they were using drugs. We don't do illegal drugs in the Air Force. These young men that were discharged were not hard-core addicts – they were just recreational drug users. Although they went through all of the training, they did not leave their old life behind and then they went back to their old ways. They were wearing the uniform, but they weren't living as Airmen.

As broken Christians, we must realize that we can't go back to our old ways. When we sign up to follow Christ, we sign up for a new way of living.

Being broken is the first part of Christian basic training. If we don't accept that we are messed up, that we can't get good on our own, and that we are signing up for an entirely new way of living, then we are NOT ready to be in the service.

Being broken down is absolutely essential for our entry into Christian combat. If you aren't willing to be broken, then go home and quit trying to be a Christian because it's not going to work. If you try to wear the uniform without going through basic training first, you will at best be a poser wearing a uniform that's not yours.

And the truth is, if you are a successful poser, you will find after some time goes by that you are not just a poser, but a traitor.

So suppose I'm willing to let God break me down. Do I then wallow in brokenness? Not at all. Once my old self is broken, it's time to get built back up with the basics. What are the "basics" of Christianity?

DAN MARUYAMA

## 2-2. LEARNING THE BASICS

Afghanistan, 2005. Our helicopter rescue crews were on alert, waiting for notification that someone needed saving. Suddenly, the computers came alive with messages about a young lady that had a serious head injury. She had shown up at an Army Forward Operating Base (FOB), and the field medic there determined that she needed immediate evacuation. Vital signs came across the computer.

In order to determine the priority of the mission, I asked our rescue doctor how critical her condition was. "She's fine," our doctor said. I asked him what he meant. "Head injuries bleed a lot, and they hurt. This girl just showed up at the FOB, screaming and bleeding and looking like a mess, so the young medic up there is thinking, 'I've got to get her help right now.' But her vital signs say she is doing just fine. Bandage her up and give her some painkillers, and she'll be good until morning."

"Morning" makes a lot of difference. The base with the injured woman was at high altitude. It was a moonless night, making it hard to see even with night vision goggles. If we launched our alert crews, they would be going on a fairly high risk mission – something we were trained to do in a minute given the need. However if the injured Afghani was actually alright, it didn't make sense to risk the lives of 12 of our airmen for what would amount to a late-night trip to the doctor.

I told our higher headquarters that we didn't need to go tonight and that we could go in the morning. The general disagreed. Now was the time to go. I launched our crews, even though I didn't think that was the smartest course of action. Thankfully, our helicopters completed the mission uneventfully.

Why did I risk my crews? Why did the crews risk their own lives when I told them to go on a mission of questionable practical value? They did so because they were following a code that they had learned in basic training. In the military, you follow the legal orders of your superiors.

Basic training is not all about being broken. The breaking down is just the first step of a longer process. Recruits are not broken down and left haggard and listless by the side of the road. Instead, once they are broken, the recruits are built back up with the attitudes and values that they need to be part of the service—values like "follow orders." After being broken, recruits are taught the basics of what it means to be in the military.

The same thing has to happen to us Christians. We are broken when we realize that we need a savior to save us from all of our shortcomings, but after being broken we need to be built up in the ways of Christ. We see this in Acts, Chapter 2, where the people listening to the apostle Peter's speech were "cut to the heart" – broken—and then were told to "repent and be baptized." Repentance and baptism are elements of Christian basic training – they are some first steps in establishing the attitudes and actions of a follower of Christ.

It is in being built up that we become Christ's warriors – men and women who are capable of blessing our world by taking the fight to the enemy.

If "follow lawful orders" is a key element of military basic training, what are the key elements of Christian Basic Training? I'm sure that smart theologians could get into a long and tedious discussion about what should be on a list of "Christian basics," but such a list (and such a discussion) is probably way too much for my small brain. I tend to keep things simple, and so I love what Pastor Alistair Begg of Parkside Church in Cincinnati likes to say of the Bible: "The main things are the plain things and the plain things are the main things."[2] Looking at the main things, I think you can boil the basics of Christianity down to two tenets: 1) believe in Christ as savior and 2) follow him as Lord.[xxiv]

I expect that if you are reading this book, you probably already call yourself a Christian and so you probably already have a handle on the basics. However, I want to go through the basics anyway. I'm not going to do it to bore you. I think there is value in looking at the basics because the plain things really are the main things. We have in our 21st century American society something that I call the "university mentality." We tend to think that the depth of our Christian discipleship is measured the same way that a university measures our educational prowess: the more I know, the better I am. We have a strong tendency to think, "If I only knew a little more, then maybe I could _____[fill in the blank with something impressive]." Our "heroes" in modern Christianity tend

---

[2] http://www.goodreads.com/quotes/447719-the-main-things-are-the-plain-things-and-the-plain

to be the guys and gals that are really good speakers and that have "Dr." preceding their name or a long list of books that they have authored. Our university mentality focuses on words and education. However, I believe that the Bible teaches a "technical school mentality." At universities, we learn grand ideas . . . like what the chemical makeup of steel is or how to calculate the force exerted by a man climbing up a staircase. At technical schools we learn how to weld steel into a staircase so a man can actually climb up. That's the way Jesus taught. He didn't really expound on the pros and cons of balancing grace with discipline. In effect, he just said, "Love your neighbor . . . now go do it . . . ." Christ didn't really clearly explain what hell or heaven is like, but he made very clear how to go to the one and to avoid the other. I don't think it was an accident that Jesus was a carpenter and not a professor. And this is very pertinent to why it's worth taking time to discuss the basics here, because it's the basics – not the deep theologies -- that are the fundamentals of Christian combat.

## Fundamental #1: Christ Is My Savior

**savior** (seyv' · yer) noun 1. A person who saves, rescues, or delivers

I grew up in and around the church (protestant and Catholic). I heard countless sermons and knew all of the major Bible stories. I thought Christ was worth following because his teaching made sense, but I did not know him as my savior. He was my leader (of sorts) or my guru or my guide, perhaps. However, it was not until my early twenties that I came to know him personally as *my* savior. I'm continually amazed at how many people I encounter that were or are in the same boat that I was in: knowing Christ as a great religious leader or an epic teacher but not as the one who saved mankind.

The brokenness that is so important to our initiation into Christian discipleship is the brokenness that comes from realizing that we have blackness in our hearts. It is the brokenness of knowing that even my best is not good enough – of knowing that even when I know the right thing to do, I frequently don't do it. When you come to that place in your life that you realize you have a soul-disease that you can't get rid of, that is when you realize that you need to be *rescued.* Christ is my savior because he has saved me from all of the judgment that justice says I deserve. "Who will rescue me from this body that is subject to death? Thanks be to God who delivers me through Jesus Christ our Lord!"[xxv]

I have known many, many people who call themselves Christian but who appeared to have no real comprehension of their need to be saved. They acknowledge "sin" as a violation of rules, but they aren't burdened by it.

I once received a speeding ticket for going 10 miles over the speed limit in a very remote part of Texas. In the 'location' block on the ticket, the officer had to write "15 miles east of Dickens." Now to my mind, if the best you can do for landmarks is "15 miles east" of something, there is no reason why anyone needs to be worried about speeding a little. When I got that ticket, I knew I had broken the law, but I didn't think I had done anything wrong. That's the way some of us look at our own sins. It is a true blessing when our view of our sins goes from "I broke a rule" to "I am dung," because that is when we realize we need saving and when a savior becomes important to us.

Even as I came to my desk to write this paragraph, I struggled with my sin. I know that God knows the blackness in my heart. I know He has seen the many times that I have lied, the times I have stolen, the times I have looked with lust (committing adultery in my heart), and the times I have looked with hate (committing murder in my heart). He knows the real sins I committed just this morning. I am, truly, unworthy to write these words that hopefully point to an awesome and pure God. It makes me wonder if I should even write.

And yet, Christ paid for my sins already. He ensured justice was served by voluntarily taking the punishment for all that I've done. So when God sees me, He does not see my sin . . . they are as far from me as the east is from the west.[xxvi] Because I have put my faith in Christ, God does not see my sin. He sees the righteousness of Christ. I am saved from my own sin!

And so are we all, who believe in the Lord, Jesus Christ, our redeemer.

That's the first basic principle of following Christ.

**Fundamental #2: Christ is My Lord**

For the most part, we're a bunch of individualists in America, and so the concept of having a "lord" is a bit foreign. Yet we all understand the idea of lordship – a "lord" is someone who has authority over us. Accordingly, in a voluntary relationship, if I call someone "Lord," I give that person authority over me. I serve them. In *Mere Christianity*, C.S. Lewis notes that it's illogical to say, "No, Lord." If someone is truly our lord, we ought to say, "Yes sir."

So when we talk about "Christ as Lord" we are really talking about a question of authority. If he is my Lord, I will do what he says. Do I? Do you?

Of course to answer those questions, at some point we need to know what he says we are to do. Christ told us that all of God's commands could be summed up into two maxims: Love God and Love Others. But for now, the specifics of what we are to do can wait. The essential idea is that we have to be obedient when we realize we are told to do something. That's Lordship.

I was talking to a fellow a few years ago, and he was telling me about the fact that his family always sat in the 5th row in one of the big denominational churches downtown and that they went to church most every Sunday. A few minutes later, I heard him sharing a tale of having had wild sex with his girlfriend the previous weekend, and then sometime later he was railing about the way the "niggers" behaved. Now keep in mind that this conversation happened in the rural south, where it seems everyone is "born Christian" and pockets of racism still flourish. Suffice it to say, he may have been a fan of Jesus, but Christ certainly was not his Lord.

Obedience is not an option—it is fundamental to being a Christian. Christ is either our Lord or he is not, and this means we are either doing our best to be obedient to him, or we are not.

I think it's awesome that these two fundamentals –Christ as savior and Christ as Lord—are all tied up with each other. When we realize what Christ did for us, his enormous sacrifice and the incredible deliverance that that sacrifice brings, we naturally have a desire to love him because of what he did for us. And we find in the Bible and in life that obedience and love are completely interrelated. Some would say, "Love is not obedience, love is adoration" or maybe "love is a feeling," but that's just not true. Here are a few verses to consider:

"If you love me [Christ], you will keep my commandments."[xxvii]

"This is love for God: to keep his commands."[xxviii]

"The man who says, "I know him [God]," but does not do what he commands is a liar, and the truth is not in him. But if anyone obeys his word, God's love is truly made complete in him."[xxix]

Certainly feelings are a part of any love relationship, but actions are much more an indicator of the depth of that love. What do you think of a husband that gushes, "I adore my wife!" and then spends all Saturday watching football instead of doing things with her? He might be genuine about what he thinks he feels, but true love goes far deeper than feelings. True love acts. Doing what God says to do--following His orders--is inextricably linked to loving Him. So as we respond in gratitude to what he has done to save us, we will love him, and in loving him, we will do our best to be obedient to Him and treat Him as Lord.

These are the fundamentals that we learn after we are broken: Jesus is our savior, and he is our Lord. But what if someone doesn't get the fundamentals?

In military basic training, some folks fail to meet standards. Should we expect anything different as we follow Christ? What do we do then? That's the subject for the next section.

## 2-3 ATTRITION: WHEN STANDARDS MATTER

I started basic training with about 1400 other cadet recruits at the Air Force Academy. Four years later, when I graduated, there were just less than 1000 of us remaining. We had lost over one quarter of our number. During the much shorter and somewhat less demanding regular Air Force enlisted basic training, about 6-8% of people wash out.[3] An astounding 80 to 85% of trainees fail to make it through the extraordinarily demanding Air Force pararescue training program.[4] Some folks quit and some folks are kicked out. Why don't people make it through these programs? They don't make it because the Air Force demands a standard of performance, and some either could not or would not attain that standard. Generally speaking, the more demanding standards result in higher washout rates.

In the military, they call these losses "attrition." They plan for attrition because they know some folks just won't make it. When you hold people to a challenging standard, it is natural to expect some to fail to meet that standard. When you begin basic training, you expect some won't finish.

Are those that follow Christ required to meet a demanding standard? Absolutely. Jesus says, "Go and sin no more . . . ."[xxx] The apostle Paul says that we should "run in such a way as to get the prize"[xxxi] and admonishes us to, "keep living by that same standard to which we have attained."[xxxii] And the apostle John says, "whoever claims to live in him must live as Jesus did."[xxxiii]

As Christians, there are standards to be met, and failure to meet those standards causes attrition. Just as it does in military training, Christian attrition happens (or at least it should happen) in two ways: quitting and cutting. Let's look at both of those.

### "I quit"

Some military recruits just up and quit. People quit an activity when the cost of doing that activity seems like it is greater than the reward of sticking with it. Ultimately, we quit when we think that

[3] Officials: Longer BMT Reduces Washout Rate, June 18, 2010, http://www.airforcetimes.com/article/20100618/NEWS/6180333/Officials-Longer-BMT-reduces-washout-rate
[4] The Hardest Air Force Jobs, May 25, 2010, Rod Powers, http://usmilitary.about.com/od/airforcejoin/a/hardjobs.htm

"not doing" a thing is preferable to "doing" that thing. The military recruit who quits thinks that it is preferable to not have to follow rules, to wear whatever clothes he likes, to avoid specific standards, or to escape certain hardships. Quitting is easier because it provides near-term pleasure and avoids near-term pain.

Christian recruits experience the same things. Some get to a point where they think the near-term benefit of quitting outweighs the long-term reward of sticking with it. Nobody gets dragged into the kingdom of heaven – folks only come voluntarily. It stands to follow that if I can choose to follow Christ, I can also choose not to. Do people really start down the road to a relationship with God and then turn back? Yes. Jesus told a story about seeds scattered on the ground. In that story, some of the seeds fell on shallow soil and sprouted quickly and then dried up because they had no root. Jesus explained that these seeds represent believers who hear the word of God with joy but then quickly dry out because they have no root. When troubles come, these people fall away.[xxxiv] In effect, folks like these say, "I quit" because they don't think that sticking with it is going to be worth it.

So what things might make someone say, "Following Christ is not worth it"?

To begin with, a "new recruit" to Christianity might not think that the reward of following Christ is worth the costs of following Christ. So let me ask you this: What rewards make following Christ worth it?

If you were brought up in a mainstream Christian church, your off-the-cuff answer might be like mine: "blessings" or "the abundant life" or "joy in all circumstances." While these are all good things that do attend following Jesus, they are not the main reason. The main reason is that following Christ saves us from the eternal consequence of our sins—we get to spend eternity with God in heaven. However, to the young, healthy, or confident "heaven" often seems like a far off reward. So maybe it is helpful to look at the flip side of that coin: following Christ saves me from hell.

Isn't it funny that the threat of something bad generally holds our attention more than the promise of something good? If you are walking in the woods and I say, "If you walk long enough, you will see the rarest and most beautiful bird," you are liable to say, "Ok cool." However, if I say, "If you walk long enough, the mountain lion will surely find you," you will probably be much more attentive. Many people decide following Christ is not "worth it" because they don't realize how cursed we are without him. When confronted with a Christian recruit that wants to quit, one of our tasks as believers is to help that person realize that following Christ is the *only* thing that matters. If you are in a plane that is crashing and you don't know that it is, you might pass up the offer of a parachute and go smiling to your death. However, if you looked out the window and saw that the engine was on fire and half the wing was gone, it's guaranteed you are not going to pass on the offer of a parachute. It's absolutely critical that we believers understand the gravity of the consequences of our own sin.

A prospective believer may be tempted to quit because they do not know that the reward of following Christ is epically awesome, but they may also quit because they believe that the near term costs of following are too great. What are those costs? Perhaps someone is involved in an inappropriate relationship (e.g., adultery, homosexuality, sex outside of marriage) and they realize that they will have to change if they follow God. Perhaps a prospective believer is involved in habits or circles (e.g., drunkenness, drug use) that are at odds with Christian discipleship. Maybe someone has their whole life built around a self-centered pursuit (e.g., fame, wealth, success) that will have to change if they become God-centered. To follow Christ, we must all be willing to move from the driver's seat to the back seat. We have a hard time doing that . . . a very hard time!

So what should we do to encourage people in these situations? I think there is really only one central argument: God's way is the only way that is truly good.

*Am I involved in an inappropriate relationship? That will end – either through separation, divorce, or death. What then? What do I have when that person that is the center of my world is no longer there?*

*Am I involved in some bad habits that I don't want to give up? What do they really contribute in the long run? Do I really think I'm giving them up for emptiness, or am I trading them for something different (and maybe better)?*

*Is my life all tied up in money-making or fame-getting? Where does all that fame or fortune go when I am on my death bed? What good is it to me when I am old and infirm and sitting in an assisted living home at the end of my life?*

I may want to hold on to what I have now because I think it is better than holding on to Christ, but it is not. Our job as believers is to remind the new and the interested of these things – to encourage them to have a big-picture and eternal perspective.

In basic training, I wanted to quit. There were many times when going home to my loving parents and friends just seemed so much better than staying in basic training and getting hollered at. I think probably everyone who goes through basic <u>thinks</u> about quitting. But when you have those thoughts, it is a tremendous encouragement when someone reminds you why you are there in the first place and that you <u>can</u> make it. There is a light at the end of the tunnel that is getting brighter all the time. You press on and before too long, you are in full sunlight and enjoying the ride. Clebe McLeary, a Marine who was severely crippled during combat in the Vietnam conflict and an incredible Christian encourager, likes to say, "FIDO . . . Forget It, Drive On!"

Sometimes unexpected challenges or costs can be the most daunting because we feel blindsided. When our Christian friends tell us about "the abundant life" and are always talking smiles-and-sunshine, we can be easily derailed by the potholes in the road of life. Maybe our pastor had an affair . . . is that the abundant life? Maybe we lost our job just as we are coming to know the Lord . . . is this what I should expect? Maybe our family is ostracizing us due to our newfound belief . . . shouldn't they all be cheering and following?

Preparing for and then entering into combat is not for the fainthearted. Christ told us to expect trials and hardships.[xxxv] Following Christ does not take us out of this fallen world (at least not until we die). In fact, the Bible is clear that God uses hardships to refine His followers.[xxxvi] Giving up your old life to take on the life of Christ is tough work. The apostle Paul put it this way in the midst of his walk with God: "We are afflicted in every way, but not crushed; perplexed, but not driven to despair; persecuted, but not forsaken; struck down, but not destroyed."[xxxvii]

The question is not whether we can face challenges – the question is whether we will face them with or without God's help.

We must remember that we can "forget it and drive on" because we are in the hands of the One who will never let us go.<sup>xxxviii</sup>

As we discuss ways to keep people from quitting their pursuit of Christ, we must acknowledge that some will quit, and we must also acknowledge our role with respect to that. Our job is to encourage them, not to prevent them from quitting. There is a keen danger in trying to avoid attrition. Since attrition is a natural consequence of having standards, the only way to keep people from quitting is to lower standards—to try to hide or obscure or get rid of those things that cause people to desire to quit.

Immediately following World War II, the US Army was understandably exhausted after years of conflict and many Americans had no desire for further war. As a result, the United States military eased off on its standards. Out of a desire to make things more pleasant for people, a culture developed that to some extent tolerated lax standards of fitness and combat capability. The consequence was that when the Korean War started, many units were ill-prepared to fight effectively and losses were much higher than they might have been.[5]

We can easily be tempted to fall into the same trap in our preparation for Christian combat. Fewer people will quit if we tell them, "Following Christ makes you rich." Fewer people will quit if we tell them, "You don't need to give your money . . . that's Old Testament stuff." Fewer people will quit if we tell them, "You don't have to hold people to standards of conduct; you just need to love them." The problem with all of these things is that they are not true. While these statements may reduce attrition, they will leave us unprepared for combat (and alienated from our Commander), and our losses in combat will be far greater than if we hold to standards and allow people to say, "I quit."

I have a good friend who, years ago, was at least considering Christianity. He came to church with us one Sunday to check things out. Providentially, on that Sunday the pastor chose to preach in part on the Biblical mandate against homosexual conduct. Now my friend's sister was a practicing homosexual, and when he heard the message my friend was turned off and never came back with me again. My initial response was to ask, "God,

[5] For a more detailed discussion, read "This Kind Of War," T.R. Fehrenbach, Brassey's, 1963

33

why couldn't you have that message on some OTHER Sunday?" But as I reflected on the situation, I realized that my desire to lower the standards ("Can we just pretend homosexuality is OK?") was like a used car salesman's strategy to sell a lemon: "I'll just lure the customer in, and he won't know what he's really bought until he's already driven it off the lot. . . " If my buddy is going to follow Christ, he will to have to come to grips with the fact that God unequivocally says homosexual conduct is wrong. It was inevitable that he would have to choose to follow God or not to follow God. And while it makes me sad that he "quit," I am glad that I was not permitted an opportunity (as I so wanted at the time) to convince him to follow a god that wasn't really God.

**"I got kicked out"**

Quitting is not the only way that people leave basic training. Some folks get kicked out. Those who will not uphold standards are not allowed to remain in the military because our Armed Forces know that letting standards slide today will result in losses on the battlefield tomorrow.

Do folks get "kicked out" of Christianity as well?

Before I answer that, let me make something very clear. I believe that no person is the arbiter of another person's salvation. Salvation is a gift of God, based on His grace alone, and salvation is neither earned nor given by any human being. With that said, God has clearly established standards for His followers, and He has told us that those who claim to believe in Him must attempt to uphold those standards to the best of our ability. When I speak of getting "kicked out of Christianity," I am not speaking of a person's salvation. I am speaking of being separated from the community of believers. This discussion is not about telling someone that they cannot be saved by God's grace. This discussion is about telling someone that they are NOT following God and so should not identify themselves as someone who is.

So, do folks get "kicked out" of Christianity? Yes. Or at least they are supposed to be.

The military rarely discharges a recruit because he or she is a top-to-bottom loser. Normally a recruit is discharged for failing to meet a *few* of the many military standards--not *all* of them. He may be a hard worker but fail to maintain fitness standards. She may have a wonderful personality but be unable to consistently show up on time. Because these people are "good people" who don't meet standards, it is rarely easy to say, "You have to go." However, when the standards are clear and someone fails to meet them, the military discharges them.

Christian "discharges" are similarly difficult, but maybe even worse. How do you, in a spirit that honors Christ, hold people to a standard? If someone is deliberately going against God's ways, you can only do so by reflecting that God's ways are the very best for everyone, and that they are on a downhill track headed for a collapsed bridge.

Before we go a step further on this topic, I need to point out a huge difference between a military discharge and a Christian discharge. In the military we discharge for failure to perform. In the church, a "discharge" is only appropriate with a failure to try (and it might be even more accurate to say that it is for "failure to die"—die to yourself, that is). Say a man comes up to me and says, "I want to be a follower of Christ, but murdered someone and I regret it. I've asked for forgiveness from God and the family of my victim, and I'm turning myself in to the police." My Christian response should be, "Let me pray with you, my brother." However, suppose a man comes up to me and says, "I'm putting my faith in Christ and will go on the church mission trip next month, but I'm not going to separate from my live-in girlfriend." If this man is unrepentantly and intentionally embracing sin, my Christian response should be to expel him from the fellowship of believers (albeit in accordance with the process outlined by Christ in Matthew 18:15-17).[6]

The misguided belief that "love others" is the same as "be nice" leads inevitably to arguments against this idea that being a Christian should require exclusive conduct, so let me address the chief ones that I know of:

**1) Who are you to judge others?** One of the great heresies Satan sows in the modern church – and which is encouraged by those outside the church – is that we are not supposed to judge at all. This lie centers on reading the verse "do not judge so that you will not be judged"[xxxix] without considering its context in the Bible.

---

[6] Note that this man may still be "saved," but he is at great risk and puts the church at risk if allowed to stay.

The Bible in general and the New Testament in particular are replete with admonitions to exercise judgment. The key is that our judgment must apply God's standard, and not our own, and our heart in judgment should be one of mercy, not condemnation. Taken to its logical conclusion, the statement "we should not judge" leads necessarily to "murderers should not be convicted." No judgment = no conviction. That, of course, is ludicrous. When God says something is wrong, it is wrong, and it's OK to point that out.

Let me provide a parallel illustration to help drive this point home. Let's say you have two teams playing basketball, and they appoint one of their players to be the referee. Now if that referee stands on the court and allows some players to run with the ball and requires others to dribble or allows some players to take free throws from 5 feet away and forces others to shoot from the normal free throw line, that ref is wrong. He is judging the game according to his own standard. However, if that referee enforces the accepted rules of the game, then he will be doing what is right. As Christians, we are no different. We don't claim to be the makers of the rules, or the perfect keepers of the rules, but we can (and should) claim to know the rules and apply the rules.[xl]

**2) Doesn't this mean that we have to work for our salvation?** We do not have to work in order to merit salvation. Salvation is a gift of God given by grace alone, and there is nothing we can do or say that can make us good enough to earn God's forgiveness. We are all fallen sinners and the only thing that saves us is His unmerited grace. However, the Bible says we do have to WORK OUT our salvation.[xli] God tells us that salvation comes from our confession of Christ and our belief in Him.[xlii] Our conduct always flows from, and therefore gives evidence of, our belief. For example, if I say that I believe the stove is cold but refuse to touch it for fear of being burned, I don't *really* believe the stove is cold. Similarly, if I say that "Jesus is Lord" but willfully and consistently refuse to do what he tells me to do, I do not *really* believe that he is my Lord.

This is not to say that to be Christian we must be sin-free or perfectly obedient. The apostle Paul's discussion in Romans 7-8 and numerous other passages in the Bible[xliii] tell us that even as followers of Christ we struggle (and often fail) in the face of temptation. The key question is whether my life is characterized by a pursuit of obedience or disobedience. If I try to follow Christ but often fail, I am right where the Bible says I should expect to be. But if I say, "I believe" but don't try to follow (or if I follow only in compartmented parts of my life and refuse to follow in others), my "belief" is meaningless and my faith is dead[xliv].

So although we do not work to earn our salvation, our salvation necessarily is evidenced in works. Someone who calls himself "Christian" but refuses to follow Christ is not a Christian at all – regardless of how many times he has said a "sinner's prayer." Put another way: Works do not save, but the saved work.

**3) God is love. How can we "love others" and kick them out of the church?** Maintaining God's standards is an act of love. As the apostle Paul notes in 1 Corinthians, we should expel the immoral believer so that person is restored to right conduct and thereby to fellowship.[xlv] If you believe that "God is love" (as the Bible says He is),[xlvi] you have to come to grips with the fact that the Old Testament records where He killed a lot of folks[xlvii] as well as the fact that the prophesy in the book of Revelation says that He will kill a lot more.[xlviii] Does this mean that God is not loving? No, it means that true love has standards—love is not arbitrary, and it involves a lot more than hugs and soft words. Imagine a world where "loving parents" never disciplined their children or where "loving judges" refused to sentence murderers. How would that work out?

I hope not to belabor this point because it will come up again later, so let me come to the bottom line: people should sometimes be "kicked out" of Christian community just as some soldiers get kicked out of the Army. Folks that don't have the will to follow Christ must either quit calling themselves followers, or they should be asked to stop doing so.

Whether we lose Christian recruits due to their own decision to quit or due to their unwillingness to try to maintain God's standards, we are supposed to see attrition. If we don't, we have no standards. It is supposed to mean something when we say, "I follow Christ."

In the military, a soldier has to learn fundamentals and has to meet standards, but those things in themselves don't make a soldier ready to fight. Our military puts its members through training in combat skills to prepare them for battle. You could say that we Christians go through the same thing. But what does Christian "combat skills training" look like?

## 2.4 COMBAT SKILLS TRAINING

On May 2, 2011 the United States killed the terrorist leader Osama Bin Laden in a small compound in the country of Pakistan. Under cover of night, American combat specialists flew to the compound, secured the area, located their objective, and killed Bin Laden when he attempted to fight back. The combat pros who executed that difficult mission deep inside another country did not get up that morning, discuss the latest fashion trends, and then say, "Hey we just found Bin Laden. . . let's go get him." On the contrary, after completing basic training, these warriors trained for years to be proficient at their combat crafts, and then they trained extensively to be ready to execute every critical detail of that specific mission.

To be successful in physical combat, you have to be trained, and Christian combat is no different. Those recruits who decide to remain committed and who do their best to maintain military standards move from indoctrination into basic training and on to combat skills training.

**Basic Combat Skills Training**

As a pilot in the United States Air Force, my basic combat skills training took well over a year. I had to learn to how fly slow and to learn how to fly fast. I had to learn to do loops and rolls and also how to fly in formation with other airplanes. The skills I learned in my early training would serve me well through different airframes, different missions, in different countries and different theaters of battle. Everything built on these basics.

In the same way, our lives as Christians depend on basics. Beyond the fundamentals that we learn in basic training, we also need to learn combat skills to be effective. When you are learning to fire a rifle, we speak of READY-AIM-FIRE; we can apply this same construct to Christian combat.

**1) READY: You've got to prayerfully read your Bible.**

When you are on a firing line preparing to shoot a rifle, the first step is to make sure that you and your weapon are ready to go. When your barrel is pointed toward the target, a bullet is in the chamber, the bolt is closed, and the safety is off, you are physically prepared to shoot the weapon. If any of this is not squared away, your attempt to engage the target is going to be a failure.

Christian combat is not about firing bullets; it is about firing the Truth. "The weapons we fight with are not the weapons of the world"[xlix]. Our weapons are those that allow us to defeat the enemy. If Satan's primary weapon is deception and lies, then our weapons are those that can counter those lies. What prepares us to counter lies? Truth. We need regular, intentional study of God's word—both alone and corporately—so that we know the truth. We need regular prayer, so we can hear the One who is Truth when He points out lies to us. Staying in the Bible while staying in prayer are the ways we keep our weapons ready for the next engagement.

Most of us know that the Bible is important, but sometimes we fail to remember how critical it is to all that we do. I think sometimes we have a tendency to think of it as a "religious book" full of good stories and ideas about God but not really a handbook for how we do life. In Christian combat, our primary weapon is the word of God, and our primary source for the word of God is the Bible. In the Bible, God tells us that His word is the "sword of the spirit"[l], that it is "alive and active"[li], and that it is effective for "teaching, reproof, for correction, and for training in righteousness."[lii] Christ set the example for us as he used scripture to fight the temptations of Satan in the fourth chapter of Matthew's gospel. We find in Christ's words directly, in the Bible in general, and in the testimony of over 2000 years of faithful Christian disciples that scripture is the fundamental key to right service to God. Other than the Holy Spirit, the Bible is the only reliable gauge of truth that believers have in this world, and it illuminates so many of the things that cause us problems.

We need to read the Bible. A lot. I've been told that the most oft-quoted verse in the Bible is "heaven helps those who help themselves," but the funny thing is that this isn't even in the Bible at all! In fact, that statement is basically contrary to what the Bible teaches. I'm always amazed at how many Christians say "Christian" things with absolutely no knowledge of whether it is actually in the Bible. You don't need to be an Oxford Bible Scholar, and you don't have to memorize everything, but you do need to regularly be reading your Bible. If you are a lousy reader, read a few lines a day. If you are a voracious reader, read the Bible five or 10 times per year, but do read it. When you hear a sermon about a passage in the Bible, look it up and read it yourself. When you are trying to find an answer to one of life's troubling questions, go to something like Biblegateway.com and do a search for the topic at hand. When you are struggling with a temptation or sin, look up in the Bible and see what God says about it. If you don't know how or where to start, ask someone who does to help you.

Having trouble with a relationship? Try Matthew 7:3-5 and 1 Corinthians 13 on for size and see if they don't shed some light on things. Wondering about disciplining your kids? Take a look at Ephesians 6:4 and Proverbs 13:24, 19:18, 22:15, 23:13, and 19:17. Financial trouble? Consider Malachi 3:10, Proverbs 22:26-27, and Matthew 6:25-30. Worried about your health? Check out Ecclesiastes 12:6-7, the book of Job, or John 9:1-11.

I used to go to the Bible like I go to a dictionary. . . looking for data to help me with life. However, some years back, by the grace of God and some great counsel from wiser Christian men and women, I began to catch on that the Bible is not just data. It is the primary way that my Lord speaks to me. I don't go to the Bible so I can memorize a great "zinger" to silence the next atheist I meet on the street. I don't go to the Bible so that I can find another nice encouragement to make me feel good about myself. I go to the Bible because that's where I hear God speak truth to me—truth that is relevant and living and effective for making life awesome. What is your perspective as you go to the Bible? Is it a book of good info or is it a message from your loving Father?

We don't just study the Bible because it is a Christian thing to do. We study the Bible because it contains keys to understanding life, to knowing our God, and to being prepared for the work He has for us. . . it can be absolutely critical to winning our next battle because it is not just a book *about* God. It is a book *from* God.

There are tons of books, articles, web pages, and videos about how true, reliable, accurate, trustworthy, and beneficial the Bible is. My intent is not to reproduce those here. However, I do want to encourage you. Read the Bible prayerfully. It is our basic doctrine, our fundamental combat weapon. It is the most frequent way that God directly communicates with you. God wants you to know how to be successful in combat. Read what He has given you.

You don't need to know all of the Bible to be effective in combat, but you do need to know enough to get to work doing God's business. I don't know all of Air Force doctrine, but I do know the specifics of how to employ a rescue helicopter in combat. Likewise, I don't know all of the book of Romans, but I do know that it says "all have sinned and fall short of the glory of God." I'll keep trying to learn more, but it will only be by the grace of God that I retain any of it. However, I do know that God speaks most often to us through the Bible and if I try, God will be faithful to keep me learning what I need to know.

Read your Bible every day. Really. That's how you get READY.

## 2) AIM: Know what you are trying to hit.

Once when I was doing my annual Air Force rifle qualification, I was on a firing line of about 20 people. I'm a big fan of firearms, so I'm a fairly proficient shooter. When we went down to score our targets, I had excellent on-target groupings. However, there was one problem: my target was missing four bullet holes. The person next to me was not very proficient with a rifle (I believe it was the first time she was qualifying), and she had holes scattered all over her target. "Coincidentally," she had four extra holes. . . right near the center of the target. You see, when you are on a firing line, all the targets are only a foot or so apart, and they all look the same. During one of the courses of fire, somehow I had failed to check the target number and had lined up my sights on her target. Bang-Bang-Bang-Bang. Four bullets on target. . . but the wrong target.

In Christian combat, you need to be sure you are aiming at the correct target. So what is your target? What is it we are supposed to do as Christians? What are we aiming for?

Some folks are aiming for salvation. As long as they get into heaven, they are good to go. They will tell you that salvation is the measure of Christian success.

Some folks are aiming for public righteousness. They'll tell you that if people respect you and know you are a "good Christian," then you are a good Christian.

Some folks are aiming for comfort. This might be relief from pain caused by life's events. It might be the happiness of living in community with others. It might be the confidence that people love you. It might be release from the treadmill of "gotta prove myself" religion. All of these are different sides of the same glass jewel — they are all just different ways of saying that the goal of Christianity is to be happy or joy-filled.

Some folks are aiming for knowledge. They believe if you just study the Bible enough and contemplate God enough and focus on doctrine, Bible study, and books enough, then they will have hit the target.

But all of the above are wrong.

Our "target" is to glorify God. Put in different terms, our target is to serve Jesus, our Lord. If I get on target, I receive the gift of salvation[liii]. If I get on target, my life reflects righteousness[liv]. If I get on target, I have the power of God that can sustain me in the most difficult times and provide joy even in the midst of tragedy[lv]. If I get on target, the Holy Spirit works in me to provide wisdom about things that the world calls foolish.[lvi]

The problem with aiming for the wrong things is that, although we might hit what we are aiming for, we are of no use in the war.

During the war in Afghanistan, an F-15 fighter pilot dropped his bomb exactly on the coordinates he was given. It was a perfect delivery. Tragically, his ground controller had mistakenly given the pilot the WRONG coordinates, not that of the target. So even though the delivery was perfect, the outcome was the death of 3 friendly soldiers.[7]

There are a lot of leaders in the church that are like that ground controller. They tell God's people to follow Christ so that they can be happy. Then when God calls those people into difficult circumstances, the people turn away – for they've been taught that surely a good God wouldn't want them to suffer at all. Some pastors tell people that they need to look good for the world and "be a light on the hill." Then when those people fail and fall, they are disheartened and leave their light quenched. Some preachers preach the message that "it's all about the Bible" – more Bible studies, more sermons, more Sunday school. Then when God presents an opportunity or a challenge, people say, "I don't know enough . . . I'm not smart enough . . . I haven't studied that yet."

Where you aim is critical and fundamental. Our point of aim must be to glorify God. Period.

## 3) FIRE: DO something.

As I type this, I'm on an airplane. The guy on my left is sleeping. The woman on my right is playing solitaire on an iPad.

---

[7] Steven Morris; "Soldier describes directing fatal air strike by US jet on British troops"; The Guardian; Apr 23, 2010; Accessed Apr 14, 2014 at http://www.theguardian.com/uk/2010/apr/23/military-afghanistan

Am I supposed to witness to them? I've prayed at least 5 times this flight for God to provide an opportunity for me to do that. Is simply writing this book enough or am I "bringing it weak" by not inserting myself into their world and preaching Christ crucified. I'm not sure. God tells us to "go and make disciples of all nations," but is that right now, with these folks? I don't know. But what I do know is that I am supposed to do something.

If I've made myself READY by studying God's word, if I've taken AIM at glorifying God, then at some point in the very near future, I need to FIRE. Following Christ is NOT about *knowing*. It is about *believing* . . . and actions always follow our belief. What you say does not tell me what you believe, but what you do does. Knowledge is good, but it is only good so much as it contributes to right action. As I mentioned earlier, we have developed a church culture in the US that is more closely modeled after a university than a trade school, and that's bad. In our "Christian academia" we stay in our institutions of higher learning (the churches) and discuss doctrines, hermeneutics, histories, apologetics, etymologies, and Biblical truth. Occasionally a new student will come to our school, and we'll have a chance to share all of this for the first time, but much of the time we will just keep learning and re-learning, dissecting and re-dissecting.

Now don't get me wrong, we do need super-smart Biblically-literate gurus who can help us to understand the really hard teachings in the Bible, or to help us through those points where things aren't clear. But most of us don't need to be that smart. Occasionally you need a physicist to determine what kind of steel makes the best hammer, but most of us just need to pick up a hammer and get to driving nails.

Our Christian Combat basics are not "READY-AIM-AIM AGAIN." They are not "READY-AIM-MAKE YOUR WEAPONS SAFE." The right thing is "READY-AIM-FIRE." Only when you pull the trigger do you find whether your gun works and whether you are shooting properly. You must keep on firing, and in so doing, you learn what you are doing wrong. Maybe you find out that you really weren't ready . . . you forgot to disengage the safety. Or maybe you find out that your aim was not so good and you need to adjust. However, you will never find out what's wrong until you fire, and you will never get better unless you fire and fire and fire and fire.

So it goes with our faith. We have to *do*. That's a basic combat skill. Maybe today I do something, and it comes out as a complete failure. Maybe tomorrow I do something and I'm still a failure, but not a complete one. Maybe the day after I will find that I am starting to get the hang of it.

Some years ago, I felt that God was prompting me to organize a morning Bible study at the place where I worked. After literally months of hemming and hawing and procrastinating, I finally decided I was going to *do* it. So I scheduled a meeting room, advertised the study, and prepared a lesson. The big first day finally came, and I stopped off at a donut shop on my way in to work so that I would have donuts available for the attendees. 15 minutes before the Bible study was supposed to start, I nervously walked into the meeting room with my Bible and a dozen donuts. 15 minutes after the Bible study was supposed to start, I walked out of the meeting room with my Bible and 11 donuts (I ate one). Nobody had showed up! My failure? Yes . . . and no. It was a failure in worldly terms – the Bible study that I planned did not happen. However, I personally found the experience to be a spiritual success. I learned that I could try something for God, fail, and afterwards emerge with my faith, my self-esteem, and my outlook intact. That morning was a pivotal event in my life as it taught me to just be obedient regardless of the outcome. When all was said and done, I believe that God wanted me that morning to "start a Bible study" not to "have a Bible study." I believe He did this so that I would learn more about Him, about myself, and about my faith. (Interestingly, several people later expressed a desire to attend the Bible study but couldn't for various reasons. We changed it to a lunchtime event and it was a success.)

The bottom line is that living as a follower of Christ means *doing* as a follower of Christ, not just thinking, speaking, or studying as a follower of Christ.

READY. AIM. FIRE.

By the way, do you remember my quandary about whether I should witness while on my airplane flight? I wish I could say I talked to the lady sitting next to me on the airplane, and she gave her life to Christ, but that did not happen. I did talk to her, but there didn't seem to be a whole lot of response. She was amiable and we chatted for a while, but although I floated some ideas to bring the conversation to a spiritual focus, she appeared to have little to no interest in talking about Christ. And, for the record, I didn't say what I wanted to say very well. I think I learned something about me and about how to open up conversations. Maybe next time. Time for me to reload, I guess.

## Specialty Skills Training

My son is a Marine, and somebody taught him how to blow stuff up. Of course, that brings a big smile to his face, but it's not a game. The demolition equipment he is trained to use is dangerous stuff, and even though I've flown in combat with the Air Force, if you gave me that explosive equipment, I'd be like a pig looking at a wristwatch. I'd have no idea what to do with it all. I may know the basics of combat, and I'm a specialist at combat rescue, but I don't know much beyond my own specialty. Not every combatant is an expert with every weapon or in every mission. They say, "Every Marine is a rifleman," but not every Marine is trained to use plastic explosives. Every Marine is a rifleman, but not every Marine knows how to drive an armored vehicle (or a Harrier jet or a Cobra helicopter).

In the same way, every Christian follows Christ, but not every Christian needs to be an expert in every aspect of following Christ. In fact, because we serve a very big God, when we are following Him, we can be very effective even when we have very limited know-how. With the basics, we can join the fight and do very well. However, God uses us at different times for different tasks, and we often need specialty skills training to accomplish these tasks. That's why it's important to understand what specialty training is.

Specialty training is God's equipping. What does Christian specialty training look like? There are all kinds. Some folks become experts in what God says about parenting. Some focus on marriage. Others concentrate on music. Some focus on glorifying God in the business world. Yet others investigate the Old Testament, prophecy, the New Testament, or creation. Why does this matter? It matters because you don't need all of this stuff to go to war as a Christian, but you might need some of it for certain battles.

In the military a commander might say to a young soldier, "You will be my radioman . . . ," and he then ensures that the young man is trained and equipped to use the radio. God does the same to us—He specifically prepares us to be able to accomplish His purposes.

God equips us through the way He created us, through opportunities, and through His providential gifting.

**God created us in a particular way to be good at particular missions.** To one man He gives an outgoing personality that works wonderfully for sharing the Gospel on a street corner. To one woman He gives a keen intellect, equipping her to argue cogently about the faith. To a young lady He gives a spirit of empathy and caring so that she can be an incredible caregiver. To a young man He gives strong muscles so that He can bring the good news to a construction crew. God created us for a purpose— His grand purpose—that involves many smaller and sometimes temporary purposes.

**God uses experiences in our life to prepare us for His assignments.** God not only created us with an orientation towards certain specialties, but He also providentially opens opportunities for us to receive specialty training. When my wife and I were very young parents, we had an opportunity to take a class in Christian parenting. It was just a class offered at the church we were attending, and we hemmed and hawed before deciding we might as well go to the class. Although we found the video curriculum somewhat boring, the principles that were taught were outstanding. Little did we know that God was not only opening the door for us to be better parents, but also giving us wisdom that, for decades, has equipped us to share effective parenting truths with countless other parents. You never know when a class or an experience or an opportunity will turn out to be part of God's plan to equip you for certain types of spiritual combat.

**God supernaturally gifts us with ability and power.**

It is important for us to remember, however, that our effectiveness does not come strictly through training. In fact, our effectiveness in Christian combat comes most significantly through God's gifting. So God not only creates us for certain special purposes and trains us for certain special purposes, but He has also given us the gift of the Holy Spirit to accomplish special purposes with His power. We often call His divine empowering "spiritual gifts."

This idea of "spiritual gifts" is frankly taught very poorly (or not at all) in a lot of Christian denominations. It is also a huge topic, so

I am only going to scratch the surface of the subject here as it pertains to specialty training. The fundamental principle is that God supernaturally empowers people to do things that they could not do otherwise. He does so because His Holy Spirit lives with us and in us. Now there are some folks that teach, "God calls those He has equipped" and there are others who teach "God equips those He has called." Both statements are right, and if they include "only" (i.e. "God *only* calls the equipped" or "God *only* equips the called") then they are both wrong. God is sovereign. If He wants to spend 30 years filling me with a specific spiritual gift so I can do one thing supernaturally, He can do that. If He wants to spend three seconds filling me with a spiritual gift so I can do one thing supernaturally, He can do that too. Put more simply, God can make me better wherever and whenever He wants. Maybe God has gifted me to be a teacher. I might teach throughout my whole life. Or maybe God has called me to teach tomorrow, and though I have never had success teaching before, He equips me to be outstandingly epic tomorrow and tomorrow only. God can do either, and He does so at His pleasure.

So how does this relate to the idea of "specialty training?" It is absolutely imperative for us to realize that all of our skills (or lack thereof) and all of our training (or lack thereof) can be overcome at a moment's notice by God's equipping. I am a teacher by nature and am pretty "Type A" (I like to plan and focus on details). However, there have been many notable times when God has diverted me from my well-prepared teaching plan in the middle of a class to pursue a "rabbit trail" that turns out to be hugely impacting for one or more of my students. Those times are examples of His gifting.

So God prepares us for special combat assignments by the way He creates us, by the way He trains us, and by giving us what we need to carry out those assignments.

If God has given you a love of prophecy and exposure to effective teaching on prophecy, then He has equipped you to be especially effective in sharing the beauty and truth of His prophetic scripture or in prophesying outright. Pursue what He has inspired in you, and don't let someone (other than God) convince you that you need to be an expert on creation science as well.

If you have spent your life training to be a great auto mechanic and you love being a great auto mechanic, don't think that you are supposed to become an African missionary or a youth pastor just because you are now sold-out for Christ. Perhaps God has given you a special assignment to bring His love to the world of auto repair (Lord knows, most of us have stories about the pain of dealing with unholy mechanics . . . and the blessing of finding honest ones). Seek to grow in greatness at the assignment God has called you to.

By the same token, if you have never spoken to a group before and you are convinced that God wants you to share something for Him, don't flinch because you lack sufficient training. He will give you what you need, when you need it.[lvii]

We don't all have to be experts in everything to be effective combatants, and yet I've seen a lot of people that don't want to enter Christian combat because they don't know it *all* or have it *all*. If you've got Christ, you have what it takes to join the fight.

I was visiting with Dave, a friend of mine who is a devoted follower of Christ, who I hadn't seen in awhile. Dave was telling me about how things were in his life and about how busy he was with work and family. In the course of the conversation, I learned that he was attending church but not very active in any of the church's formal ministries. My first thought was, "I should encourage Dave to follow God more." However, as I talked with him, I heard about the employee that he had helped out of a tough financial position. I heard about the son that Dave was growing up in faith through example and instruction. I heard about the tremendous financial benefit that Dave's business success was bringing to the church through his generosity. Shame on me—I had been caught in Church-ology: "Ya gotta be doing stuff at church to be doing stuff for God." My friend's ministry is through his life and business . . . and I'd venture to say that he is having a more direct positive impact glorifying God than most of the people who are regulars at church programs. Dave's "specialty training" was in how to bring Christian combat through the business world, and he is fully engaged in the fight.

It has been my experience that "specialty training" comes pretty naturally. God opens doors and opportunities for us and, if we are obedient to follow His leading, we find that He is preparing us for a subsequent task.

Specialty training is good – it prepares us to be spiritual-ninjas in some of the arenas of Christian Combat. However, we must beware the deception that we have to be a ninja to join the fight. With God on our side, who can stand against us?[lviii] Embrace the specialty training that God gives you a passion or an opportunity for, but don't let a lack of training keep you away from the battle if God is calling you forward.

So is a specially trained soldier ready for any and every battle? Not hardly. There's more to it than just our own ability, and that's the subject of the next section.

## Unit Tactics

Air Force pilot Captain Scott O'Grady was shot down over Bosnia on June 2, 1995. Once he was shot down, US satellites picked up his homing signal. Intelligence specialists disseminated his location. Fighters and bombers stood by to take out any hostile enemy in his vicinity. Marine rescue helicopters flew in to recover him. Captain O'Grady was rescued from enemy territory not by one superhuman hero, but by a team working together to get the job done. Each asset had unique strengths and weaknesses and each had a particular role to play in the successful mission. None could do it alone.

From the very earliest days of basic training, soldiers are taught to work together as a team. They are taught to subordinate individually to the unit, and they are taught to rely on each other for success.

We who follow Christ are the same. We have special gifts, experiences, and training to act together as part of a unit. Maybe I have a gift of communicating. Maybe you have experience in marketing. Maybe someone else has a gift of making money. Yet another has been building things for years. Together, we could come together and organize the building of a church or the completion of a mission trip or coordinate community service. Together we can work to do things that we could never do alone. This is God's design. In the book of Ephesians, Paul talks about how all the different members of the church are different parts of the body working under the headship of Christ.[lix] This is how we are supposed to be.

There is a critical and dangerous tendency to think we are supposed to be like Christian Rambos. This line of thinking says that each of us should be able to preach, teach, nurture children, lead mission trips, mentor youth, cook perfect holiday cookies, and play guitar. We are especially bad about expecting this of our pastors. Such a mindset is ludicrous and dangerous.

In one of my military training classes, I was told a story about a fighter bomber unit that was tasked to fly a special mission during the war in Vietnam. The fighters were told to fly at high altitude, to only engage certain targets, and absolutely not to deviate for reasons that could not be disclosed. Given these orders, the pilots realized that the tactics they were told to employ were foolhardy ways to destroy the enemy and a number of them decided to disregard the instructions. They executed their missions wrongly but safely and returned to base. However, it was only when they got back to base that they were told the real reason for their instructions: they had been a diversion for a top-secret rescue mission at the North Vietnamese Son Tay Prisoner of War camp, and they were supposed to have flown as ordered to divert enemy attention from the low, slow, vulnerable rescue helicopters. By good fortune, the fighter pilots' disobedience did not impact the rescue mission, but their attempt to "fly solo" could have been devastating.

As we follow God, we frequently want to be like those pilots. We want to try to go things alone, to do things our way. However, every good Christian, like every good soldier, should know that the only way we win is if we work together.

I've heard "solo soldier" statements all my life (and said some of them myself): "My religion is just between me and God" . . . "I believe in God; I just don't think you need to be part of a church" . . . "My religion is a private thing."

There is an element of truth in these thoughts. My salvation is between God and me. I don't have to be part of a church to be in relationship with the Lord. My faith does have a private aspect. However, there is an element of falsehood as well. My relationship with God is most certainly personal, but my following Him is unarguably public and corporate.

Imagine a bride or groom who said, "I'm married, but I don't ever let anyone know . . . it's just between me and my spouse." That would be weird and dysfunctional. Or suppose someone said, "I'm on the San Francisco 49ers football team . . . but I won't ever suit up, practice, or play with them." You would say, "What are you talking about?" You can be legally married and never tell anyone, and your name can be on a football team roster even though you never play football, but these situations don't make any sense. Married people go through life together. Football players play with their team. Christians follow Christ together.

The Bible is not even remotely silent on this concept. In the Old Testament, God gives us models of corporate worship.[lx] He tells us that wisdom acknowledges the need for others.[lxi] He reminds us that it is pitiable for a person to be alone.[lxii] In the New Testament, Jesus models corporate relationships with his disciples and through his teaching. The apostle Paul tells us how to meet together [lxiii] and reminds us that we are together the body of Christ.[lxiv] The writer of Hebrews encourages us not to give up meeting together[lxv], and Jesus' brother James tells us to support each other.[lxvi]

With so much in the Bible encouraging us to follow God together, why do so many of us want to be "solo soldiers?" If my own life is a good indicator of how things are with others, I suspect that two things, as much as anything else, encourage this false way of thinking: pride and past history.

It is a rare person who isn't bothered when he or she is shown to be weak, wrong, fallible, or incompetent. Our pride hates to admit to our faults. Yet this is one of the key revelations of the Bible – we ALL have fallen short of the glory of God, and we are ALL hopelessly weak, wrong, fallible, and incompetent. When we embrace Christianity, we acknowledge this in theory . . . but do we acknowledge it in fact? It is (relatively) easy for me to stand up in front of a bunch of people after a moving sermon and say, "Yes, I agree that I need a savior," but it is another thing altogether to live and work with people on a daily basis and let them in on all of my shortcomings and failings. It is far easier for me to say, "It's just between God and me" and then not let anyone know the real me. By soldiering solo, I get to pretend like I'm a Christian Rambo, I can hide behind my fake-façade, and I can say all of the things in private to God that I think I'm supposed to say without having anyone there to hold me accountable to do all the things I've told God I'll try to do. I get to play Christian with no one to call me on those places where I'm just paying lip-service.

To this natural tendency to be proud, we get to add on all of the fits and failures of the past history of the institutional church. Make no mistake about it, the institutional church in America today is failing. We don't do what we say we should. Many of our leaders preach erroneous doctrine, and most of our followers don't really follow. Church leaders famously (or infamously) end up plastered on headlines for sodomizing children or cheating on their wives. "Christian" congregations publicly embrace doctrines that are explicitly contradicted by the Bible. Lay leaders split churches due to petty disputes and personality conflicts. Christ told us to judge by fruit, and judging by the fruit of our churches, we're not doing well. To paraphrase one theologian, if even 25% of America was actively Christian, wouldn't you think that 1/4 pound of salt would flavor 1 pound of meat a whole lot more?[8]

Is the church all bad? No, we are not, but we are goofed up enough that ANYONE with a self-centered motivation can use us as a good excuse why they shouldn't be part of a church.

However, ultimately these are just excuses. God said to live life together and to follow Him together. He didn't say "encourage one another" *if* people are good enough. He didn't say, "Love your neighbor" *if* they are worth loving.

When all is said and done, the reason people try to be solo soldiers is because it's a lot easier than working together in community. It's easier, that is, until you actually face the enemy. We say we're ready to go to battle as part of the army, but what we really mean is that we're ready to go to battle if the army does what we want it to. That's the problem. We think that conflict should only be with the enemy.

In Hollywood, Rambo saves the day. In *real* battle, people acting like Rambos will lose the war. In Christian combat, Rambos get defeated as they either wear out or prove their inadequacy (or both).

We need to realize that God calls us to work together as a team and equips each member of the unit so that we are effective when we work together. We need to realize that He calls US, meaning more than just me.

---

[8] Quoted by Dallas Willard, The Spirit of Discipline, (Harper Collins: San Francisco, 1990), p. 23.

Do you want to win the battle for Christ? Do you want to see people blessed, to see innocents protected, to see people freed from spiritual bondage? If so, then it is time to lash up with your Christian brothers and sisters.

In Christian Combat, the only solo soldiers are those that are dead or dying.

# PART 3: LIFE DURING WARTIME

It was pitch dark, around 0300 (3:00 AM, for you non-military types), and I was on a well established air base in Kandahar, Afghanistan. It was near the middle of the night shift, and my eyelids were feeling heavy, so a friend and I walked a few hundred yards from our tactical operations center to go get a coffee at the 24-hour "Green Bean" coffee stand that was on base. As we walked up the dimly lit boardwalk, built to keep boots out of the mud during the wet season, two soldiers walked up in full "battle rattle"—helmets, body armor, weapons, and web gear. They walked ahead of us, entered the coffee shop, and proceeded to the counter to order mocha lattés. There is nothing quite so incongruous as being in a combat zone in the middle of the night and watching a fully-armed soldier in combat gear order a latté.

Such a situation just doesn't meet your expectations, but that's what life during wartime can be like in the 21st century.

If we Christians are engaged in a war, what should our expectations be for life during wartime? What are your expectations?

Our expectations can shape both our perceptions and our responses, and so our expectations are important. Do your expectations line up with the fact that you and I are living life during a spiritual war? These next few pages will help you answer that question.

## 3-1 EXPECTATIONS OF THE MILITARY

I've had the chance many times to bring friends onto an Air Force Base for the first time in their lives. Sometimes people are kind of surprised after you come through the gate. On a given day at an Air Force base here in the States you might not see anyone with a gun (other than the police). You probably won't see any groups of troops marching in formation. You likely will not see guys riding in Humvees with machine guns mounted on top. A few of the airmen are tall and look like iconic Hollywood super-soldiers, but most of us are short or dumpy or a little overweight or in some other way underwhelming. People are often surprised that the men and women on base aren't all engaged in martial activity like they've seen on television, and they might wonder if something is wrong.

This is a classic example of wrong expectations. There is nothing at all amiss . . . people just don't look like what we think they were supposed to.

Sometimes we have some very wrong expectations about Christian combat forces as well, and at times our wrong expectations can set us up for trouble. What should we expect from our Commander in Chief (God)? How about from our platoon leader (Christ)? How about from our air support (the Holy Spirit)? How about from our fellow soldiers (other Christians)?

### The Commander in Chief

While in the Air Force, I worked for a senior officer named Craig. He is tall, commanding, has piercing blue eyes, is amazingly articulate, incredibly smart, and unflappable. I worked for another senior officer named Chad. He is short, somewhat reserved, a little dour (especially before his first cup of coffee), and won't hesitate to bite your head off if you aren't doing things to standards. Both of these men were radically different in presentation, but both were of sterling character and were among the best leaders I've ever worked for. Just because a leader is not like we expect doesn't mean he is a bad leader. In fact, it is very important that we understand how our leader really is if we want to follow well.

Christians, by definition, follow God. But who is this God that we follow? Now that's an epic question that I can't answer, at least not completely. I'm not dumb enough to try to give a finite description of an infinite God, but I am dumb enough to try to highlight some of the places where we typically expect something from God other than what we ought. God is our Commander in Chief. He's in charge of this war that we are engaged in, and while we could never understand Him fully, there are some things that a good Christian soldier needs to keep in mind:

**1) God is who He is, not who you want Him to be.** I have several good friends for whom I have been praying for years to come to a saving knowledge of Christ. When we talk about God, we invariably end up discussing something along the lines of "I can't believe in a God who _____." Fill in the blank with whatever you like: "allows kids to be molested," "doesn't want homosexuals to love each other," "would allow a tsunami to kill 100,000+." The point is, these friends are not looking for God; they are looking for their god. Imagine if I went up to a plainclothes police officer and said, "You aren't a police officer because you don't look like I think you should." That's totally illogical. In the same way, it's illogical for us to go to God and say, "You're only God if you look like I want you to."

That's what a lot of non-believers do, and frankly, that's what a lot of believers (including yours-truly) do as well. We say, "I believe in God," but when we read Bible passages where He smites men, women, and children, we make up excuses or ignore those passages or pretend like He didn't do that.

Or maybe we read the part where God says through the apostle Paul, "I do not permit a woman to teach"[lxvii] and think to ourselves "that doesn't mesh with my 21st century image of gender equality." So we either ignore that passage thinking "He didn't really mean it" or "we're so much more enlightened now than they were back then."

We cannot remake God in the image we'd like for Him and still be effective warriors.

During the Allied North African Campaign during World War II, some commanders decided not to follow orders of their superiors. Why? They thought that surely they knew better than their commander what was best for their unit. So instead of carrying out their directive exactly, they delayed, lost the initiative, and lost the opportunity for victory in that battle. What happened?

They would only let their commander command if that commander was doing things in line with what they wanted.

We can do the same with God. If we don't allow God to be who He is and if we only see Him as we want Him to be, we will miss missions that He has for us or will be disobedient when He calls us to act.

If it were up to me, I'd contend with God about how He gave Job up to Satan for a time. I'd contend with Him about Jepthah sacrificing his daughter to God.[lxviii] I wouldn't let all the families get swallowed up by the earth in Genesis 16:32. I wouldn't put women in submissive roles as God does in 1 Timothy 2:12, Ephesians 5:22, and 1 Corinthians 11:5-7. I would have stopped Hitler when he was a young man. I would have made it okay to get drunk every once in a while.

But it's not up to me. I'm small and stupid, and I know God's plans, intellect, and character are infinitely better than my own. So when He and I disagree, I try to do my best to change my mind and get it right.

The Commander In Chief is who He says He is. A good soldier accepts this and follows, even when he doesn't understand why.

**2) God is absolutely sovereign.** The four-wheel drive system on my truck is not working right, and I need to get it checked out. This might cost $100 to fix, or it might cost several thousand. My natural tendency is to worry about the "several thousand" possibility. But why do I worry? I have money in my bank account, and if God wants me to spend it on fixing a truck instead of on retirement, isn't that okay? If God is who He says He is, isn't it just as possible that I'll come into a financial windfall this year that makes my repair bill look like a pittance?[9]

My anxiety comes when I forget that God is absolutely sovereign, which means He is in control of everything. Nothing happens except as He allows and intends. If I get rich, it is at His will. If I become poor, it is that same will. If my wife and I live to be very old, that is God's will, but if one of us dies this afternoon, then that is His will. He is in charge of everything.

So if God really is sovereign, doesn't that mean a soldier can

---

[9] Interestingly enough, several weeks after I wrote this, I received a completely unexpected (and large) check from an insurance policy.

just sit back and wait for the victory parade? No.

God is in control of all things, but He has seen fit to give us the blessing of choice, and choice means nothing if choices don't have consequence. My choices in this battle have real consequences on those around me and myself. Returning to my broken truck example, I can choose to ignore the warning signs that something is wrong. However, that choice might result in me really destroying something expensive in the drive train. In that case, what was going to cost a few hundred dollars to fix might cost a few thousand dollars. So would that mean my inaction thwarted God's plan to fix my truck? Not hardly, but it might mean that I have a big (rather than small) repair bill. You see, God can give me wide latitude to choose, and realize the consequences of those choices, without sacrificing His sovereignty. Let me give you a couple of examples that help me to picture how God maintains control even as He allows me to choose.

When my children were small, I would sometimes take them to dinner at a restaurant. My "sovereign" will was to feed my family, and within my budget I had the power to make that happen as I saw fit. However, if my initial plan was to go to Applebee's, and the kids started asking for McDonald's, I might take them to where they wanted to go. Even as I let them have choice, I maintained my sovereignty to meet my overall goal: that they be fed.

Here's a similar example: When our kids were still at home, we would often go hiking as a family. If my children wanted to climb on trees or rocks as we hiked, I generally let them. If they fell, they had skinned knees or bruises and some pain to cry through. However, if they started to get too high or too dangerous, I would stop them so that we could avoid yet another trip to see our friends at the local emergency room. Our children could hike away from us and take risks, but I wouldn't let them go so far as to get lost. Even as I allowed them to exercise choice, I exercised sovereignty (at least as far as is possible for a human being).

These situations help to illustrate how God allows us to choose even as He is sovereign. His sovereignty matters a lot in Christian Combat.

When we are in battle and it seems all hope is lost, it isn't. God is still there working all things to his good end. When it seems like God has given us a task that we could never accomplish, we just need to do our best. If the task needs to be done, He will make sure that we are successful. To me, one of the most amazing miracles of life is that God, in His sovereignty, has chosen us to help carry out His plans. This means that what we do makes a real difference in real lives of real people. When we engage in combat, lives are saved. That's awesome!

I came to know Christ as my savior because God asked someone to bake a loaf of bread, and they did. You see, I visited a church one Sunday as a young man. Though I liked the preaching, I didn't feel connected to the church and had decided not to go back. However, that next Wednesday someone (I don't know who) came and left a loaf of bread and a note on my doorstep that said, "Thanks for joining us at church . . . ." That loaf of bread was enough encouragement to get me to come back the next Sunday, which led to me getting involved, which led to me meeting my wife, which led to me being nurtured in Christian community, which led to me finally understanding the gospel, which led to me choosing to believe in Christ and confessing him as my Lord and Savior, which has guaranteed me eternity in heaven! Someone *chose* to bake a loaf of bread, and God used that as part of His sovereign plan to love me.

God is in control of it all, even as He gives us freedom to choose.

### 3) God is not in the business of working for us.

As a squadron commander in the Air Force, I was afforded a certain degree of positional privilege that went beyond just my rank. Usually, when I would walk into parts of my squadron, people would stand up or call the room to attention. It can give a guy a big head, but the respect I received was not really about me. It was about acknowledging that the person in charge must have authority if the military job is to get done right. It would have been a major faux pas for a young airman to say to his commander, "Sir, take that trash out, would you?"

Do you ever tell God to take the trash out? Do you ever tell God to do anything? In my stupid moments I sometimes do . . . but I try not to, because it's not right. God does NOT work for us.

You may have heard of "name it and claim it" theology or you might have heard Christians say, "we just need to pray it with enough faith and God will make it so." Hogwash! We do need faith—it is critical—but that is faith *in* God, not faith that God will do *our* bidding. At times, we do need to be more faithful in believing that what He has dictated will come to pass at a certain time or place or in a certain way. However, it is not faith to conjure God like a genie or to say to the Creator of the Universe, "Thou shalt heal me now"—that's pride, not faith.

The Christian soldier works for God in whatever circumstance and in whatever way and to whatever end God has given Him.

I started looking for a new job last year because my retirement from military service was coming up. I looked for seven months with absolutely no luck. During that time, my tendency was to say, "God give me a job now," but the right thing to pray was "God, your will be done" and "God, I know that your plans for me are awesome . . . give me faith and patience." A year later, in hindsight, I can see that He was working things in just the right time to bring my wife and I to just the right place that He has us today. There have been many consequences to waiting for His plan (and she and I will both admit that it was a tremendous struggle for us to wait for His plan). We now find ourselves plugged into a great community, supporting an exciting ministry, having learned much about our faith and about our God, and living in a way that is much deeper and more meaningful than we have experienced before. However, the road to this point was tough on us, partly because of pride, partly because of impatience; from all those things that the 'fallen' side of us is prone to hang on to. However, because we let Him be in charge, we are now in a place to engage in certain skirmishes that we are convinced God has prepared and equipped us for, and we are thankful to be in combat where He wants us.

Soldiers in the field don't get to decide where their unit goes, what their unit gets assigned, or whom their unit fights. If we want to be soldiers for the Commander in Chief, we need to make sure that we're letting God be in command of everything.

### 4) God cares about us.

"His men would do anything for him."

You may have heard this in movies or books or histories about any number of military commanders. It's a common sentiment, and in our American culture it implies that men would do anything for a commander because they love and respect him. In my 22 year military career, the most loved and respected leaders I encountered were invariably the ones that loved and respected their subordinates. You might find a General that was an incredible speaker or a Colonel that was a fantastic administrator or pilot, and people would speak well of them, but the ones that get the "do anything for him" accolades are the ones that truly care for their troops.

God truly cares for us. We miss that point sometimes. When you suffer, He hurts for you. When you rejoice, He rejoices with you. When you worry about how things are going to turn out, He says, "Trust in me because I want to bless your socks off." All of the deistic religions of the world posit a god who somehow requires us to earn his love, respect, or admiration to get to the afterlife. They all require a sacrifice, whether a physical sacrifice like an animal or a personal sacrifice of action, to earn a place with God. All except for one. Christianity is the one and only religion that says, "God loves you enough that He sacrificed Himself for you so that you can be with Him." Christianity is the only religion that offers grace—an unmerited gift—instead of a path of toil to righteousness.

In his book *Night*, Jewish Holocaust survivor Elie Wiesel writes of a time in a concentration camp when he witnessed Nazis hanging a young Jewish boy. Too light to have died quickly on the gallows, the boy hung and kicked for more than half an hour. A man behind Elie said, "For God's sake, where is God?" Elie writes, "from within me, I heard a voice answer: "Where He is? This is where—hanging from this gallows . . . ."[10]

Some 2000 years prior to that boy's death, God hung on a gallows of sort—hung by nails—and personally experienced all of the tragedy and pain that boy did. He was with that boy as he hung there, and while God understood the hurt, He also had provided a way for victory even over death. God sacrificed Himself so that we would have a way to God that did not depend on our own unworthy actions. That is love: ultimate sacrifice for another. God loves us!

I have a friend that was raped when she was a young lady. She described how during this unconscionable act God had taken her emotionally out of the situation and had protected her spiritually

---

[10] Elie Wiesel; "Night"; as quoted on Goodreads.com; Accessed Mar 18, 2014 at http://www.goodreads.com/work/quotes/265616-la-nuit

even as her body was violated. She said it was like she was watching things as a third party and not feeling despair or crushing demoralization. Long after this dastardly deed was done, God used her experience to help her assist others through their own tragedies. Does this make her rape any less horrible or tragic or wrong? Not at all, but it does show how God's love can be in action even in the most trying human circumstances. His love never fails.[lxix]

For us in battle, we can *never* forget the backdrop of our Commander in Chief's great love for us. When the enemy is on all sides and death seems imminent, we must know that God has not forgotten us. He has not left us to final defeat. If we experience a loss, it is temporary, and we know that in the end we are absolutely certain to share in victory, because He is all-powerful and He loves us dearly. When it seems we are crushed, abandoned, exhausted, or without options, when it seems we could never do what needs to be done, when we see good appear to be failing all around us, when it feels like the easiest thing to do is to raise the surrender flag and just give up, then we soldiers must remember who our Commander is. God loves us; He will never let us be destroyed or taken from Him. Any setback is only temporary; physical death is not an end, but a glorious beginning. It is good to be loved by the King of the Universe, and it is good to serve under a Commander in Chief who truly cares about us.

When we see our Commander in Chief as He really is, we will have right expectations about Him and about how we follow Him. We will say, "I will do **anything** for Him," and we will say, "I am absolutely secure in Him."

However, the Commander is not the only one that we need to have right expectations about. What are your expectations about our "Platoon Leader," God's son?

## Our Platoon Leader

Lieutenant Mike Murphy received the Medal of Honor for his actions taking care of his SEAL team in Afghanistan. After his team's location was compromised, "Murph" led his men in a fierce battle in which they were incredibly outnumbered. His small squad was cut off from the outside world, and their only hope was to get word out that they needed assistance. Their only means of communication was via satellite phone, and in the steep terrain of the mountains of Afghanistan, you have to be out in the open to get a decent signal. Knowing this, Murph exposed himself to enemy fire so that he could call for reinforcements and evacuation. His heroic actions cost him his life, but ultimately led to the survival of one of his team members.[11]

Success in battle depends on courageous and competent leaders. We Christians have one of those, and his name is Jesus.

You can read the Bible and say that Jesus should be looked at as a General or even a Commander in Chief (CINC). There is truth in both of those images of Christ. However, I think in our day-to-day combat it is more helpful to look at him as our platoon leader, so that's what I'll do here. A platoon is a small unit and the platoon leader is the guy that is right there, side-by-side with his fellow soldiers, leading them in the middle of the battle. Generals and CINCs are usually back at Headquarters strategizing and moving armies, but in the life of the Christian, Jesus is right there with us, fighting with us. So who is this Jesus that we follow?

Jesus is God, so I'll say again as I said in the section above about God the Father: I can't tell you everything about Jesus. How do you fully describe the King of all kings, the Lord of all lords, the beginning and the end, the only son of God, the savior of all mankind, Emmanuel (which means "God with us")? The answer is that you don't, but I think it might be helpful for us to consider two things about Christ that will be of some benefit with the idea of Christian combat:

**1) Jesus is an active leader.** A friend of mine was participating in a meeting chaired by a general officer. The meeting was about all of the computer-based training that we had to complete to get our airmen ready to deploy to combat theaters. Some of this stuff was sensible – like first-aid training – but some of the preparations were redundant and irrelevant – like doing "cultural awareness" training for a country that you'd been to a myriad of times. As this meeting progressed, the general was listening to some of the comments and then said something like, "Well at least we've really reduced the redundant training." There was a pregnant pause, and then someone said, "Actually sir, we've increased it."

---

[11] The official Medal of Honor Citation can be found at http://www.navy.mil/moh/mpmurphy/oc.html

"I thought we got rid of all of that," the general said.

"No sir," came the answer.

The general was wrong about reducing training—just the opposite had happened. This senior officer was out of touch with what was happening to the common airman because he lived in circumstances very different from the average Joe.

Jesus is not like that general. He is supremely aware of what we go through every day. He understands our victories and our disappointments because he lived them himself. He is not a detached deity; he is with us, encouraging us, rooting for us, looking out for us. The Bible tells us that Jesus, through the Holy Spirit, continues to counsel us and to give us power and aid.[lxx]

It is easy to think of Jesus as being "out there" or "back then" living some 2000 years ago, but thinking that way is a mistake. It is right to think that Jesus is right here – he is with us in Spirit and cares very much about what is going on right now.

Generals give orders like "*you* go take that hill over there." Platoon leaders give orders like "*let's* go take that hill over there." And while you are charging up the hill in the face of the enemy, your platoon leader might yell, "take cover" because he's right there to see the threat.

Now if you are a "detail person" like I am, you are right now thinking "but Jesus isn't here with me; the Bible says he is in heaven at the right hand of the Father."[lxxi] You are right, of course, from a physical standpoint. However, spiritually speaking, Christ is with us in our battles through the power and the presence of the Holy Spirit (more about this in the next section). From a practical standpoint in spiritual combat, Christ is *with* us.

I spent many years looking at Jesus as more of a general than a platoon leader. I'd take my orders (basically speaking, the Bible) and then go out and try to execute them. The big problem with that way of thinking is that it depends entirely on *me* to carry out God's plan – and my personal history has shown that I'm not bright enough or capable enough to do a good job at that. The Bible tells me that is true of you, too.[lxxii]

I can remember one time when I knew that I needed to go talk to an acquaintance who was exhibiting some behaviors that looked very much like she had an addiction problem. I genuinely wanted to see if I could help her, and I knew that it was the right thing to address whether there was a problem. I still believe that to this day.

I felt like those were my "marching orders" from God and so I went and took care of it. Suffice it to say that the discussion turned into a confrontation and things did not go well at all. The lady I was talking to became very irate and hostile and basically threw me out. I wonder now if things would have gone better if I had been following my platoon leader instead of stepping off on my own. If my eyes had been more focused on Jesus than the "orders" in my hand, perhaps I would have seen him give me the "pause, wait" signal. Or perhaps he would have said, "Okay Dan, here's how you do this in a way that it will have a positive impact." Maybe things would have been no different, but I know that if I had focused on following Jesus step-by-step instead of just carrying out a set of orders, I would have had the best chance of making a positive impact.

There's a really funny (albeit vulgar) animated video clip on Youtube about "Leeroy Jenkins." In the video, a bunch of gamers are playing some sort of video game online, and they are discussing strategy about how their whole team is going to go rushing into this room full of monsters to slay them all. All of a sudden, this one player, Leeroy Jenkins, totally disregards all the planning and goes running in on his own and everyone just follows. The end result is that all of their characters are killed. We need to not be a Christian Leeroy Jenkins. We not only need to engage in battle, but we need to engage at the time, place, and bidding of our platoon leader, Jesus Christ.

He's here in it with us; we need to make sure we're paying attention to him all the time. We don't want to get out in front, and we don't want to lag behind.

### 2) Jesus is not cuddly.

I once worked for a commander who was too nice. The level of discipline in our unit was low because our boss was too easy-going. If your performance was sub-par, you might get a talking to, but you wouldn't really get in trouble unless did really badly. At our squadron social events, the commander spent more time trying to be "one of the guys" than he did trying to set the example or show leadership. It's very pleasant to have a nice-guy for a boss, but if he's so nice that he won't enforce standards, things are going to go downhill quickly.

Our popular 21st century image of Jesus is that he is a nice guy.

Too nice, that is, and not at all like the Jesus of the Bible. We picture him with a lamb or a child in his arms. We picture him sharing good news with a woman at a well. We picture him riding a little donkey and healing blind men and forgiving an adulteress. All of these pictures are good and true, but they are only half the picture.

Do you picture Jesus whipping people in the temple? He did.[lxxiii] Do you picture Jesus turning to his friend and saying angrily to him "Get behind me, Satan"? He did.[lxxiv] Do you picture Jesus publicly calling the most respected religious leaders of his day "snakes" and "whitewashed tombs"? He did.[lxxv] Do you picture Jesus killing armies of men so that birds can "gorge on their flesh"? He will.[lxxvi]

This isn't your Sunday-school flannel-graph Jesus.

When we talk about our Lord and Savior Jesus Christ, we are talking about a guy tougher than a Navy SEAL or John Wayne. We're talking about a guy who can love better than any of us can and who can take out Chuck Norris with a single punch. We're talking about a guy who could (and would) entertain your grandma with his wit and caring, and then turn around and make Simon Cowell look like an uplifting guy.

Christ is not cuddly. As C.S. Lewis said, "He's not safe, but he's good."[12]

As we follow our Platoon Leader, we need to understand that he can beat down the enemy. He is the best combat tactician, the best hand-to-hand fighter, the best rifleman, and the best demolitionist. We also need to understand that he will call us to task if we don't do what he orders.

There is a great scene in the movie *Glory* where civil war soldiers are practicing their rifle drill. They are generally having a good time until their colonel comes up. The colonel starts pressuring one of the soldiers and pulls out a pistol, firing just behind the frazzled soldier's head as the young man struggles to shoot his rifle. The colonel then explains that that is what it is like in real combat, and admonishes these soldiers to get their act together and start training for war rather than just playing with guns. In this scene, the colonel is not nice, but he is very good.

In Christian combat, Christ will sometimes make very big

[12] C.S. Lewis; "The Lion, The Witch, and The Wardrobe"; as quoted by goodreads.com; accessed Apr 16, 2014 at http://www.goodreads.com/quotes/10569-he-s-not-safe-but-he-s-good-referring-to-aslan-the

demands of us. He will sometimes chew us out, in a manner of speaking, so that we get things right. That's how he keeps us in good spiritual health as we engage in spiritual warfare.

Maybe Christ wants you to spend *all* of your free time right now to get ready for the next battle. Maybe he wants you to spend *all* of your extra money (and some that's not extra) to be prepared for the next engagement. Maybe he's hounding your conscience or telling you to leave that sinful habit behind because he knows that those are chinks in your armor that the enemy will exploit.

Jesus is a warrior. He will hold you when you need to cry on his shoulder when you've just taken hits from the enemy, but he might also make you suck it up and stand strong, injuries and all, when he knows that you are able to do so.

Jesus is "Emmanuel" – which means "God with us." Keep your eyes on the Platoon Leader and trust that he is there in the fight with you. Even if he isn't physically next to you, he is there in the battle. How? Through the Holy Spirit . . . what we might think of as "spiritual air support."

## Our Air Support

I once flew my helicopter to a remote location here in the United States to pick up a man that was having a heart attack. We landed, loaded him in to the back of our helicopter on a gurney, and started flying at best speed to the nearest hospital. This man was an older fellow who had served in the Vietnam conflict and while en route, the medics in the back of the helicopter put the man on a headset. He came up on the intercom and said, "Man, I haven't been on one of these birds since Vietnam! When they came down out of the sky to get us out of there, it was like seeing angels . . . !"

The vet in the back of my helicopter was expressing a soldier's appreciation for air support. In modern war, "air support" does all kinds of things for the soldier on the ground. Helicopters will evacuate the wounded. High-flying airplanes will act as radio relays so soldiers can maintain communication and call in reinforcements or artillery. Fighters and bombers can precisely hit the enemy with bombs and bullets – what one Marine called a "rain of hate." Transport planes deliver needed supplies to troops in the field. Unmanned drones pinpoint the enemy and reveal his actions.

In Christian combat, the Holy Spirit of God is like our "air support." The Holy Spirit is not a thing, but rather is a "He" and is part of the Trinity of God (Father, Son, Holy Spirit). He is the present and powerful presence of God here on earth, and we who are believers in Christ have the Holy Spirit in us. He is why we can embrace the perspective that Christ is with us even as Christ is in heaven, because the Holy Spirit is our advocate and messenger from Christ and the Father.[lxxvii]

The Holy Spirit is in some ways hard to wrap our thoughts around. It is hard to conceptualize Him in part because He is intangible spirit. He cannot be seen or touched or put in a box. Christ, the Son, took the physical form of a man and so we can picture him clearly in our brains. The Father has physical parallels: we view Him as a great Father and Judge and King. But the Holy Spirit has no direct physical parallel in this world, so this makes it harder for us to know what to expect from Him. The Bible compares the Spirit to a wind[lxxviii]— something we cannot see directly, but can perceive through its impact (e.g. we feel the wind or see leaves blowing).

It is also sometimes hard to understand who the Holy Spirit is because He is inseparable from God the Father and God the Son. Whenever we talk about the Holy Spirit, we are talking about something that the Father and Son are doing. So it is easy for us to just talk about Christ and about God the Father and kind of ignore the fact that there is a third person in our one, triune God.

Yet to be ready for Christian combat, it is critical for us to understand, at least in part, what we should expect from the Holy Spirit. A right understanding of the Holy Spirit helps us to comprehend how God's Kingdom is not just coming, but is here today. We aren't just waiting to get to heaven . . . we who know Christ are working with God, through His Holy Spirit, right now.

- Our Commander in Chief can give us orders, right here right now, through His Holy Spirit.
- Our Platoon Leader can give us weapons for the fight, right here and right now, through His Holy Spirit.
- Our Commander in Chief can rescue us, right here and right now, through His Holy Spirit.
- Our Platoon Leader can protect and strengthen us, right here and right now, through His Holy Spirit.

In this discussion of spiritual combat, I think there are three key

70

things that we should expect of the Holy Spirit:

**1) The Holy Spirit communicates.** There are large parts of Afghanistan and Iraq that are very remote, and Afghanistan has soaring mountain ridges and deep valleys. Both distance and terrain make radio communications very difficult in parts of both of these countries, and so soldiers on the ground can easily be cut off from communication as they move about. When you are part of a small combat team working in a hostile country, it is easy to be outnumbered or overwhelmed if you cannot call for assistance, so communication is imperative. Accordingly, the US flies planes and drones (and even uses satellites) as radio platforms to maximize the ability for soldiers to communicate no matter where they are. That way if there is critical intelligence about enemy forces or the need to call for reinforcements or bombs, the soldiers on the ground can do so.

In spiritual battle, communication is arguably even more important than in physical battle because our weapon in Christian combat is Truth, not bullets. As believers in Christ, we are in constant contact with God through the Holy Spirit. Jesus said that he was sending the Holy Spirit "to guide you into all the truth."[lxxix] God has not left us alone, flapping in the breeze, dependent on our own wisdom, Bible memorization, or education to fight off the enemy. He is *with* us.

What does the communication of the Holy Spirit look like in practical terms? There is no one way or format through which He communicates (He is God, after all!), but here are some examples of what He does:

The Holy Spirit speaks through the Bible. Have you ever read a passage from the Bible and had a verse almost jump off the page? That's the Holy Spirit prompting you. Have you ever had a big problem going on and found just what you needed during your daily Bible study? That's the Holy Spirit encouraging you or reminding you of God's Truth. I had an opportunity to teach a particular Bible study several times over the course of several years. Each time I went back through the study, looking at the same Bible verses and the same study questions, I found that God brought new aspects of truth into focus. He took the exact same verses and used them at different times and in different ways to show me how His truth was specifically applicable to my life right then. When we realize that God speaks not only with the words on the pages of our Bible but *through* the words on the pages of our Bible, our time spent in the Bible is transformational.

The Holy Spirit also communicates through our conscience and feelings. Have you ever been "cut to the heart" by a truth you've heard? Have you ever been listening to something and been overwhelmed with a feeling of "God you are so incredible" or a feeling of "God forgive me for what I've done?" Often that is God prompting you to listen to what He is saying and to internalize His truth. It's important to remember that not *all* feelings are from the Holy Spirit, but it is equally important to realize that when He touches us, He frequently does it through our feelings (or maybe it's more correct to say that His touch generates feelings in us).

The Holy Spirit communicates with us directly. God's communication isn't reserved for old-guys with long beards and camel-hair robes or for super-spiritual gurus. God is in everyone who believes in Jesus Christ. Jesus said that this is true[lxxx], so you should expect to hear from God. One time God woke my wife up in the middle of the night and the Holy Spirit told her, "Go where I am working." We had been planning to start a ministry of our own, but (as future events would confirm) God wanted us to abandon those plans and help with a ministry that He already had going. This was just one of many examples of when the Holy Spirit has spoken. Now neither my wife, nor I, nor anyone else I know has a running dialogue with God that is just the same as conversing with another human being. Sometimes I've been wrong thinking God said something when the truth was that I just thought something. However, the fact that my perception is imperfect does not negate the truth that the Holy Spirit can and does communicate directly with us.

When believers go into spiritual combat, they aren't going alone. God is with us, communicating His Truth and arming us for each skirmish and battle. Don't believe it when the enemy says, "You are all alone in this." The Holy Spirit is right there with you. Speak to Him. Listen for Him. He not only brings Truth, but power as well.

What kind of power? Read on.

**2) The Holy Spirit empowers.** A fighter pilot I worked with received a medal for flying a high-risk mission in Afghanistan. A ground convoy came under attack on a high mountain pass. The convoy was pinned down and in danger of being overwhelmed by enemy attackers, so they put out a desperate radio call for assistance. Flying an A-10 Warthog, a fighter jet with a massive 30 millimeter cannon and tons of rockets and bombs, my friend received the call and had to work his way through low clouds and bad weather to find the stricken convoy. When he arrived on scene, he opened up with his deadly ordnance and decimated the Taliban aggressors, saving the convoy. He brought air power to the fight, and it made the difference in defeating the enemy.

Like an A-10 fighter, the Holy Spirit brings power to our spiritual fight—God's power. He brings natural power and supernatural power. His is the power to overcome Satan's minions, and His is the power to overcome our own selfish selves. His power can tear down the strongholds of the enemy, sending evil in full retreat, but His power is not just to destroy. His power sustains us, gives us strength when we are suffering, and gives us endurance to run our race to the finish.

Suppose our Platoon Leader, Jesus Christ, says, "The children in our community are struggling, let's bring the truth to them." You and I might say things like "I don't know any kids" or "I'm not much of a teacher" or "I don't have patience with children." All these statements may have an element of truth in them, but the truth is God and when He calls, He empowers. "I don't know any kids," but God can suddenly introduce me to kids. "I'm not much of a teacher," but the Holy Spirit can make me a fantastic teacher in the blink of an eye. "I don't have patience with children," but the Holy Spirit can fill you with patience that you didn't know you had (because before He showed up, you didn't have it!). The apostle Paul talks about fruits of the Holy Spirit and gifts of the Holy Spirit, and he gives us lists of those in Galatians[lxxxi] and Ephesians[lxxxii], respectively. But God's power is not limited to a list, so don't limit what you believe God's Holy Spirit can do in you. He can make you a great prophet[lxxxiii] *and* a great refrigerator repairman. He can give you "joy, peace, and patience"[lxxxiv] *and* insight into how to teach your children to use the internet wisely.

Suppose your church just "blew up." The pastor and the elders got into an argument and now the church has split. It may feel like all is lost and Christianity is a sham. The devil intends this situation to be the end of faith for you and many others, but the

Holy Spirit is *with* you. He can give you the strength to endure the barbs of former friends who have become enemies. He can give you the wisdom to know if sides must be chosen and who to side with. He can give you the patience to wait until resolution occurs. He can take this whole messy situation and use it as a refining experience so that your church comes out stronger, more faithful, more alive.

Do you have a big challenge coming up? The Holy Spirit is with you and can give you the strength to prevail.[lxxxv] Do you need to confront someone who is doing something wrong? The Holy Spirit is there to give you the right words to speak the Truth in love.[lxxxvi] Are you trying to figure out what God wants you to do with your life? The Holy Spirit is there to answer, and He will in God's good time.[lxxxvii] Are you ready to give up because of a bad relationship, a death, a financial catastrophe, or a bad diagnosis? The Holy Spirit, God, is in you with all of the love, peace, patience and hope that any human being can handle.[lxxxviii]

A couple of months ago, I was asked to lead a big grading project for a Christian camp that is under construction. I didn't know anything about moving dirt – I'd never done it and never seen it done. So when we had this opportunity with volunteers and heavy equipment (that I didn't even know the names of), my first thought was "there is no way we are going to be able to do this." Yet God had opened the opportunity and was bringing things together. So with some good encouragement from a Christian brother, I pressed ahead. Guess what? The Holy Spirit showed up. He provided advice from a professional dirt mover. He provided equipment operators, including one with 38 years of experience. He provided good weather, good teamwork, and some "lucky" guesses on how to solve some of the problems that came up. At the end of our week, we had finished the project ahead of schedule and under budget, and three people on the team had made professions of faith in Jesus! I couldn't do that, but through the power of the Holy Spirit we could do just what God asked us to do, and more.

If Jesus is your Lord, the Holy Spirit is in you and He has God's power, so *you* have God's power. You have what you need to be victorious. God's Holy Spirit is even better than air support, so don't be afraid of combat.

**3) The Holy Spirit is God.** In 2002, some Air Force pilots crashed a helicopter on the side of Mt Hood, Oregon. They were doing their best to rescue an injured hiker and were operating at their maximum altitude. The helicopter flew over the injured hiker and dropped off a rescue medic and then departed to wait until the medic had the hiker ready for evacuation. A short time later, the medic told the helicopter to return and so the pilots flew over the exact same spot where they had dropped the medic off. However, as they secured the survivor to their hoist line, the helicopter began to descend uncontrollably. The pilot and crew were barely able to get clear of the hiker before impacting the mountain side and rolling downhill seven and a half times. Fortunately, no one was killed in the crash.

What happened? The wind shifted, robbing the helicopter's blades of the lift required to hover over the high mountainside. Because of their successful first approach to the mountain, the crew was lulled into thinking that they had enough power at their disposal, but they were tragically wrong.[13]

It is easy for us to be like those helicopter pilots and think that because the Holy Spirit is in us, we have all the power we want. That's not true. The Holy Spirit is God, so He is not ours to command. What is true is that we have all the power we need, but as I discussed before, when talking about God the Father we need to be careful about moving from the idea that "God is with us" to the idea that "God is working for us."

What does that look like in real life?

Suppose God has given a Christian man a spiritual gift of being able to prophesy. He starts off tentatively sharing what God is saying to him, humbly acknowledging that his words come from the Holy Spirit. After some success, he becomes confident and begins to share with more boldness. Then after more success, he makes a subtle transition to where he is no longer speaking God's words, but is instead assuming that when he speaks, he speaks for God. In this scenario, a man has gone from being a vessel of the Holy Spirit to being a commander of the Holy Spirit (and of course it's just a matter of time until some "prophesy" is proved false).

[13] Ed Darack. "Calamity on Mt Hood." August 2014: Air and Space Magazine. Accessed on Aug 10, 2014 at http://www.airspacemag.com/military-aviation/calamity-hogback-180952139/?no-ist

Imagine another scenario: Suppose last year a Christian woman started a student ministry that absolutely took off. She used a particular curriculum and style and format, and it exploded. So she does it again this year, but it flops. What's going on? Perhaps last year, the Holy Spirit was prompting her to use what worked for last year, and this year He is prompting her to use something totally different. However, she thinks last year's success was due to the Holy Spirit's response to her good choices rather than her response to the Holy Spirit, and so she doesn't stop to ask Him what to do this year. She is unwittingly trying to command God's power, instead of inviting the Holy Spirit to take her where He intends to move in power.

These examples demonstrate that we cannot fall into the trap of believing that the Holy Spirit is ours to employ, and this truth is critical for two reasons. The first reason is that many people in the church don't really believe in the Holy Spirit's present, supernatural power because they don't see Him do what they want when they want it. They might say something like "God, heal my son" and when healing doesn't come, they unintentionally internalize the idea that God doesn't really heal. The truth is that God does heal supernaturally (there are countless examples), but He does so in His time and His place, not ours. Why didn't He heal when I asked? I don't know. But that doesn't change the fact that God can heal people supernaturally and at times He does heal people supernaturally.

The second reason we must understand that the Holy Spirit is not ours to command is so that we don't adopt a wrong notion that *we* are the key determinants of God's power. Such a notion leads inevitably to a doctrine of works. Continuing the above example, suppose my son is not healed when I ask for his healing. Some will teach that this is "because I didn't have enough faith." Translation: I need to be a better believer so that God will approve of my request. Others will teach that my son was not healed "because I didn't pray in the right way or often enough or with fasting." Translation: I need to be a better believer so that God will approve of my request. While it is true that unrepentant sin can come between God and me and make my prayers ineffective[lxxxix], this is not the same as saying "if God doesn't do what I say, I must be in unrepentant sin."[xc] Likewise, it is true that a lack of faith can cause God to withhold His power,[xci] but this is not the same as saying "if God withholds his power, it's because of my lack of faith."

God does what He wants, when He wants, and He invites us to be a part of that and to be vessels through which He blesses the world. But He does *not* invite us to be His boss.

Believe that the Holy Spirit can and does move with power in our lives, but don't forget that our plans are not His plans (His are so much better) and that He is not ours to command. When we call on Him for help, He is always there. When we call on Him for help, He responds in love. The way in which He responds is not always what we are looking for, but He will always respond with what we need.

We must have the right expectations of the Holy Spirit; He is the power to win our spiritual battles. We must also have right expectations of our fellow soldiers, because we rarely fight our battles alone. But what should we expect of our fellow soldiers?

## Our Fellow Soldiers

I knew a senior Air Force officer who was on temporary duty with the Army in Afghanistan. A highly experienced Electronic Warfare Officer trained to employ high-tech equipment on airplanes, this man was attached to Army ground convoys to assist them with electronic jamming of Improvised Explosive Devices. He helped the soldiers he was with to understand the theory and practical application of using advanced electronic equipment to prevent friendly deaths caused by roadside bombs. One day his unit stopped and was clearing an enemy weapons cache that had been discovered. Being an Air Force guy, he wasn't really familiar with the items that were found in the cache, but wanting to be helpful, he helped load the captured equipment on the back of a truck. As he was placing some odd-shaped metal objects in the truck, a Sergeant yelled abruptly at him, "SIR! DON'T STACK THE LAND MINES!"

Wouldn't you think that a highly trained, college educated, combat seasoned senior officer would know better? Out of ignorance, a good officer doing his best to help made what could have been a big mistake. We see the same kind of thing in all aspects of our lives, and working with other Christians is no different. "Nice" guys are sometimes jerks. "Competent" pastors sometimes make huge mistakes. "Great" teachers occasionally lose their way and teach things that are wrong. "Caring" ladies at times will say the most offensive things. This is the reality in which we live and work, and this is the reality that we contribute our own shortcomings to. So what should we do about it?

What do most people do about their odd-ball younger brothers, their crazy aunts, and their goofy parents? They deal with them as they are. When our family has problems and shortcomings, we work through them. There are, of course, cases where families tear apart, but most of us just enjoy the good stuff and put up with the bad stuff. Why do we do that? We do it because we don't consider *not doing it* an option. We're stuck with them, and they are stuck with us.

We should have the same view about our community of believers. Like soldiers in a platoon, we don't get to choose whom we share our foxhole with—we must do our best to make things work. And like a platoon, we will quickly find that together we can win far more fights, both individual skirmishes and collective battles, than we ever could alone.

Truthfully, one of the big things that influence our perspective of our fellow Christian soldiers is whether we believe we are at war. In peacetime, folks get flighty and go their own way because they don't have to put up with their fellow soldiers. They can be self-centered with no real consequence. But I've seen more than once that when troops are put in a place where the going is hard and they face a determined enemy, people naturally close ranks and come together because each man knows that he needs his brothers.

Your fellow Christian soldiers are just like you. They aren't Biblical supermen or superwomen. Some are tall, broad, muscle-bound and square-jawed, but many are short and dumpy. Some stutter. Some are blonde and stunning, others are gray haired and unimpressive. Some fellow soldiers aren't real bright, and others have accents or personality quirks or idiosyncrasies. However, they are all part of the good-guy team, and they are doing their best to do what they can to win the battle, just like you are.

Somehow it's easy to get captured by the lie that Christians are supposed to be perfect (or nearly so), supremely competent, and unflappable. I'm none of those. Neither are you. Why do we expect others to be any different? What makes a Christian soldier a Christian soldier is his or her commitment to the cause of Christ.

As I've noted above, there are a tremendous number of people out there who call themselves Christians but aren't really following Christ. They are fake Christians, and they make it hard to figure out what to expect from the true soldiers. It's not that our job is to ferret out the "true believers," but in Christian Combat, it is critically helpful to know what to expect from our fellow combatants. Here are some key points to help you have right expectations so that you don't buy into the enemy's lie when he says, "You are alone in this fight."

**1) Your fellow soldiers are imperfect, just like you.** I have a very good friend who crashed a helicopter in Afghanistan. It wasn't due to hostile fire—it was due to pilot error made in some very difficult flight conditions. Fortunately no one was killed in the crash, but he wrecked a $20 million helicopter. Is he a bad pilot? No. He's a better pilot than I am, but he's a human pilot. But for God's grace, I would also have at least one crash in my 22 year flying history. I can think of several instances where Providence rather than my own good piloting skills resulted in me returning to a safe landing.

All people make mistakes, and it is absolutely essential that we remember this as we interact with our fellow Christian soldiers. Sometimes "good people" make selfish decisions. Sometimes "good people" make bad choices out of ignorance. Sometimes the best effort of "good people" is just not good enough. Those are the facts of life in a fallen world.

I have watched pastors make stupid decisions or succumb to pride or misprioritize important things. I've listened to my fellow Christian friends rail at God during tough life circumstances. I've seen well-intentioned people try to teach a Bible lesson and in so doing create a new standard for ultra-boredom. Situations like these are all just part of life and can be very frustrating. However, I've found that my frustration dims considerably when I remember that, as a Christian disciple, I have: 1) made stupid decisions, 2) succumbed to pride, 3) misprioritized, 4) fussed at God, 5) taught boring lessons, etc., etc., etc.

The early church is filled with examples of disciples showing their human side. The apostle Paul admitted to his shortcomings[xcii]. Peter, the one on whom the church was built, had to be corrected about legalism[xciii]. Barnabas and Paul went separate ways over an argument about a companion[xciv].

The point here is that you don't expect perfection from yourself, so don't expect it from anyone else. Know that in combat people are going to goof up, sometimes with pretty significant consequences. Thank God that He is in charge of everything and that there is nothing we can mess up badly enough that He can't fix it.

I once spoke with a lady in our church who called the pastor a "teacher of false doctrine" because he made one comment in one sermon that could be taken to mean that the Bible was fallible. This woman was correct in her statement about what the pastor said: his statement could be interpreted that way – he had made a mistake in choosing his words carefully. However, it was just a mistake. The pastor didn't believe the Bible was fallible, and he certainly didn't intend to teach that. However, this poor woman wouldn't allow the pastor to be human.

All of God's soldiers make mistakes. We should expect it. Knowing that He is in control, we can deal with the setbacks of our fellow soldiers, and we can do all things without arguing and complaining[xcv], in all things striving to build others up[xcvi].

**2) You are surrounded by new recruits, seasoned veterans, and everything in between.** The most dangerous and challenging rescue mission I ever flew was a rescue attempt on a moonless night in rainy weather in Afghanistan. We took off from our base and flew over the local town. The town's sparse electrical lights gave just enough illumination for our night vision goggles to allow us to see well enough to fly. However, as soon as we flew away from the town, we found ourselves in inky-black nothingness, unable to clearly differentiate the ground or mountains from the night sky. I was in command of the mission, so I ordered our formation to turn around and go back to base—there was just no way to get to our objective without crashing into the side of a mountain. On that mission, my copilot was navigating—he was young and on his first deployment. My formation had a mix of seasoned flyers and rookies. If we had had a formation full of ultra-experienced aircrew, maybe (and just maybe) we could have made it, but the reality was that we were not all supermen and so we had to deal with the situation in light of that fact. We didn't accomplish the rescue that day, but 12 brave airmen lived to fly many more rescue missions.

It is imperative that we are cognizant not only of our human propensity to make mistakes, but also of our differing levels of ability. We should recognize both the strengths and weaknesses of those around us. In Christian combat, we need to be sensitive to the abilities of those around us so that we have reasonable expectations.

Have you ever been in one of those conversations or lectures where someone says something like "and of course we all know the lesson of Balaam . . . "? If you are like me, you might go, "Who the heck is Balaam, and how do you even spell that?" The point is not that the story of Balaam is irrelevant; the point is that we need to be careful about assuming that others know our point of reference. Sometimes we get frustrated with our fellow Christians when they won't help us "take the hill," not realizing that they don't even see the hill. I've known some absolutely devoted and on-fire new Christians who have very limited Biblical knowledge.

When God calls us to combat, we might need to spend a lot of time preparing and encouraging the spiritually young. We might need to pursue wisdom from the seasoned veterans. Having right expectations about our fellow soldiers helps us understand how we can best encourage each other and employ each other's strengths in complementary ways.

**3) Cooks are not nurses, and nurses are not snipers.** One of my deployments was to a NATO airfield which had very limited facilities. We had about 200 people of all ranks and job specialties at this base. Several times, the most sought after and important person on the base was a very young officer. Why? Because he was in charge of "comm"—our communications. Without him and his people maintaining our satellite communications, we had no phones, no internet, no radios. Despite having a few hundred million dollars worth of aircraft on our ramp, with no comm we were essentially dead in the water. That young lieutenant was not better than the others at our camp; he was just special. In his or her own way, so was just about everyone else. All of the parts of our organization had to function mutually for us to be combat-effective. The same goes for God's people. No one of us is irreplaceable, but to be combat effective we all need to work together with our special functions and abilities.

Our churches are filled with dysfunction caused by the "everyone ought to be like me" mentality. The evangelist wants everyone to be fired up about going to the street corner every week to talk to strangers about Christ. The musician can't understand why everyone doesn't want 45 minutes of worship each Sunday. The older lady can't stand that the youngsters like Christian rap music. The men don't see why it is so important to spend so much money on decorations for the church.

God uses all of us for various different functions at various different times, and He uses us together to carry out His plans. We don't need a church full of administrators or of pastors or of musicians or of teachers. We need communities that have all of these gifts.

So what is the practical combat application of this point? Suppose Bob believes he has a calling from God to evangelize at the local college, so he goes to Sue and says, "Let's go do this." Now Sue is an introvert, and open-air evangelism is as scary to her as fire is to a scarecrow. Satan knows this and so he encourages Bob to push Sue to get on board with this great idea, and he encourages Sue to start avoiding Bob. Pretty soon, both Sue and Bob are angry, nothing gets done, and Satan has won that battle.

But what if Bob had been paying attention to Sue's strengths and said, "Can you pray for me while I do this?" Maybe Sue would say, "Yes, absolutely. By the way, do you know Steve? He has a heart for evangelism like you do. Maybe he could help." Chock one up in the win column for God's people.

Know your fellow soldiers. God put them with you for a good reason, and it probably wasn't so that they could be just like you.

**4) Good soldiers argue.** In an Air Force unit, the First Sergeant is the commander's right-hand man. When I was in command of an Air Force squadron, I had a First Sergeant that I respected and valued tremendously. One of the things that I valued the most was the fact that he would come into my office, close the door, and tell me why I was wrong about a decision I'd made (or was about to make). Sometimes he'd tell me so forcefully that it would hurt my pride a bit (not that that's hard to do). I'd find myself thinking, "Hey. Wait a minute. I'm the boss!" But my First Sergeant would always respectfully but forcefully let me know if he thought I was making a mistake. Sometimes he was wrong and sometimes he was right, but he'd always let me know if he felt strongly about something. Once I'd heard him out and made a final decision, we would open the door and, whether he agreed with me or not, he would back me up 100%.

Dissention and contention are a tremendous asset to decision making. Healthy argument is something I wish I saw a little more of in my military career, and it's something I wish I'd see a lot more of in the Christian community. Unfortunately, Satan's been pretty successful in convincing us that a wussified version of love is what Christ promoted. We often feel like we should be "nice" in church rather than "good." "Nice" is for politicians and strangers. We brothers and sisters must strive to be good. This means we often should say something, albeit lovingly, when we disagree.

I was once participating in a strategic planning retreat as part of a board of church elders. We spent a good part of our weekend being nice and generally agreeing on things, and then something happened. One of the elders said "we have to stop ignoring the elephant in the room," and we started to uncover the sharp edges of disagreement. Some of us voiced concerns that we were not functioning well. Some voiced concerns over our relationship with the senior pastor. The discussion got mildly heated, went very deep, and before the weekend was over we were a closer board with a better relationship with our senior pastor and a better course for our future.

Every Christian organization I've ever been part of has exhibited various levels of incompetence. The same is true of every secular organization I've ever been part of. At times, I've been a big part of that incompetence. The question is not whether we will encounter incompetence and dysfunction. The question is what we will do about it. Sometimes we have to let minor things ride as we prioritize relationships over performance; this is love. But often we have to confront even minor things as we realize that the deepest relationships are honest and not just surface-nice. This also is love.

It is with God's grace and the Holy Spirit's wisdom that we can discern when it's time to "speak the truth in love" and when it's time to remain silent. However, don't be one of those soldiers who thinks that being agreeable is the essence of Christian love. This fight we're in is important—important enough to get passionate about. If something is messed up, speak up. If someone is wrong, let them know. If someone tells you that you are wrong, listen and pray and judge whether they are right. Just be careful to do everything in love; not squishy-pop-culture-love but Jesus' love.

**5) Some of the soldiers in your unit are most likely spies.**
On November 5, 2009, US Army Major Nidal Hasan concealed a pistol, drove on to Fort Hood in Texas, walked into a deployment processing center full of his fellow soldiers, shouted "Allahu Akbar," and opened fire. Thirteen GIs died that day at his hands and 30 were wounded.[14] Hasan was a traitor wearing the US Army uniform; acting like one of the good guys but working for the enemy. A sadly ironic fact is that members of the military in the US are not allowed to carry weapons on base unless they are specifically designated as military police or in active combat training. Properly certified soldiers could be armed to protect themselves at Walmart but would literally have to stop by home to drop off their weapon before coming on base. Hasan knew that all of his victims would be defenseless, and they were so because the US Army refuses to acknowledge that the enemy is in its midst.

Sometimes it seems easier to deny that the enemy is with us. We can be happier in the short term if we keep our head buried in the sand and pretend that our world is just full of friends, roses, and blue skies. However, that's a fool's gambit. As the Army found out at Fort Hood, and as we are likely to find out in Christian combat, if you pretend like there is no enemy, he kicks your tail when he shows up and finds you are unprepared.

The enemy is in our midst. Some of the most famous pastors in the US are working for the enemy. Some of the folks at your church are most likely working for the enemy. Some of your friends and family may be working for the enemy.

Don't believe me? That's OK. Believe God. This is what He tells us in the Bible:

"Beware of false prophets, who come to you in sheep's clothing, but inwardly are ravenous wolves."[xcvii]

"For false christs and false prophets will arise and perform great signs and wonders, so as to lead astray, if possible, even the elect."[xcviii]

"I know that after my departure fierce wolves will come in among you, not sparing the flock; and from among your own

---

14 "Soldier Opens Fire At Ft Hood; 13 Dead," CBS News, November 5, 2009, 3: 33 PM; accessed 4 Jan 14 at http://www.cbsnews.com/news/soldier-opens-fire-at-ft-hood-13-dead/

selves will arise men speaking twisted things to draw away the disciples after them. Therefore be alert!"[xcix]

"Some false believers had infiltrated our ranks to spy on the freedom we have in Christ"[c]

" . . . There will be false teachers among you, who will secretly bring in destructive heresies, even denying the Master who bought them, bringing upon themselves swift destruction."[ci]

"For certain people have crept in unnoticed who long ago were designated for this condemnation, ungodly people, who pervert the grace of our God into sensuality and deny our only Master and Lord, Jesus Christ."[cii]

So does this mean that we are supposed to treat everyone with suspicion and distrust? Not at all. We have two truths that can keep us from being manically distrustful: First, God is in charge, and He is big enough to protect us even when "wolves" slip in. Second, Christ tells us that we can know those who are subversives by the "fruit" that they produce. In other words, if you see someone in your faith community that acts like a cheeseball used-car salesman, pay attention. Maybe he's just one of those frustratingly overly-positive guys, or maybe he's a spy. If your pastor seems like he just uses every Bible verse as a justification to talk about what he wants to talk about, pay attention. He may be a really poor preacher, or he may be a spy. The difference between a "faithful Christian with issues" and a "spy" is seen in the fruit they produce.

The European Spindle is a plant with a brightly colored fruit that looks inviting to eat. However, the fruit is laden with poison that can cause liver or kidney damage or even death. That's a bad fruit. If you've never seen a European Spindle and you are hungry, you might eat one to see how it tastes. That would be a bad day for you. However, if someone teaches you what it looks like and warns you that it's poisonous, it poses no threat because you know what "bad fruit" looks like.

So what does "bad fruit" in the church look like? What would help identify wolves-in-sheep's clothing, a.k.a. the traitors-in-our-midst, a.k.a. spies? God has given us His word, the Bible, so that we have a standard by which to judge. This is another example of why it is imperative for us to know and search out the Bible. Like a book that shows you a picture of a European Spindle, the Bible points out "bad fruit." Additionally, the Holy Spirit points out bad fruit to us. So once again it is important for us to be in prayer so that we are aware when God is trying to tell us something.

A very well known Christian pastor was pressed on national television to answer the question "Do you have to believe in Christ to be saved?" and he would not.[15] He just kept dodging the question. That's bad fruit right there. There's always the chance that the man fell short under the pressures of the moment, but the consistency with which he dodged means it's most likely that he is a spy hijacking Christianity to his own ends.

I know a woman whose husband was teaching a class at church while secretly having his second affair. That husband was a spy.

Another friend witnessed a woman move to another state, ditch her husband for selfish reasons, and then start an intimate non-marital relationship with another man while once again participating in a church community. The leadership at her church refused to confront the woman's sin and simply welcomed her back. Those leaders are growing bad fruit.

So when is "bad fruit" a mistake born of our sinful nature or an indication of treasonous Christianity? I think it has to do with the consistency of the fruit. I grew up in California and we had a lot of plum trees in our yard. Most of the plums were delicious, but every once in a while, I would pick a fresh plum and find that it was diseased or rotten. It was a good plum tree, but a random bad fruit. Like those plum trees, we all produce bad fruit sometimes. The question is whether that is consistent or an anomaly. In the examples I gave above, consistent denial that "Jesus is the way," unrepentant cheating on your wife, or consistent refusal to call bad conduct "bad conduct" are all indications of trees that are producing bad fruit. There we will find the spies among us.

However, even if you are pretty good at identifying spies, my experience has been that you will still have times when they sneak in and do damage. Expect it. Don't let it destroy your unit when a spy rears her or his ugly head—stay in the battle. Don't say, "Just look at what that church-guy over there just did. The whole church is worthless." One of the ploys of both human spies and Satan himself is to use the acts of one or two traitors to destroy trust, confidence, and cohesiveness between our fellow soldiers and us.

[15] "Osteen denies Christ on national TV," Steve Lumbley, accessed on Jan 6, 2014 at http://www.apostasywatch.com/Wolves/WolfReports/JoelOsteen/OsteendeniesChristonnationalTV/tabid/169/Default.aspx

Spies are a fact of life. Jesus said so. Watch out for them and be prepared for them. When they show up, deal with them. When they do damage, don't let them win by tearing apart your fighting unit's trust.

Fighting as a unit is what Christian Combat is all about. We need to have right expectations about our Commander in Chief, our Platoon Leader, our Air Support and our fellow soldiers. If we don't, we'll end up fighting alone or not fighting at all, and if we do, we'll be equipped to take the fight to the enemy and to bless those around us.

Knowing your own army is just part of being prepared for battle. We also need to know what going to war is like. If we have wrong expectations of what it looks like to be at war, it can set us up to be unprepared for the enemy or discouraged by what we see. And we don't just need to know what to expect in direct combat, we also need to know what to expect when we are getting to the fight. So what does it look like to be at the war, but not yet on the battlefield? Read on to find out.

DAN MARUYAMA

## 3-2. EXPECTATIONS FOR LIFE IN GARRISON

I can remember my first time in a combat theater. I didn't know what to expect and so everything seemed new and different. I found myself on a main operating base, "in garrison" meaning at home base and not at the front, with no direct combat exposure other than an occasional poorly-aimed mortar attack on the base. When you are in that sort of situation, it's easy to lose focus on what's important for combat operations and to focus on less important things. I can remember one situation where my boss said something to the effect of "Your guys did a great job on that combat mission last night, but let's talk about how they were out of uniform when they were in the dining hall." My boss had fallen into the "garrison mentality"—focusing on not-so-important things and losing focus on combat operations.

I constantly struggle against an in-garrison Christian mentality. I find myself focused on the non-essentials: my next big firearm purchase, a movie I want to see, something great for dinner, conserving my money, our next family vacation, and so on. None of these are bad, but they are not the most important things. In a combat theater, our time in garrison is best spent on one thing: preparing for battle.

When we're not fighting with the enemy, we need to be preparing for the next engagement. As a Christian, sometimes this means developing a "battle-rhythm"—that is, ordering your life to be prepared for combat. At times this means collecting intelligence so I'm prepared for the next battle. Sometimes this means taking the time to relax and recharge my batteries so I'm equipped emotionally and physically for conflict, but always my perspective should be that I am in a war and so I should be preparing for combat.

### Developing a Battle Rhythm

In the military we use a term "battle rhythm" to discuss the general flow of day to day events. A combat battle rhythm might be "on duty at 0500, situation brief at 0600, mission preparation at 0630," and so on. The battle rhythm can change at any time based on the enemy's actions or on changing conditions, but we usually try to establish some sort of routine so that we are ready for the next mission.

Christian living is the same way. While at war, we do well if we establish a battle rhythm. Like soldiers, we find that our battle rhythm changes depending on our situation. What is your battle rhythm? Many of us don't have a battle rhythm. We have a battle spasm: when we get the urge, we spasm into action for God. When the urge is past, we go back to living life our own way. Looking at our Master and at the historical Christian masters, we see that a great case is made for living according to a battle rhythm.

In the Bible we see in Jesus' life a habit of taking time to go off to pray to God[ciii], and he explicitly instructs us to do so.[civ] Do you have such a habit? I have consistently found that things go better in my own life when I regularly make time to deliberately pray to God. It makes sense, doesn't it? If Jesus is my Lord, I ought to acknowledge that daily. If God is with us, shouldn't we spend time talking with Him? My experience is that it's a best practice to do that first thing in the morning so that you start your day with God. There are a thousand books on ways to spend "quiet time" or "devotional time" with God, but here's the key point: we need to do it. That's an essential part of our battle rhythm.

Jesus also went to the synagogues and the Temple. He met regularly with his disciples. He lived in community with people and the Bible says clearly that we should do the same. Do you? Is going to church a once-in-a-while event or is it an intentional part of your battle rhythm?[16] I used to go to church out of duty or out of self-centeredness. My question was "what am I going to get out of today's service?" But I've found that, while that might be a valid question, it is not the driving question. I go to church because it's part of my battle rhythm. It's an opportunity to fellowship, to worship, to focus on God, to serve, and to learn. Soldiers at war typically have a "standup" or "roll call" to check in, check up, share info, and make sure everyone is ready for battle. Our participation in our faith community is the same way. It's an absolutely essential part of our battle rhythm.

## Collecting Intel

The modern military uses an amazing integration of technologies — unmanned flying vehicles with cameras,

---

[16] The phrase "going to church" means a different things to different people – here I mean "participating in a community of believers."

planes/boats/submarines/satellites with electronic detecting equipment, interconnected computer networks, highly trained analysts – to develop a clear picture of the battlefield. Before a convoy leaves a base or an aircraft ever takes off, the soldiers and airmen executing the mission have usually taken time to get a picture of the threat and the situation. Although these new technologies have revolutionized the way we execute a war, they are just new ways of applying the age-old principles of knowing the disposition of the enemy and adapting to the situation.

When you are in combat, your motivation to assess the situation is obvious: failing to do so may result in disaster. If we Christians want to be ready for spiritual battle, we need to assess our situation as well.

In chapter one I talked about knowing who the enemy is. Here we will look a little more specifically at what the enemy is doing. What is the enemy doing around your life, right now? The Bible says he is prowling around like a lion, looking to devour someone. Do you know where he is? We frequently don't take the time to think about such things.

Right now, in my life, Satan has taken most of the folks I work with captive with false ideas. He has distracted many of my Christian friends with things that are absolutely meaningless. He is tempting me with crap on the Internet, with treating guns as idols, and with a desire for a life of ease. He is trying to convince my kids that their lives are about fulfilling their desires. He has quite successfully taken over the standard of morality in the public schools in my neighborhood. When I finish typing these sentences and walk out to talk to my peers, he will be trying to convince me that this is no place for a spiritual discussion.

Do you collect intel, or do you just wait until you (or your loved ones) are under attack and then go "there he is, that old devil!" How often do you take the time to assess the situation you are in? What is the spiritual terrain? Is there someone close to you that needs to hear the gospel? Is there someone in your life that you might be able to help if you share or show the truth? Should you be studying about Jehovah's Witnesses so that you can help your next-door neighbor break free from a cult? Should you be changing churches because your current pastor has decided to add to the gospel things that are not true? Are your kids surrounded by music, media, and friends that are opposed to Christ? Are you regularly putting yourself in a position that makes you an easy mark for the deceiver? We must take the time to assess our situation so we are ready when God calls us to put on our body armor and engage in combat.

Don't just take time to observe the enemy. "Collecting intel" means looking at what you and your fellow soldiers are doing as well. Do you ever take stock of what positive impact you've had on the people in your life? Do you pause to consider how awesome it was when you followed God last week or last month or last year? Do you ever make an assessment of all the things that He is doing in your life? Collecting intel in this way can be a great encouragement and reminder to you of the tactics that are working on the spiritual battlefield.

Let me take time to give some really specific examples of what I mean when I say "collect intel." Assessing your situation is not just taking five minutes to think about things and then going back to watching *American Idol.* Assessing your situation means you aggressively gather information to find out where the enemy is working and where God is working.

I know a man who was living an extremely successful Air Force career. He was a squadron commander, a Lieutenant Colonel, and was making a name for himself. Suddenly and with very little warning, he put in for retirement and within a few months he was out of the military. What happened? His teenage daughter was in a bad spot. Although I don't know the specifics, I do know that she was on a destructive path. The enemy had her in his sights and was using his tricks to take her down. Her father saw this, he realized where the enemy was, and he aggressively (and at some personal cost) pivoted his entire life to be in a position to fight the enemy.

Contrast him with a Christian woman I met some years ago. As a young lady and pastor's daughter, she had heard the gospel all her life. Yet in high school she fell prey to the iconic "cheerleader" temptations—gossip, obsessing over looks, flirting with all the boys. This led to more: drugs, sex, more obsession, and more lies. She became a pastor's wife, had kids, led Bible studies, drank alcohol and did drugs until finally one day her life exploded. I met her in a rehab clinic. What would have happened if, as a young teen, she had taken a hard look at where the spiritual fight was coming?

Collect intel. It's a lot easier to defeat the enemy when you know where he is, when you know what he's up to, when you know where friendly forces are, and when you can come at the devil with a can full of smackdown. No one in combat wants a fair fight—you always want to engage the enemy with overwhelming force. It's hard to do that if you get caught in a surprise attack.

Collecting intel is important, just as developing a battle rhythm is important. Yet even life during wartime is not all about constant work. In between skirmishes, there is a lot of downtime. Is it okay to use some of that just "for fun?" You'll find that in the next section, and the Bible's answer might surprise you.

## R&R

During World War II, over 500,000 soldiers were removed from the battlefield due to combat fatigue. After killing and seeing friends killed, living for days at an extremely high stress level, and encountering numerous situations where continued life was uncertain, these heroic warriors had to be pulled back from the front to rest, get perspective, and recharge.

The military talks about "R&R"—Rest and Relaxation, and acknowledges that it is essential to success in long-term combat. Hear that now: R&R is not just "fun time." It is an absolutely critical part of being a warrior. Part of the traditional military battle-rhythm is ensuring that there is time for R&R so that personnel are as prepared as they can be to endure the rigors of combat when it's time to fight. Studies have shown that fatigue can be as physiologically impairing as being drunk,[17] and continued sleep deprivation is a strong contributor to physical and mental health problems[18].

R&R is no less important in Christian combat. In fact, God commanded R&R in what we've come to know as the Sabbath—the day of rest that is captured in the 4th commandment. A more detailed study of the Bible reveals other rest and relaxation commands: the Feast of Trumpets[cv], the Day of Atonement[cvi], the Festival of Tabernacles[cvii], the Sabbath year[cviii], and Christ's encouragement for people to come and receive rest in him.[cix]

---

[17] Shives, Lisa, M.D. *Driving drowsy as dangerous as driving drunk, studies show*, Nov 9, 2011. http://thechart.blogs.cnn.com/2011/11/09/driving-drowsy-as-dangerous-as-driving-drunk-studies-show/. Accessed 14 Nov 13.
[18] Peri, Camille. *Coping with Excessive Sleepiness.* http://www.webmd.com/sleep-disorders/excessive-sleepiness-10/10-results-sleep-loss. Accessed 14 Nov 13.

Yet rest and relaxation are almost anathema to contemporary Christian living. Without getting into arguments about "how" or "on what day," it is true that very few of us "honor the Sabbath and keep it holy" (other than perhaps by making it more busy with "church activities"). In fact, many of us regard nearly all rest as sloth or laziness. Added to this, elements of the church have successfully branded "fun" as a non-Christian activity, and the resultant cultural image (albeit bolstered in part by the devil's deceits) is that Christians don't know how to rest and relax.

So what does R&R look like for the Christian soldier? Rest doesn't happen naturally in our microwave-oven fast-food cell-phone society. We must be very intentional about rest, and I have three suggestions for doing so.

1) For starters, why not try obeying the 4th commandment: "Remember the Sabbath day, to keep it holy" —not as a means to salvation but as a way to experience God's greatest blessings. When we structure a whole day each week toward resting in God, we automatically do two things. First, we make our week's schedule revolve around Him—it is always good when we place God at the center of our life. Second, by setting a whole day of the week aside, we are forced into a dependent-on-God attitude. When everyone else around us is taking 7 days to get life's business done and we only take 6, we are automatically pushed into an attitude that says: "Okay Lord. I need you to take care of me because I'm trusting that I can rest in You one day each week." My experience over and over has been that following the Sabbath commandment is a tremendous blessing, not a burden.

Now don't go getting legalistic on me. I'm writing this on a Monday, and yesterday was my normal day to rest. However, due to a church potluck, an imposed meeting with someone about a business concern, an evening interfaith event, and an invitation to come over to a friend's house, life's circumstances combined yesterday to minimize the opportunities to rest and relax. Could I have been more intentional about resting yesterday? Perhaps, but it seemed to me that the things God put in my life yesterday were less my choices and more obligations or opportunities for good. My wife and I will frequently decline invitations to go out and eat on Sunday out of deference to God's Sabbath commandment, but at times we accept because it seems that there is an important opportunity or relationship that we shouldn't miss. My point in bringing this up is to reinforce the idea that observing a Sabbath rest is a means of living for God, not of observing a rule. We live under grace and not the law of the Sabbath. [cx] I believe that God is okay with the fact that yesterday was a little busier than normal, but I wouldn't be surprised if this week is just a little bit harder physically, emotionally, and spiritually since I didn't recharge much this Sunday.

2) A second way to be intentional about rest is to sleep. That probably sounds kind of stupid, but the truth is that sometime around the time that our mom and dad stop saying "go to bed," many of us adopt an attitude that sleep is what we have to do when we can't stay awake any longer. Televisions, computers, light bulbs, and caffeine make it easier and easier to completely disregard normal sleep patterns; but what if your attitude was, "I need to sleep so that I'm fresh for tomorrow's work"? I wonder how many times I've missed or failed in one of God's appointments because I was so sleepy that I had neither the perception nor the energy to engage in someone else's salvation or personal need. Athletes typically go to bed on time before a big game. The Air Force has regulations that require pilots to get a minimum amount of sleep before flying. People will often be deliberate about sleeping before a job interview or an important test. They do this because they want to be ready for the big event. What is your big event tomorrow? Will you be ready for it, or are you going to spend another hour on Facebook before you turn in tonight?

3) A third way to be intentional about rest is to limit your and your family's activities: after-school sports, work, shopping, haircuts, visits with family, Sunday school, small group gatherings, church meetings, time with friends, birthday parties, hobbies, lawn care, cleaning the house, laundry, dining, hunting, football games. None of these things are bad. Some are really good. But, they all take time. Are you tempted, like me, to run around like a frantic frog and get everything done? If you do, you'll find (as I have) that the exciting things become less good and the chores become a drag. We enter that season-less world where everything is blandly busy, and our spiritual and personal relationships suffer. More importantly, we find we don't have time to rest in God—to

prepare for the next battle. It's okay to say no to Mom if she asks you to visit, to the pastor if he asks you to be part of another church thing, to your spouse when they want to go out to eat, and to your kids when they want to go to Johnny's house—even if the only reason is "because I don't want us to be too busy." Is sloth and laziness a danger? Yes—the Bible tells us so.[cxi] But laziness is no more a danger than busyness. Both sins ignore that we are supposed to do exactly what God says (whether it is "Don't just sit there, do something" or "Don't just do something, sit there").[19] Be intentional about your rest so that God can remain the center of your intention.

Rest and relaxation are essential. God modeled it on the seventh day of creation, and we need to be intentional to follow His model. If we aren't, we might find ourselves ill equipped to fight in the next battle that He calls us to join.

Developing a battle rhythm, collecting intel, and taking time to R&R are all things a Christian warrior needs to keep in mind when waiting for the next battle. However, war is not all about being in garrison. Sometimes we foray out to find the enemy, and so we need to have right expectations about life in the field.

---

[19] Thank you to Dr. Blackaby and his insightful sharing of these phrases in the study "*Experiencing God*."

## 3-3. EXPECTATIONS FOR LIFE IN THE FIELD

Soldiers like baby wipes. That seems kind of incongruous, doesn't it? When you are "in the field" (away from a safe, built-up base), you don't have ready access to showers, toilets, and the like. If you want to keep some modicum of sanitation (or at least want to keep the enemy from smelling your approach), you can use those disposable, pre-moistened towels we call "baby wipes" to clean up. It's not a shower, but it's better than nothing.

That's life in the field: You are in hostile territory, on the move, and away from the comforts of home. If you go into the field expecting showers, you are at the very least going to be disappointed, and at the very worst are going to do things that make you vulnerable to enemy attack. Soldiers have to go into the field with right expectations.

Christian soldiers have to do the same, but it's more challenging to tell when I am "in the field" as a Christian soldier. Our world of Christian combat is defined on spiritual lines that can't always be seen. However, even though the lines may be blurry, it is still helpful to know what to expect when we find ourselves in the field but not yet engaged in direct combat.

### Ruck Marches

Before Marine recruits can graduate from basic training at the Marine Corps Recruiting Depot in San Diego, they have to complete "the Reaper." This challenging task involves hiking up a 9.7-mile long hill with a 70-pound pack on your back. Even though the task never involves actual fighting, it is physically and mentally exhausting. The Marines know that it is not only valuable to conquer a physical challenge; they also know that getting to the battle at the right time is sometimes more important than how you fight. This event is what the military calls a "ruck march"—hiking with a heavy pack ("a ruck") on your back to get to battle.

Unlike in the movies, soldiers don't just show up on the battlefield. A lot of time has to be spent getting to the place of combat. Ruck marches are not exciting. They are not glorious. They are not usually particularly fun. Could you imagine a four hour Hollywood movie that had 3 hours and 45 minutes of hiking down a road followed by 15 minutes of an actual combat sequence? That wouldn't exactly be a blockbuster. It's easy to get discouraged or diverted during the times of marching to battle, but if you never get to the battlefield, you'll never win the battle. For the Christian soldier, it is important to remember that getting to the battle is as important as engaging the enemy. Our ruck march is what gets us to battle at the time and place of God's choosing.

In the Bible, the story of Joseph (Genesis 37-50) is fascinating. Most of Joseph's life is his "ruck march." He goes from being sold into slavery, to being cast into prison, to being put in charge of a kingdom, but still not fulfilling his ultimate destiny. All of this happened to put him a place to fulfill the purpose that God had for him—to save his family from famine.[cxii] How easy it would have been for Joseph in slavery or in prison to say, "I give up!" We may be tempted in the same way.

You might ask, "Why am I still in this stupid job?" Perhaps God will have you in that "stupid job" for another 5 years so that you can meet and minister to one lost soul who doesn't know Christ. Is that okay? Are you willing to keep up the ruck march? I watched my friend Pete faithfully labor through an unsatisfying job as a Junior ROTC Instructor for several years, until just the right time when God molded both Pete's heart and his circumstances to make that job into what he considers the best job he's ever had—and one in which he has a daily positive impact on a huge number of high school students.

You might ask, "Why am I not doing something really big for the kingdom?" What if you aren't prepared yet to do something "really big" or what if the time is not yet right for someone to be helped by you? Will you keep plugging along in your anonymity and mediocrity until God gets you to His chosen field of battle? John Wesley, founder of the Methodist movement in Christianity, was willing to keep at it, and after toiling through an unfulfilling and insignificant pastoral effort in America,[20] he went back to England where God used his experiences to make him one of the two people most responsible for the 18th century Christian revival in England.[21]

---

[20] *John Wesley*, posted Aug 8, 2008.
http://www.christianitytoday.com/ch/131christians/denominationalfounders/wesley.html. Accessed Nov 18, 2013.
[21] Severance, Diane, Ph.D. *Evangelical Revival in England*.
http://www.christianity.com/church/church-history/timeline/1701-1800/evangelical-revival-in-england-11630228.html. Accessed Nov 18, 2013.

You might ask, "Why does my spouse/child/parent still not believe?" Is it possible that God is positioning you to be there at just the right time with just the right words to help your loved one come to a saving belief in Jesus Christ? Will you keep plodding along for another few decades until the time is right? I once heard a talk by a man who had been involved in the mafia and gone to prison. His mother prayed and prayed for him. It took 40 years for God to take this man to a place where he was willing to humble himself before God, but his mom's prayerful persistence paid off and she was able to see her son get right with his Savior before she passed away.

Joshua stuck it out in the wilderness for 40 years with the unbelieving Israelites, and only after that was he able to lead his people into the Promised Land. That was a long "ruck march!"

I wonder how many times souls have suffered because believing Christians wouldn't stick with God's plan and get to the battle. We may never know what victories we sacrifice when we are diverted by immediate pleasures or when we go rushing off toward what look like closer opportunities. We always want to see near-term results of our efforts. We want to be resting or we want to be in combat. It is important to remind ourselves that often success in the war depends on us staying with the march. We have to get to the battle that God has prepared us for, and it may be a long ways away. Only then will we have the opportunity to fight.

We need to understand the need to stick with our ruck march, but we also need to understand what it's like when we stop along the way. We're not always moving to the battle. Sometimes we stop and wait for the right time to continue our march or for the battle to come to us. Let's take a look at what we should expect for those times when we are living "in the field."

## Field Conditions

I slept with another man once. No, it wasn't like that. We were in survival training and were out in the mountains of Colorado trying to evade from instructors that were "the enemy." It was freezing cold, we had no shelter, and I couldn't stop shivering. So two of us crawled into one sleeping bag (back to back) until we could warm up. That was weird and uncomfortable for me, but worth it.

We were living in "field conditions" away from the comforts of a home. In America, Christians don't normally have to endure field conditions due to their faith—at least not physically. However, there are some strong spiritual parallels that are worth noting.

When you are living in field conditions, comforts are largely absent. You may not have running water. You won't have a shower. Your chow tastes marginal at best (and horrible at worst), or you might be short on rations. You might not have a bed or a roof over your head.

Although I've never been in a foxhole in combat, I would imagine that the discomfort of laying on the ground is hardly noticed when there are bullets whizzing over your head. However, when you are in field conditions, you aren't necessarily in the middle of a fight—you are just enduring discomfort as you come from, wait for, or go to battle. If you don't see the necessity of being in field conditions, when these discomforts come you'll grouse and complain to no end.

We Christians can do the same. As we wait to engage in an obvious spiritual battle, we may have to wait in discomfort. We may have to make decisions to pull ourselves out of our comfort zone with absolutely no immediate tangible result. If we fail to realize that this life in "field conditions" is necessary, then we may shirk back from the battlefield or never be where we need to be in order to return fire on the enemy.

Practically speaking, here is what this looks like: My close friends (we'll call them Bob and Sue) have some neighbors that are part of another faith, a cult actually. Bob and Sue cultivate relationships with their neighbors so that they might have an opportunity to someday share the gospel and deliver their neighbors from the deception of that cult. However, these relationships are sometimes hard in that they are awkward, they can be uncomfortable as the neighbors share about their beliefs, and they are emotionally scary. Bob and Sue are developing truly loving friendships with their neighbors, all the while realizing that those relationships may one day be destroyed if they come to a point where friendship is irreconcilable with the differences in faiths. The easy thing for my friends to do would be to just hang out with other Christians and keep their neighbors at arm's length. Fortunately, Bob and Sue have chosen to live in "field conditions" and are accepting their discomfort so they can be ready to engage the deception of the enemy.

For the Christian, "field conditions" can look like a lot of things:

• We might have reduced financial flexibility because we are using our money for God's things.

• We might have difficult relationships as God positions us to do good—with folks in the church that we don't "gel" with or, like Bob and Sue, with folks outside of the church that have oppositional beliefs.

• We might have stressed family relationships as we move to follow God's calling.

• We might have very little free time as we respond to opportunities God has presented.

• We might be ostracized from some relationships in our life because we choose to hold to God's standards.

Keep in mind that in all of these situations, we might see absolutely no fruit. When you are in field conditions on a military patrol, you might not ever engage the enemy. When you are in field conditions in spiritual battle, you might not get to see someone give their life to Christ or thank you for your caring or grow closer to God. At least you might not see that today or tomorrow or for a few years. However, what you are doing still matters, and inevitably if you stay in the field long enough, the Commander will put you in direct combat.

It's important for us to remember that service in God's army is not about body counts. It is about obedience. So when we feel like we're suffering the discomforts of the field without getting to actually engage in battle or to witness victory, we need to remember that, like soldiers, God just has us in field conditions, and He has us there because He's taking us to the place and time where He wants to use us to crush the enemy. Likewise, if we think we should go into the field but aren't sure we want to go through that discomfort since we can't see the enemy, we need to remind ourselves that the life of faith is not about our glory, it's about His.

Life in enemy territory—with its ruck marches and field conditions—can be difficult, but staying in those conditions is necessary if we want to save the lost or defend the saved. Such trials are part and parcel of being in God's army. Another thing that is inherent in being in His army is responding to orders. But what do those orders look like? Is there a difference between an "order" and a "suggestion?"

## 3-4 ORDERS

While I was commanding a rescue unit in Iraq, I received an urgent report that an Army helicopter had crashed about an hour away from us. I immediately told my crews to prepare to launch and contacted higher headquarters for clearance to send my airmen on the rescue mission. My orders were that I could only launch with headquarters' approval. Within minutes, my crews were in their aircraft, ready to launch. We talked with headquarters and waited. And waited. And talked and waited. And waited. And talked some more. And waited. Finally, headquarters tasked a different team from a different service to rescue the downed crew, about two hours after we could have done so. Frustrated, I stood our crews down, and we watched the reports from the other team as the rescue unfolded. (Fortunately, the delay did not result in any deaths in the downed crew.)

The "why's" (why did we wait, why did headquarters delay, etc.) in this story are not important to this discussion. What is important is that we had orders, and we followed them. It made total sense to immediately launch on our rescue mission, but the powers-that-be did not want us to go. The practical thing would have been to execute the rescue in contravention of orders, but the right thing was to obey. That night, with lives potentially on the line, it was hard to follow orders. Some orders are easy to follow and some aren't.

As I discussed in Part 2, following orders is fundamental to our service in the military, and it is fundamental to our service as Christians. If we don't follow orders, our missions will surely fail and the enemy will win. As we consider our Christian combat, there are four aspects of God's orders that are worth highlighting here.

### Orders are both EXPLICIT and IMPLIED

When a general tells his tank battalion commander to "take Hill 151," he is giving an explicit order. The tank commander knows that he is to take possession of the hill. However, along with that explicit instruction are countless implied orders. These are orders that go along with taking the hill, orders like "arm your tanks," "feed your men," "travel to Hill 151," "assess the enemy positions," etc.

God's orders are the same. When God says, "love your neighbor," He is giving an explicit order. Compliance is not optional. Along with that explicit order are all kinds of implied orders: "Get to know your neighbor," "learn his or her name," "be in a state of health and mind and responsibility where it is possible to love your neighbor," etc. As we go through life as Christian soldiers, we need to remember that the implied orders are just as important as the explicit ones.

Here's an example: Philippians 4:8 says, "if anything is excellent or praiseworthy, think about such things." That's an explicit order. So what is implied in that? Well one thing that's implied is "don't think about crap." Yet so many of us struggle with the idea that we should limit intake of media that is full of unhealthy content (sex, drugs, violence, language, or God-dishonoring themes), whether in movies, video games, television, or the internet. One of the reasons that we struggle so hard to be good is because we fill our minds so full of evil. Because we don't follow the implied orders, we have a very difficult time being successful in battle.

Another example: God says, "You shall not commit adultery."[cxiii] That is our explicit command, and you will find very little argument or thought within the church that "adultery is OK." But what are the implied commands? One is "Don't expose yourself to temptations," but how many Christian men and women are happy to put themselves, without second thought, in situations (one-on-one business lunches, private meetings, flirtatious conversations) that expose themselves? Another implied command is "love your spouse well enough that they don't want to seek love in an adulterous relationship," but many Christian women regularly ignore the sexual desires of their husbands and many Christian men regularly ignore the emotional desires of their wives. There is no explicit order from God that says, "have sex this often" or "tell your wife you love her this many times a day" but both of those orders are certainly implied.

It is a form of legalism to only focus on God's explicit orders and to ignore those that are implied. In Christian combat, it's important to know that God's orders are not intended to constrain our behaviors, but rather to give us victory. That means that we need to pursue not only the letter but also the intent of His commands. Doing so will ensure success on the spiritual battlefields of life.

**Orders aren't just about WHAT, they also specify WHEN**

The military has a number of different terms for different types of orders. Sometimes you will receive a "PLANORD" or planning order which directs you to prepare plans for some task. At other times you will receive a "WARNORD" which is a warning order to let you know that you are probably going to be required to execute a task. You might also receive an "EXORD," or execute order, which tells you to do something at a specific time. Sometimes you'll receive a PLANORD and then a WARNORD and never have to actually do the required task. At other times, you'll be sitting fat-dumb-and-happy and receive an EXORD without any preparatory WARNORD, which means everyone starts jumping through hoops to make things happen right now.

The military uses different types of orders because the timing of an order is often just as important as the specific task that is ordered. God gives us different timings for orders too, even if He doesn't name them like the military does. It's critical for us to understand that timing is part and parcel of effectively carrying out God's orders.

Are you familiar with the story of the nation of Israel as they tried to enter the Promised Land the first time? You'll find it in Numbers chapter 14. God told the Israelites to go into the Promised Land, but they were scared off and refused. So God essentially said, "Fine, none of you get to go into the Promised Land except for the two that weren't scared, Joshua and Caleb." The Israelites' response was to say, "Oh, no, in that case we will go into the Promised Land right now." They did so and got a proverbial butt-kicking.

The Israelites did exactly what God said they should – they went into the Promised Land – but they did it at the wrong time, and so it didn't go well. God's timing was part of God's order.

There are a number of ways that this concept is critical to our Christian combat.

First, we need to realize that sometimes God prepares us before He asks us to act. Just last year, I had to find a new job. In the midst of my job search, in times of prayer and Bible study and during discussions with fellow Christians, I was repeatedly confronted and impacted by the verse from Genesis where God tells Abram, "Go to the land that I will show you."[cxiv] When confronted with that verse, I asked, "Where am I supposed to go God?" However, it wasn't until several weeks later that I had a job opportunity come up where God was clearly providing an opportunity. We ended up leaving our home and going to the job without knowing what we were exactly going to be doing, how much we were going to be paid, or how long we would be at the job. God's "Go to the land that I will show you" was a warning order for me to be ready to respond when the "execute order" finally came in.

It's easy to think that every thought from God, every movement of the Holy Spirit, and every opportunity is an "execute order." However, sometimes God says things and does things in our life to prepare us for the future—not to impact the present. When He wants us to act, it will normally be clear. It is a profound truism that we should not cease doing what God has last told us to do until we are sure that He has given us a new task.

Second, we must remember that today's order will not necessarily be the same as yesterday's order. Parenting offers great examples of this truth. God says, "Do not withhold discipline from a child . . . punish them with the rod and save them from death."[cxv] Most days, if a child is willfully disobedient, he or she deserves corporal punishment, and a competent parent will follow God's command in this proverb. However, there are some days when there are other things going on or where a bigger lesson needs learning, a lesson like "mercy triumphs over judgment."[cxvi] There are times when we should punish and there are times when we should withhold punishment in the name of mercy. If we are not sensitive to God's timing we will *always* punish or *always* show mercy. In such cases we are law-followers, not God-followers, and our children suffer for it. However, when we are open to hearing from God each time we confront a situation of disobedience, we can parent effectively, showing both discipline and mercy, just as God does with us.

We can do the same thing in ministries. We note that some bible-study or sermon or event or effort had miraculous results last time we did it. So with best intentions we repeat the recipe for success and have a partial or even abject failure. Why? Because the recipe for success is following God, not just our effort. Last time God said, "Do it this way" and it worked. Maybe this time He is saying, "Do it *that* way" or maybe even "Don't do it at all." That's the lesson the Israelites learned in Numbers chapter 14, and from both an individual and corporate perspective, it would be a good one for us to learn as well.

Third, we must remember that because the battlefield is fluid, orders change. When I first took command of an Air Force squadron, I was convinced that God had called me to that role not only as a job but also as my primary area of ministry. Accordingly, I was very intentional about not getting deeply involved in "church activities" that would sap my time and focus. However, after about a year in command, an opportunity opened for my wife and I to lead a youth group at our church, and we felt certain that God wanted us to do so. We ended up pursuing the opportunity, and it turned out to be a blessing for our youth group and us. The point is that for a season God's orders were "focus on your command" and then later His orders changed, "now lead the youth group as well." If I had assumed that His first order was eternal, I would have missed out on being obedient to His second one.

I wonder how often I have missed out on God's greatest blessings because I have forgotten to keep going to Him to see if He has new orders. How many parents are stuck in the old orders of focusing primarily on their children even though their kids are either mostly or fully grown? How many ministry workers are still doing the same ministry at the same place because "that's where God called them," but they can't see that His present, different calling is just as valid as His first one was? How many Christians are mired in going to Bible study after Bible study after Bible study because God first said "I need you to become strong in my Word"? Now that they are, God is calling them to do something with that word, but they are still trying to study.

One of my favorite scenes in the Bible is where God takes Moses and removes him from leadership of the nation of Israel.[cxvii] For forty years God's command to Moses has been, "Lead the Israelites." Now, at the edge of the Promised Land, God gives new orders: "Pass on the torch." It appears from the Bible's account that Moses had no qualms with that and was ready to pursue God's next set of orders. Would that we could all have the wisdom of Moses to following the timing of the Order-Giver.

## Opportunity Is NOT an Implied Order

On April 14, 1994, two US F-15 fighters located some

unidentified helicopters flying in the Iraqi "No Fly Zone" during Operation Provide Comfort. Convinced that the helicopters belonged to the enemy, the fighter pilots misidentified them as Russian-made and in violation of the no-fly zone, so they shot them down. Tragically, they turned out to be two United States Army helicopters. The 26 Americans and allies onboard were all killed. Subsequent investigation revealed that there were a series of mistakes, omissions, and miscommunications that led to the shoot down.[22] A root cause, however, was that the lead F-15 pilot had seized on an opportunity for combat and violated rules of engagement.

Opportunities can be very deceptive. In aviation safety, we talk about a phenomenon called "strength of an idea." Strength of an idea refers to the psychological tendency for us to see what we want to see or what we expect to see. That F-15 pilot was looking for hostile helicopters, and when he found some helicopters, he was predisposed to accept the facts that indicated they were hostile and to disregard the facts that indicated they might be friendly. This type of thinking can happen to us in any situation, especially in Christian combat.

How many times have you seen a friend who is longing for an intimate relationship seize on an opportunity and wind up enmeshed with a loser? How many times have you seen someone buy something that really wasn't a smart purchase just because that person was dying to have that something? (Maybe you are like me and answer, "Yes, I've done that.")

In Christian combat, we need to remind ourselves that opportunities do not mean God is giving us an order. As one great pastor said to me, "Saying no is as important as saying yes . . . the good can be the enemy of the best." I had the opportunity to help lead a men's ministry some years ago. I seized the opportunity and the ministry was pretty much a failure. Why? I think it failed because God wasn't telling us to do it, and frankly I suspect my "strength of an idea" was that we needed a more robust men's ministry.

Perhaps God is preparing to use your church to conduct a full-out assault on one of the devil's local schemes. If you seize a lesser

22 "1994 Black Hawk Shootdown Incident," accessed Jan 20, 2014 at http://en.wikipedia.org/wiki/1994_Black_Hawk_shootdown_incident

opportunity and go running out ahead on your own, maybe you will so dilute the resources at your church that the major assault will fail. Perhaps God is preparing you to have a tremendous impact in someone's life 237 days from now, and He needs you where you are and doing what you are doing to be prepared to make that impact. If you go launching off on a new venture, you won't be ready and available for God's plan.

One of the greatest places where we fall into the "opportunity trap" is in prayer. Christians tend to ask God for those things that they desire most. When something shows up that looks like an answer to those desires, we automatically assume "God is answering my prayer." Maybe He is. Or maybe the Prince of this World is trying to work his deception. Don't assume that every opportunity is from God. When God speaks, He will use some combination of prayer, circumstances, the Bible, and His people to let you know that the opportunity is truly from Him.

So does this mean that the only time we should act is when we are absolutely, positively 100% certain of God's orders for us? No. Such an approach leaves no room for faith. But what this does mean is that we should never act until we have asked God two questions: "Lord, do You want me to do this?" and "Lord, do You want me to do this now?" If, through prayer and God's word, you think His answer to these questions is yes, then move out and do not doubt.[cxviii] If you've misread the order, God is big enough (and loves you enough) to call you back.

When opportunity knocks, don't assume it's an order. Ask God what His orders for you are. *Ask* God what His orders for you are. He is good and is not going to let you stumble off into mayhem if you are asking sincerely for His guidance.[cxix]

Life in the field of Christian combat can be hard if we don't have our expectations right. We need to be prepared to endure "ruck marches," waiting to get to the battle where God wants to use us. We need to be ready to put up with "field conditions" as God gets us ready for our next engagement. And we need to pay attention to God's orders—in terms of both what and when—to ensure that we are engaging the enemy at the time and place that the Commander in Chief has instructed. When we get our expectations right, we get closer to the truth the apostle Paul was expressing when he said, "I have learned to be content in whatever circumstances I am."[cxx] The difficulties we face in the field are all part of what we go through as we fight for peoples' eternities.

Life in the field is full of challenges, but those challenges lead us to the "tip of the spear." They lead us to combat where we can engage the enemy. What does that look like? Read on as we discuss actual combat.

# PART 4: COMBAT

During the summer of 2006 in Iraq, a United States soldier had gone missing during an engagement with the enemy, and his unit thought he might have been blown into the Euphrates River. We were called to search with our helicopters for the missing soldier. The mission required us to do a low and slow search during daylight hours in the midst of enemy-held territory. This flight profile was one of the most dangerous we could fly given the potential threat of men with AK-47s and rocket-propelled grenades. However, it needed to be done if we were to have a chance at a successful rescue. Door gunners had fingers on triggers, pilots were ready to aggressively maneuver if fired upon, all eyes were out, and adrenaline was flowing. This was combat.

We were both successful and unsuccessful that day. We did our job despite the risks and didn't get shot down, but we weren't able to find our missing soldier.

It's been said that combat is hours of boredom punctuated by moments of sheer terror. Being a soldier is not about shooting or getting shot. It's not about fearlessness or combat skills that would shame a ninja. What marks a soldier is that he or she does the job to defeat the enemy—no matter what the risks or circumstances.

Everything I've discussed thus far in this book leads to this point: we Christian soldiers must engage in combat. It's boring. It's terrifying. It can be incredibly difficult. It can be unexpectedly easy. But we need to make like a Nike commercial and "Just Do It."

The key question is "How?" How do I engage in combat? How do I fight? Who do I fight? Where do I fight? To answer these questions, we must first understand our weapons and then we must understand our battlegrounds.

## Weapons of Christian Combat

God tells us in the Bible that "For though we live in the world, we do not wage war as the world does. The weapons we fight with are not the weapons of the world. On the contrary, they have divine power to demolish strongholds. We demolish arguments and every pretension that sets itself up against the knowledge of God, and we take captive every thought to make it obedient to Christ. And we will be ready to punish every act of disobedience, once your obedience is complete."[cxxi] Our goal in Christian combat is not to put bullets in enemy brains. Our goal is to destroy the lies, arguments, and pretensions of the enemy.

So how do you destroy lies? With the Truth. To be effective combatants, we must know the Truth, and we must share the Truth with both our mouths and our actions.

Knowing the Truth means knowing God. That goes back to what I talked about in the section about Basic Training: We put our faith in Christ, and we pray and read the Bible so we can hear the truth that He wants us to use. I don't need to be a Bible scholar to be an effective combatant, but I do need to be listening to God. Consider how the apostles Peter and John engaged in combat after Christ died. When confronted with the lies that Jesus was not the Savior, these two relatively uneducated men simply trusted in God to give them the words to say— and He did so.[cxxii]

Sharing the truth is done through both our words *and* our actions. Jesus' brother James says, "Show me your faith apart from your works, and I will show you my faith by my works."[cxxiii] Too often we Christians identify ourselves by denomination, by doctrine, or by credo. Christ said that Christians are supposed to be known because of their love for one another.[cxxiv] 19th century British evangelist 'Gipsy' Smith said, "There are 5 gospels: Matthew, Mark, Luke, John, and the Christian. Most people will never read the first four."[23] If we want to defeat the lies of the enemy, we don't need a Chuck-Norris-life-ending-karate-kick—we need to speak the truth and live lives that reflect our faith in that truth.

Now that last statement is so incredibly broad that it's almost not helpful. It's like saying, "We need to do good." Duh. So to try to make this discussion at least a little helpful, we need to talk about battlegrounds and how we can fight on them.

## Battlegrounds of Christian Combat

Every battleground in Christian combat is centered on truth and deception. Each battleground consists of battle lines that are drawn where truth ends and lies begin. We see the consequences of spiritual battle physically: Atheists came to power in Russia and so over 15 million people were slaughtered. Teens in America are convinced that they originated randomly from "primordial soup" and so suicides naturally increase. Men are taught that their sexual appetite is an unstoppable part of their DNA and so adultery, fatherless children, and sexual immorality skyrocket. All of these things—slaughter, suicide, sexual immorality—are the physical consequences of losses on the spiritual battlefield. All the physical consequences start with a departure from a spiritual truth. Fever is a physical symptom of infection. It is not bad to treat the fever, but if you treat the fever and not the infection, the patient may die. In the same way, the physical chaos in our world stems largely from spiritual malaise. If we think that our battle strategy should be to combat the physical consequences, we will never eradicate the root cause, and so all we will be doing is delaying final destruction. Our grand strategy as Christian combatants must be to attack the root deceptions that obscure Truth. So our battlegrounds are where these truth-battles occur in our lives.

There is no Biblical taxonomy for battlegrounds. Nor do I have any uniquely special revelation from God about our spiritual battlefields. However, when I look at real life in America, I see six areas—six battlegrounds—where deception is rampant:
- The Battleground within Us
- The Battleground at Home
- The Battleground of the Church

[23] Quoted by Robert D. Papa at http://www.theprisonersweb.org/wp-content/uploads/2012/04/December-2013-Letter-website1.pdf

- The Battleground in Education
- The Battleground of Media
- The Battleground in Politics

Almost every Christian man and woman in America finds him or herself on these battlegrounds regularly, and so it may increase our combat-effectiveness if we look at each one.

## 4-1 THE BATTLEGROUND WITHIN US

I have a friend—a fighter pilot—who worked in the US Air Force headquarters during the first push into Iraq. My friend is a supremely competent fighter pilot, and so he was a little disappointed to be working as a staff officer and not "in the fight." However, his job as a planner gave him a unique perspective as he watched his fighter pilot friends go to and return from real combat, most for the very first time. When the "safe" switches were turned off and these men and women were able to launch destruction against a real enemy for the first time in their lives, true colors came out. Some pilots were as professional as ever. Some pilots struggled with the real act of destroying fellow humans. And a few pilots uncapped a hate that they kept hidden daily and revealed a killing side that my buddy found profoundly disturbing. With these men, when the Air Force said, "You may now kill" their Mr. Hyde inside said with gleeful rage, "Free at last!"

The truth is, Mr. (or Ms.) Hyde is in each of us. Perhaps your Hyde wants to run greedily after stuff; perhaps her Hyde wants to be the center of everyone's attention; perhaps my Hyde wants to chase after every lust; perhaps his Hyde wants to hate and hate and hate. These are all symptoms of the battle within us. If we don't fight the battle, we will destroy ourselves and those around us.

So where are the battle lines in the Battleground Within Us? I think there are four primary lines of truth pitted against four lines of deception.

### It's Not About ME

The first battle line on the Battleground Within Us centers on our purpose. We were created for a purpose outside of ourselves. The Bible tells us "we are God's handiwork, created in Christ Jesus to do good works, which God prepared in advance for us to do."[cxxv] The opposing deception is that we are to live our lives for ourselves. This is a deception that we come to naturally. How often do you look at the world with a "what do I want" perspective?

I do it all the time: "Do I want to go to church?" "Do I want to spend time with my wife?" "Do I want to be honest on my tax return?" "Do I want to get up early this morning?" This deception is strongly bolstered by our media culture. Advertising is designed to make us say, "I should have what I want." The deception is further encouraged by the prevailing scientific theory that we evolved by chance: if we were not created intentionally, then we have no purpose. If we have no purpose, then we are all about self-gratification.

Yet God tells us that we are created on purpose for a purpose. The right attitude is not to view the world from the "what do I want" perspective but from the "what am I supposed to do" perspective. "Does God want me to go to church today?" (His answer to this question is not always "yes"), "Am I supposed to spend time with my wife?" "Does God want me to be honest on my tax return?" "Do I need to get up early this morning to fulfill my purpose?" These are the questions we should be asking.

So how do we fight the "all about me" deception? We fight this deception by understanding the truth that we are indeed made for a purpose outside of ourselves and that we are part of God's plan. Meditate on verses like Ephesians 2:10, Jeremiah 29:11, and Psalm 139:13-14. These remind us of our purpose. We fight as well by reminding ourselves that gratifying our desires never brings lasting joy. Have you ever noticed that nearly all of the things that make you feel good fade over time? If not, try this: Eat a cookie every day. The first day you'll be overjoyed at the good sweetness in your mouth. But after the 10th or 100th cookie, you'll say, "This just isn't as good as I remember."

You will also experience the deception of self-gratification if you make some money. When you make your first $1000, you feel like you are on top of the world, but days or months later, you decide you need $10,000. Then after awhile, only $100,000 will be sufficient. Then a million. Pretty soon you will realize that no amount of money will do it for you.

The only thing that brings lasting joy is being in right-relationship with God, fulfilling the purposes that He has for us. His plan might not be "fun" right now, but following through on it will always eventually take us to the place where we lay down to sleep and say, "Thank you God, my life is good." If we gratify our desires, we find ourselves always wanting more, but when we fulfill our purpose, we find contentment.

Here's a great illustration of this truth: Our church used to take an annual weekend trip to build houses in Mexico. I was always amazed at what happens when you take people on a mission service trip. I and ten or twenty other selfish and rich Americans would go live in tents, eat mediocre food, relieve ourselves in rank toilets, take cold showers, collapse into our sleeping bags exhausted at night, and then go home at the end of the weekend saying, "That was AWESOME!" Why? Because we were living with purpose—God's purpose.

The truth is that we were created for a purpose outside of ourselves. Don't believe the lie that we should live our lives for ourselves.

## We Are NOT Good

The second battle line in the Battleground Within Us is our understanding of our true nature. The world wants to tell us the lie that all humans are basically good. Left to our own devices, we'll be good girls and good boys. That's a nice thing to hear, but it's completely contradicted by experience. I think I can say without pride that I do a lot of good things, but the fact of the matter is that I also do a lot of bad things, and I want to do a whole lot more bad things than I actually let myself do. While we are all created in God's image[cxxvi], we are also horribly and undeniably flawed.

There are two crushing consequences of believing the deception that mankind is basically good. The enemy either convinces us that we are abnormally rotten, or he tells us that we are really pretty okay. Both deceptions will result in chaos.

If we are convinced that mankind is basically good and then we are confronted by the truth of our own rottenness, we will believe that we are worthless because we see ourselves as "worse than everyone else." When the enemy convinces us that we are abnormally bad, we give up on ourselves and on God. To ourselves we say, "I am worthless." To God we say, "There is no way You could love me or forgive me or use me." We are tempted to give up on trying to follow God because we are convinced that there is no point in it.

On the other hand, if Satan can't convince us that we are too rotten for God, he tries to tell us that we aren't really that bad. "You're a pretty good dude," he tells us. "You are one of the most beautiful, likeable women in this area," he says. He shows us losers at school, or murderers in the news, or liars in politics, or fanatics in other countries and says, "See: those people are bad. *You* are good!" And, oh, how we love to embrace that lie because it makes us feel good about ourselves. When I am good, I don't need a savior. When I am good, I don't really need God, or maybe I need to just help God a little in determining what's right for my life. Here's what I look like if I believe the lie that I am good:

• My life is not about following my savior; it is about following a great teacher with great doctrines.

• My life is not about leaning on others for accountability, correction, or instruction; it is about teaching others (or maybe just going it alone).

• My life is not about grace (blessing people with what they don't deserve); it is about mercy (holding back bad consequences that people rightly deserve).

• My life is not about going to God each day, each hour, and each minute for His wisdom and aid -- it is about going to God in those rare and unpleasant circumstances where I get convinced that something is actually beyond my ability to handle alone.

This deception is a big part of why so many Christians cheat on their spouses. They say, "I'm good" when they should be saying, "Left to my own devices I will be an adulterer." This is why so many churches are unloving places for so many people. When Christians should be saying, "They are just like me," they instead are saying, "Unlike me, they are messed up." The enemy wants to convince us that mankind is basically good, either to push us down with a wrong sense of worthlessness or to prop us up with a false sense of humility. But we can fight this deception by contending for the truth: "All have sinned and fall short of the glory of God[cxxvii]" and "There is *no one* on earth who is righteous, *no one* who does right and never sins.[cxxviii]"

While God is saying that *all* people are messed up, the world tries to convince us that the superstars don't have issues like ours, be they Christians like Billy Graham, politicians like the President, movie stars like Jennifer Lawrence, or maybe just our all-put-together pastor or friend. But they do. They have big issues, just like you and me.

While God is saying that we are messed up and need Him, the world is trying to tell us that we've got it all under control, that we are good enough to make it through life without God and that religion is for the weak. It's easy to carry this lie in our abundant American lifestyle. Our cars and homes and hobbies and movies and fine dining and fancy clothes can allow us to paste over the questionable parts of our lives or distract us when we start to get an inkling that maybe we are not "all that." Yet watch what happens when the doctor says, "Cancer" or death comes calling or the economy crashes or terrorists bring down a skyscraper. We are suddenly confronted with the truth of our own inadequacy. Our challenge, our fight as Christians is to keep that truth in mind even when God hasn't humbled us with tragedy.

So how do we contend for the truth that "all have sinned"? First, we must look often into the mirror that is found in the Bible; God makes it abundantly clear there that we need Him.

Second, we must remember that our worth comes from God's love for us, not from our own actions or goodness. He loves us so much that He was willing to die for us, and if that doesn't speak to how much worth you have, I don't know what does. He died for you and me even though we were still screwed up and thumbing our noses at Him. Find your worth in your own actions, and you will certainly prove to be worthless. Find your worth in His love for you, and you will find that you have worth that is eternal and immeasurable because it comes from Him.

Third, we must constantly fight our desire to make ourselves look good. When we use nice clothes or "white lies" or drawn shades to hide the truth about ourselves, we perpetuate the lie that we are better than we actually are. When we are honest about who we really are, we shatter the lie that we are so horrid that we can't stand to be seen.

The Christian life is not one of perfection on this earth—it is one of total dependence on God to use us and love us despite and through our imperfections. The apostle Paul talks about a frustrating shortcoming in himself, what he calls a "thorn in the flesh," and tells us that God was okay with that thorn; in fact God left it there because God's "power is made perfect in weakness."[cxxix] And the apostle John tells us that God "first loved us"[cxxx] even though we are sinners and thumbing our noses at Him.[cxxxi] The truth is that we are rotten—we have huge flaws, foibles, illicit lusts—but we are *all* rotten. God knows this, and yet He also tells us that we are made in His image. In Christ, right now, we are washed "white as snow"[cxxxii] despite every horrible thing we ever did or thought. And in Christ, over time (often a long time) we are brought to perfection.[cxxxiii]

Don't fall for the lie that mankind is basically good. You and I are *not* abnormally worthless, and you and I are *not* good. "All have sinned and fall short of the glory of God[cxxxiv]" and "There is no one on earth who is righteous, no one who does right and never sins.[cxxxv]" We *all* screw things up. We *all* need God. Yet despite our countless shortcomings, we *all* have immeasurable worth not because of what we do but because of His love for us.

No one is good, except in Him.

## God Is Always Right

The third battle line on the Battleground Within Us centers on what's right. This is an incredibly simple truth, but the counter-deception is everywhere. I think maybe that's because our pride hates this truth: God is always right. Always, always, always, always right.

If God said it, it is right.

If God wants it, it is right.

The enemy will convince us that our opinions or our circumstances matter. He tries to convince us that God is right, in principle, but in many cases God's version of right doesn't really apply to me. When I say that on paper, it probably sounds kind of absurd, but we think this way all the time. Consider these examples:

• God says that wives should submit to their husbands. That's unequivocal in the books of Ephesians, Colossians, and 1 Peter.[cxxxvi] Yet Christians everywhere hedge that truth based on the quality of the husband, changes in culture, changes in the role of women, or other extra-biblical teaching.

• God says that homosexuality is wrong. He says it in both the Old and New Testament, multiple times.[cxxxvii] Yet Christians everywhere equivocate as if we have some new, wiser-than-God understanding now in the 21st Century.

• God says that you should physically discipline children. He disciplines mankind throughout history,[cxxxviii] He tells us that it is an expression of love,[cxxxix] and He explicitly commands it repeatedly.[cxl] However, Christians all over the United States disagree with God's instruction to discipline based on their understanding of popular psychology, their friends' comments, or something they saw on TV.

Satan wants us to believe that God is only mostly right. The history of this deception goes all the way back to the Garden of Eden when Satan tells Eve to eat the forbidden fruit saying, "You will not surely die. "[cxli] Satan is telling Eve, "Don't be silly, God is wrong." He says it still today, "God doesn't really mean you should submit to your husband, God doesn't really mean two loving men should not have sex, God doesn't really mean that you should strike your child." And we are tempted by this lie because we want to weigh in with our opinion. We want to approve God's ways. It's a natural part of our sinful nature.

So how do we fight this battle? It's easily said, but harder done: Decide that God is always right. If God said it, it is right. If it's in the Bible, it is right. Don't weigh in with your opinion. Don't allow yourself to decide if you want to agree with God. Just agree. In military terms: salute smartly and press on.

I recently read a controversial book by a Christian pastor that teaches (wrongly) that every person who ever lived will be saved. Here's what the jacket of the book says: "'God loves us. God offers us everlasting life by grace, freely, through no merit on our part. Unless you do not respond the right way. Then God will torture you forever. In hell.' Huh?"[24] The "huh?" is the crux of the problem with that book. "Huh?" means "I don't agree with that" or "that doesn't make sense to me" or "that's messed up." Essentially, "huh?" means "God, I do not approve." Predictably, the arguments in that book are flawed because they spring from assumption that "God has to be like I think He should be."

If a successful pastor can make that mistake, so can we. That's why it's imperative for each of us to decide that God is always right before we confront the things He says that seem to us to be wrong.

Now this is not a call to be unthinking. We still need to carefully study the Bible, to search out truth as it is conveyed in the whole Bible and to examine those passages that seem challenging. But once we've done all that, if we find that God says something that we disagree with, we need to get *our* mind right, not His.

Christian warriors can't fall prey to the lie that God is mostly right. Decide right now that if you are convinced He said something, then you are convinced also that that something is right.

TIME OUT: Before we move on to the last battle line on this battleground, let me be very clear about what I mean when I wrote that "God said it." There are some difficult Biblical concepts that have been debated by smarter folks than you and I for centuries.

---

[24] Rob Bell. *Love Wins.* 2011: Harper One, New York.

Logic and scripture can reasonably end you on either side of such a debate. In cases like these, you might not be able to say with certainty what you think God said, and even if you can say with certainty what you think, you might still see the viability of the other side's position. These debatable subjects are not the battle line I'm talking about here. Discussions and arguments over debatable matters can be healthy and even faith affirming, and a myopic insistence on a single interpretation can be divisive and destructive. The battle line is on those subjects that are clear but that we don't want to agree with (for whatever reason). If God says something clearly in the Bible, we can be comfortable saying, "God said it." When something in the Old Testament is reaffirmed in the New Testament, or if God says something repeatedly in the Bible, we can be extra-comfortable saying, "God said it." You aren't on this battle line when you are trying to determine the meaning of a debatable portion of scripture, but you know you are on this battle line when you (or someone else) want to disagree with something that God has clearly said.

## Act Today

The final battle line on the Battleground Within Us is the battle line of time. People love to think long-term. We love to plan. We love to procrastinate. We love to concoct detailed long-term schemes, and we love to say, "I'll do that tomorrow." Have you ever wondered why we make New Year's Resolutions? Why not April Fool's Day resolutions or All Saints Day resolutions? I think it's because, as we mark the passing of a year and begin a new one, we realize that time is getting away from us and so we desire to do something about it.

There is an old folk story that goes like this: The devil is plotting how to destroy the church, and he asks his demons for ideas. One demon comes and says, "Burn their building!" Satan replies, "Idiot, that will only renew their appreciation for their church." Another demon comes and says, "Distract their children with things of the world." Satan says, "No, you fool. That will work for a time, but as their lives fall apart, they will realize the reason and turn back to God." A third demon comes up and says, "Master! Tell them they have lots of time!" "Yesssss!!!" responds the devil.

The truth of the Bible is very clear: We have today to deal with, and we are supposed to be obedient to God today. Jesus tells a story of a businessman who invests himself in building for the future rather than in working for God, not realizing that all of his planning is for naught because he is about to die.[cxlii] When we put off doing God's stuff today saying, "I'll do it later," we never know what opportunity we are missing, because "later" may never come. In his sermon on the mount, Christ says, "Do not be anxious about tomorrow, for tomorrow will be anxious for itself."[cxliii] God has given us today, and today is when we are supposed to serve Him. It's a very big assumption to assume that we can "do it tomorrow."

Satan's deception is to tell us that we have all kinds of time. He tells us to get busy after we've taken care of some other "important" stuff or to take care of things when we feel like it. This lie is subversive because it allows us to say, "I'm not doing anything that's bad," even as we ignore the fact that we just aren't doing anything that is good.

I have a friend who is in prison that I correspond with. He sent me a letter some time ago, and I saved the letter so that I could write him back. I saw that letter on my dresser countless times and said, "Oh, I should write Tim[25]. . . tomorrow, maybe." Tomorrow turned into next week and next week turned into next month. When I sat down to write him yesterday, I was appalled at myself— I received his letter a month and a half ago! I didn't realize the passage of time, and so for a month and a half I failed to encourage my brother, a man very young in the faith, at the time when he needed encouragement most. Epic fail! That's the tyranny of the deception that "you have time."

We can fight on this battle line daily by changing our way of thinking. Every morning, start the day by asking God what He wants you to do today. We need to ask "can I do this now?" instead of "must I do this now?" Believe that this might be your final hour or your final day. Believe that this might be your neighbor's final hour or final day. What do you (or they) need to know to secure eternity? What would you do differently today if you knew that your time was limited? God has a purpose for us – resolve to never miss out on fulfilling that purpose by waiting for tomorrow. When you wake each morning, ask yourself, "If this is

---

[25] Not his real name.

my last day, what would God have me do?" Do not listen to the subtle, sly whisper that says, "Oh, you have lots of time."

"Today if you hear His voice, do not harden your hearts."[cxliv] Don't wait to commit your life to Him. Don't wait to share His Truth with your friend at work. Don't wait to teach your children about God. Don't wait to encourage your sister. Don't wait to tell your husband you love him. Don't wait to read your Bible.

Don't wait, that is, unless God tells you to wait. At times He will say "not now" or "later." Sometimes it's okay to wait and to postpone. What is not okay is to wait or postpone something that should be done today. Success on this battle line is all about being tuned into God through constant prayer. Do everything you can in His timing, not your own.

It's hard to get the right perspective of time; in fact, it's a battle. God wants Christian warriors focused on *today*, doing His will *today*, because when we are faithful *today* people get saved for eternity!

Are you fighting on the Battleground Within You? Arm yourself with the Truth and engage Satan on each battle line:

- It's not about me.
- We are not good.
- God is always right.
- Act today.

Believe the Truth so that you can crush the lies that war within you. That's what we Christian soldiers do, and if we don't, we can't be of much service on any of the other Battlegrounds that I'll talk about below.

## 4-2 THE BATTLEGROUND AT HOME

December 7, 1941.

President Roosevelt called it "a day that will live in infamy." That's the day that the Japanese bombed Pearl Harbor and brought the United States into World War II. History tells us that there were a number of indicators that should have clued the US into the fact that they were at risk from Japan. However, for whatever reason, these indicators were overlooked or ignored, and so when the Japanese attacked that December morning, the US military was completely unprepared and badly defeated. Eight battleships, almost 200 airplanes, and nearly a dozen other navy vessels were damaged or destroyed. Over 2000 Americans died that day.

Perhaps that morning at Pearl Harbor our brave service members were thinking that war only happens away from home.

In real war, it is often a winning strategy if you can defeat your enemy at home. That's why history is filled with examples of surprise attacks, spies, and traitors. Take down your adversary at home and you will never have to meet him on a declared battlefield. Our enemy knows that full well, and that's why the Battleground at Home is the next battleground we need to talk about.

The Battleground at Home really revolves around the family—whether just a husband and wife; a husband, wife, and children; or a single parent and children. Now if you are single and reading this, you might be tempted to check out or skip to the next chapter, but I'd ask you not to. We all not only participate in families (at one time or another), but we are constantly encouraging (or discouraging, as the case may be) healthy family interaction in others. So wherever you are on the spectrum of single to married-with-kids, this battleground is relevant and you have a role in achieving victory.

The truths and deceptions that make up the primary battle lines of the Battleground at Home can be divided into three major categories: The Marital Battle Line, the Parenting Battle Line, and the Battle Line of Youth. We'll look at each one in more detail.

### The Marital Battle Line

Have you ever stopped to ask yourself what marriage is all about? The legal institution of marriage has been in the news a lot for the last several years because of the movement in the US to redefine it in a way that appeals to homosexuals, but what is marriage, really?

Some would say that marriage is about happiness. Some would say it is about Jerry Maguire's famous line: "You complete me." Some would say it is about child rearing. Some would say marriage is about sex. Some would say that marriage is just a legal institution designed by government to encourage the health of the family. There are elements of truth in all of these answers, and that should be expected since the best lies always start out with truth and then twist it.

If marriage is about happiness, what happens when you aren't happy in your marriage? The logical answer is divorce. Go find a new happy-maker. If marriage is about completion, what happens when your spouse is in a horrible auto accident and emerges as a quadriplegic? You are no longer being completed (at least not the way you thought you were). The logical answer is divorce since your substantive reason for marriage is gone. If marriage is about child rearing, what do we say to those who have no children? What if a spouse is infertile? That makes it time to find a new spouse. If marriage is about sex, what happens when your spouse puts on 50 pounds or has a physical condition or just loses his libido? Time for divorce. If marriage is about healthy families, what happens if you are married and your family is anything but healthy? The marriage has failed its purpose . . . might as well dissolve it.

Here is the biblical truth: Marriage is about union. Such union entails happiness, completeness, child-rearing (more often than not), sex, and family. But these are byproducts of the union, not reasons for it. Jesus said when two people marry, they are united, and "they are no longer two, but one flesh" joined by God.[cxlv] If you've been in the church for a while, you know this truth, but you also probably know that the divorce rate is about the same among Christians as among non-Christians.[26] How can this be? If God says that marriage is about union, how can God's people be dissolving marriage at the same rate as the rest of the world?

Some would say that this is just because we're comparing apples to apples: since many Christians are really just shallow believers,

26 "New Marriage and Divorce Statistics Released," March 31, 2008, The Barna Group. Accessed Feb 12, 2014 at https://www.barna.org/barna-update/article/15-familykids/42-new-marriage-and-divorce-statistics-released#.Uvu5RnmA270

they look just like the world. However, if you look at the stats from a survey conducted by the Barna Group in 2007-2008, you'll find that evangelical Christians only divorce about 4% less than atheists or agnostics![27] These statistics indicate that Satan's attack on the family is in full swing, but instead of dropping bombs full of TNT, he's dropping lies. Here are the three big ones:

**"Marriage is about me."** Ask any young fiancé why he/she wants to be married and you're more than likely to hear an answer that includes "she makes me feel . . . " or "he makes me feel . . . " Literature, movies, and television all propagate the image of marriage as a way for me to be happy. Satan and the world tell us that marriage is about me being blessed, me not being lonely, me having a family, me having sex. Even if we change this to us—us being blessed, us not being lonely, us having a family, us having sex—we still have not captured the truth. The truth is that the covenant of marriage is about the other person. My friend Nick likes to say, "it's not a 50%/50% deal, it's a 100%/100% deal." However, I'd take that one step further and say it's a 100%/0% deal where I am called to give 100% and be okay if I get nothing back.

Does the Bible really say this? Pretty much. Christ tells us that the only standing valid reason for divorce in God's eyes is sexual infidelity.[cxlvi] In other words, it doesn't matter whether your spouse is doing anything for you; you are to stay married. Additionally, in Ephesians 5:22 God tells wives to submit to their husbands (translation: wife give 100%) and just three verses later God tells husbands to love their wives "just as Christ loved the church"— Christ loved the church while the church was hating him and gave up his life for it (translation: husband give 100%).

So how do we fight the "Marriage is about me" deception? If you are married, anytime you think "my spouse should . . . " stop yourself and ask what you should do. If you are considering marriage, there is only one question that matters: If your spouse becomes ugly, angry, and disabled, will you stay with him or her? If your answer is "no" or "probably not," don't even think about marriage. If you know someone who is married, anytime you hear them say, "He never . . . " or "She never . . . " consider whether it is the right to time to ask your friend, "Why do you think that your

---

[27] Ibid.

spouse is supposed to do something for you?" I remember a time years ago where a man in my church told me about problems he was having with his wife and said, "I've got needs, you know." I wish I had had the wisdom then to say, "Yes you do, but why do you think your wife is supposed to supply them and not your God?"

My marriage is not about me. My marriage is about my spouse.

**"Marriage is an agreement."** This is a second big deception. This is where prenuptial agreements come from. When we buy into this lie, we say, "I'm in for marriage, but only if you hold up your part." I've known good Christian couples who keep separate bank accounts not for convenience but because they want to keep "my money" separate from "your money." I've known Christian men who won't let their wife drive "his car." I've known of Christian women who only let their husbands "get some" on a scheduled basis. But here's the truth: Marriage is a sacrificial promise, not an agreement. When I say to my wife "I, Dan, take you, Monica, to have and to hold, from this day on, for better or worse, for richer, for poorer, in sickness and in health, to love and to cherish, until death do us part," do I actually mean it, or do I mean, "*As long as you do your part*, I, Dan, take you, Monica . . . "?

God tells us to let our "yes" mean "yes" and our "no" mean "no"—we are to be people of our word.[cxlvii] And so when we vow to be in union with someone we need to be in union with someone. It's a lie to think that I should *mostly* be in union with my wife. Right now, my wife could easily destroy my finances, my reputation, my emotions, and my health because she has access to everything of mine. That is how it is supposed to be. We are not two halves in agreement. We are one whole in union. So if she ever rips away (or if I do), it's going to be miserable. That's a natural consequence of God's intent for union.

We can defeat the deception that marriage is an agreement. Sacrifice yourself to your spouse. Hold nothing back. Don't hide schedules or friends or money or plans or stuff. Don't ask your spouse to jump through hoops to get your love. Don't refuse to do things you don't like to do without first asking if doing that thing would bless your spouse. Give.

Does this mean I can never say, "No" to my spouse? Of course not. There are all kinds of good reasons to say, "No" or to disagree. But "because I don't want to" or "because that's my stuff" are not generally good reasons. Your marital vows were not an agreement; they were a sacrificial promise.

**"God wants me to be happy now"** is a third great marital deception. This is a lie that affects a lot more than marriage, but it has such a profound impact on marriage that it's worth discussing here. The truth is that the Bible does not say anywhere that God wants you to be happy now—He wants you to be faithful now so you can be happy in eternity. The "happy now" baloney is directly contradicted by history and by the life of Christ. Noah probably wasn't "happy now" when he watched all his friends die and then was stuck on an ark for a year with stinky animals. Joseph wasn't "happy now" when he was in prison. David wasn't "happy now" when his son died. Christ wasn't "happy now" when he was going to the cross. Paul wasn't "happy now" when he was shipwrecked. To be sure, God does bless us with lots of joy in this life, but that joy occurs amidst a lot of difficulty. If you are in a bad marital situation, it's very conceivable that God does not want or intend for you to experience marital bliss for quite some time (yes, men, this includes sex). God may be saying "stay the course" until you or your spouse (or both) get over whatever issue Satan is using to try to divide you.

Our response to any hardship is usually to make that hardship go away as fast as possible, but God may be saying, "I need you right where you are, doing just what you are doing, for another 20 years. That's how long it's going to take for My plan to come together. I need you to do good even though you don't feel good, and I need you to do it for Me. Sacrificially. For 20 more years."

One of my best friends—a follower of Christ—went through some serious financial hardship some years back. As his business was going down the drain, he basically decided to hide it from his wife. He dabbled in gambling. He made foolish decisions under the pressure of financial ruin. And then everything came to light. My friend's wife (also a disciple of Christ) had every justification to leave him or to hate him, but she didn't. She went through a pretty long period of "I'm not happy now" (as did he). But she stuck to truth and stuck with my friend and now they are doing great again relationally and fairly well financially. If my friend's wife had bought into the "be happy now" lie, it would have destroyed their marriage, hurt their children, and made a mockery of the statement that following Christ makes a difference.

What's the best way to fight the battle against the "be happy now" lie? First, we must understand that leaving marriage is not an option unless God specifically tells us it is. Second, we must focus on being faithful to God, not on trying to fulfill our desires. It's a truism that when we seek God, He either takes care of or changes our desires (although sometimes this takes time). Christ said that if we seek God first, everything else will be taken care of.[cxlviii] Third, we would do well to remind ourselves and others that God's plan is the very best and that all things are truly under His control. A God-centered marriage is going to get better, even if it takes some time.

To be effective on the Marital Battle Line, we Christian warriors must Trust God and deny the lie that marriage is about anything other than a commitment to our spouse.

Marriage is at the core of God's gift of family, and so the devil attacks marriages relentlessly. But what if we have a marriage that is solidly built on God? The devil can't do squat to the marriage, so what does he do? He goes for the kids. That's why we need to talk about the parental battle line next.

## The Parental Battle Line

Have you ever been in line at Walmart watching the bratty kid in front of you play his mom like a violin? He asks for candy and she says no. He wines and she says, "Don't whine." He starts to throw a fit and she says, "I'm warning you." He gets into a full-blown tantrum, and as all eyes within a 50-foot radius turn to see the spectacle she finally says, "Fine. Here!" and gives him the candy.

If there were a scoreboard it would say, Kid: 1 Mom: 0, and the Devil would point to it, wave his pom-poms and cheer.

Have you ever noticed that all of the screwed-up worldviews go after kids? Stalin indoctrinated children in communist Russia. Hitler pulled German kids into "education" programs at the earliest possible age. Progressives in America continually argue for a more robust government education system to be administered at ever-earlier ages. Education is a battleground in and of itself that I'll discuss in a later chapter, but the battle over children starts in the home. Satan knows that if he can make parents ineffective, he can easily deceive the next generation, and so we find ourselves constantly confronted with lies about the proper role of parents. Let me address what I think are three of the biggest lies that parents fall victim to.

The first lie on the parental battle line is this: Evil wants to convince you that your children are as important as—or more important than—your spouse. Certainly, in extremes, we acknowledge that it is good for parents to sacrifice for children. Who wouldn't cheer for a mom or dad who gave up her or his own life jacket and gave it to their child as their ship was sinking? But we don't usually find ourselves on sinking ships. We are typically parenting in normal, dry-land, good ol' US of A. And in life's normal activity, the truth is that our spouse is supposed to be more important than our children.

God never tells us in the Bible to prioritize our children. He tells us not to aggravate and exasperate them,[cxlix] but He does not tell us to be joined to them, to submit to them, or to love them as Christ loved the church—all of which He says about our spouses. Don't misread this and think that God wants us to disregard children—the opposite is clearly true in the Bible. However, the marital relationship has priority over the parental relationship.

How does this play out in real life? Moms: Your child's art class is a lower priority than your husband's needs. Dads: Your son's football game is a lower priority than your wife's needs. Parents: It's okay to tell the kids, "We're not going to go out to dinner where you want to go . . . we're going to go where Mom (or Dad) wants to go." If you need to move to follow your job, it is right to say to your child, "Yep, it's a bummer to move during the middle of high school . . . but here we go." It is not usually right to say, "Well, we'll just split up for two years so Jimmy can finish school in one place." Dads: It is holy to say to your son, "I better *never* hear you talk to your mother like that again!" Moms: It is righteous to say to your daughter, "Don't *ever* disrespect your father like that!"

This is the amazing thing that I've seen in my experience: when spouses focus healthily on each other, their children thrive. Keeping the right perspective on the marital relationship breaks the back of the tendency to spoil your children; they will learn very early that the world is not all about them. Keeping the right perspective also prevents festering wounds in the marriage relationship. How often have you seen someone look to their kids to fill the hole that they feel due to a relational problem with their spouse? Mothers, because God gave womankind a nurturing spirit, you are most prone to this. One of my friends had a real problem in her marital relationship and the way she dealt with it was to keep focusing on children more and more by continuing to adopt young ones. Using her kids as a retreat from the problems she had with her husband kept her from dealing with problems while they were still small, and this was one of the things that ultimately caused her marriage to collapse.

If you have little kids in the house, notice how they act when you snuggle with your spouse. You'll find that they generally like it. In fact, they will frequently try to get between the two of you when you embrace, but not to split you. They intuitively want to be in the middle of that love. The truth is that when we honor our spouses before our children, we are the very best parents we can be, and we ultimately bless our children more than we would have if we had put them first.

Speaking of putting children first, answer this question: if you are not financially strapped, is it more important to devote time to parenting or to employment? I think the vast majority of people will say that raising your children is far more important than raising a little extra spending money.

So here is the next lie on the parental battle line: The world tells us that generating luxury income is more important than parenting. When both parents work outside the home, they are, by definition, parenting part-time.

According to the Bureau of Labor Statistics, between 1970 and 1993, the proportion of dual income couples rose from 39 to 61 percent[28], and the Department of Labor reported that between 1996 and 2006 the number of dual-income families increased by an additional 31%.[29] As of 2010, over half of families with children had two working parents.[30] This means that in America, two-income families have become the norm, meaning that most families have two part-time parents.

---

[28] Bud Meyers; "Two Income Households, 'Mean' and 'Median' Income Statistics"; accessed Mar 5, 2014; http://bud-meyers.blogspot.com/2012/05/two-income-households-mean-and-median.html

[29] "Employment Status of Women and Men in 2007," US Department of Labor, accessed Mar 5, 2013; http://www.dol.gov/wb/factsheets/Qf-ESWM07.htm

[30] Bureau of Labor Statistics as quoted by Tara Struyk; "Two-Income Households, Can Making More Put Us Further Behind?"; Mar 8, 2012; accessed on Mar 5, 2014; http://www.wisebread.com/in-two-income-households-can-making-more-put-us-further-behind

Is this necessarily bad? No. Many families do well with two working-outside-the-home parents. But let me ask you a few questions: not including sleep time, who is spending more time with your kids? Is it you and your spouse, or is it the daycare or the babysitter or the teachers? Are your children alone more often than they are with you? Who welcomes your children home from school? Who spends the most time overseeing their free time during the week—you, someone else, or no one?

So often when we speak of whether both parents should work, we speak of adequacy. We ask if both parents can both work and raise kids. We ask if kids will get messed up by having two working parents. We ask if it will have any long-term significant consequences if we both work. All of these are ways of asking, "Will we be adequate parents?" However, the Biblical question to ask is, "If we both work, will we be the best parents we can be?"

The Bible does not proscribe single-income families. There is no "Thou Shalt Not Both Be Employed Outside The Home" commandment. In fact, if you read Proverbs 31, you'll see praise for a working mother. The issue is not whether we have dual incomes. The issue—and the deception—is about whether we should choose better income over better parenting.

The Bible makes a clear case that parents should parent well. By both example and command, we are taught to treasure our children,[cl] to teach them spiritual truth,[cli] to teach them wisdom,[clii] to discipline them,[cliii] and to provide for their needs (which would include financial needs).[cliv]

The Bible also makes a clear case that we are not to chase after riches. God tells us not to store up things here on earth,[clv] He tells us that greed is sinful,[clvi] He tells us not to covet,[clvii] He tells us not to seek pleasures,[clviii] and He tells us not to worry about stuff (which includes money).[clix]

I don't think any rational person would argue with the statement that when we spend more time parenting our children, our chances of parenting success are higher. If that's true, then it follows logically that if we can afford to be a full-time parent, we ought to be. I don't know how many times I've heard stories of (or been part of) situations where kids get into trouble "while mom and dad weren't home."

So the question that arises is this: when is a second income providing for our children's needs and when is it providing for our luxury? Ultimately, that is a question for all parents to take up with God, but evil certainly would like you to believe that everything is a "need" and nothing is a "luxury." Let me give you some hard facts to help defeat this deception. According to the US Census Bureau, the median annual income for a family household in 2012 was $64,053.

Here are the median incomes for different wage situations:

|  | Median Income |
|---|---|
| All Family Households | $64,053 |
| Both Wife and Husband Work | $110,357 |
| Only Wife Works | $64,699 |
| Only Husband Works | $69,400 |

Figures derived from US Census Bureau data for 2012 [31]

This means that the typical family with only one wage earner will take home more than the median income for all households and will be over twice the poverty level for a family of four. Put in simpler terms, most families on a single income will be living on the same amount of money as at least half of the families in the US. In other words most families can exist just fine on a single income.

However, by only having one wage earner you typically will be sacrificing almost $50,000 worth of luxury a year. Are children worth that? I think they are.

If these statistics are true, why do so many families feel like they have to have two incomes? Folks in lower-wage jobs genuinely do need two incomes to keep food on the table, a roof over their head, and provide adequate medical care for their children. However, many of us feel like two-incomes are a necessity largely because we live in a high-income culture. That is to say, there are many things in middle-class America that we sees as 'needs' that are really just 'wants'. Here are just a few things to consider about life in 21st Century America:

- In 1980, the average family was happy in a house that was about 1600 square feet; in 2010 they feel like they needed almost 2200 square feet.[32] How much house do we

[31] United States Census Bureau, "Current Population Survey"; accessed Mar 5, 2014; http://www.census.gov/hhes/www/cpstables/032013/faminc/finc04_000.htm

[32] "Median and Average Square Feet of Floor Area in New Single-Family Houses"; US Census Bureau; accessed Mar 5, 2014; http://www.census.gov/const/C25Ann/sftotalmedavgsqft.pdf

really need? (Also, the average house in the 1950s was 983 square feet.)[33]

• In 1980, almost no one had a cell phone bill; In 2012, a typical family of four can spend over $200 per month.[34] Sometimes we wonder if it is possible to live without cell service—yet most of us grew up without it.

• In 1990, a basic monthly cable subscription cost $16.[35] In 2011, the average monthly cable bill was $78[36] despite the fact that it is still possible to get basic cable packages for around $30.

• The average cost of a new car in 1980 was $7200; in 2013 it was $31,352.[37] However, you can still buy a new, four seat, family sedan in 2014 for less than $20,000.

• Americans spend almost half of their food budget on eating out[38] and the average adult has 4.8 restaurant meals each week,[39] but eating at home can be 2 to 10 times less expensive than restaurant food.[40]

• The bottom-line is this: Many of us have been caught by the lie that we need more money and stuff to be "good

[33] Kaid Benfield; "What's going on with new home sizes – is the madness finally over?"; Feb 9, 2012; accessed Mar 5, 2014;
http://www.census.gov/const/C25Ann/sftotalmedavgsqft.pdf
[34] Zain Asher-Ejiofor; iofor; iofor; or; v/const/C25Ann/sftoCNNMoney; accessed Mar 5, 2014; http://money.cnn.com/2012/04/16/pf/cell-phone-bill.moneymag/index.htm
[35] Geraldine Fabrikant; brikant; er One, New York.able Channels Are Losing Their Momentumatthew 26:36-46 Times; May 28, 1990; accessed Mar 5, 2014;
http://www.nytimes.com/1990/05/28/business/the-media-business-pay-cable-channels-are-losing-their-momentum.html
[36] Lauren A.E. Schuker; huker; .E. Schuker; York.rms, er; .E. Schuker; York.e Wall Street Journal; Dec 29,2011; accessed Mar 5, 2014;
http://online.wsj.com/news/articles/SB10001424052970203479104577124494272500550?mod=e2tw&mg=reno64-wsj&url=http%3A%2F%2Fonline.wsj.com%2Farticle%2FSB10001424052970203479104577124494272500550.html%3Fmod%3De2tw
[37] Comparison of Prices Over 70 Years; accessed Mar 5, 2014;
http://www.thepeoplehistory.com/70yearsofpricechange.html
[38] How much do Americans Spend on Eating Out; WiseGEEK; accessed Mar 5, 2014; http://www.wisegeek.com/how-much-do-americans-spend-on-eating-out.htm
[39] accessed Mar 5, 2014; http://www.wisegeek.com/how-much-do-americans-spend-on-eating-out.htmw.upi.com/Health_News/2011/09/19/Americans-eat-out-about-5-times-a-week/UPI-54241316490172/
[40] accessed Mar 5, 2014; http://www.wisegeek.com/how-much-do-americans-spend-on-eating-out.htmw.upi.com/Health_News/2out-5-times-a-week/UPI-54241316490172/

parents" or to be "happy" when in fact we would be better parents—and happier—if we were to settle for a lower income and keep a full-time parent at home. The truth is that God wants us to prioritize parenting over savings, extra income, retirement, luxuries, big houses, or vacations.

If you and your spouse both need to work to provide essential food, shelter, and welfare for your children, then continue to do so, and God bless you for your hard work. But if you and your spouse are both working so that you can have a bigger house, newer cars, better vacations, or a bigger college fund, you might want to examine your priorities and see if you aren't losing the battle on the line of parenting. Don't fall for the lie that your income is more important to your kids than your time.

There's one last lie that I'll discuss on the parental battle line, and it is pervasive, pernicious and aggressively forced on us. It's the lie that disciplining your children is a bad thing. Let's just get things clear right from the start: God says you should hit your kids.

That statement will, for most people, evoke a reaction, and I wrote it that way for a reason. A resistance to physical punishment is pretty deeply ingrained in us both by experience and by American culture. That's why we feel this visceral opposition when someone says, "God says you should hit your kids." So let's take a moment to unpack why we react this way. To do so, we'll look at a couple of historical trends.

In 1946, Dr Benjamin Spock wrote *The Common Sense Book of Baby and Child Care* in which he discouraged punishment and encouraged a child-centered approach to parenting with an emphasis on children's feelings and preferences.[41] Reacting to then-common notions that parents should withhold affection from children, Spock taught that children's motives are "good most of the time," that parents should avoid scolding or threats, and that spankings were unproductive and even harmful. His book sold over four million copies in its first six years and has since sold over 50 million copies—arguably impacting parenting as much as any book. In the years after the book's publishing, Spock's views were mirrored and promulgated by many so-called "experts," and acknowledging this impact, Life Magazine named Dr Spock one of

[41] Reb Bradley; "How Dr Spock Destroyed America"; WorldNet Daily; accessed Mar 6, 2014; http://www.wnd.com/2009/01/87179/

the 100 most important people of the 20th Century.[42] Whether his work was causative or just indicative of cultural trends I don't know, but we now find ourselves in a culture where parents are often unsure of whether they should discipline their children and where corporal punishment is largely discouraged or even actively opposed by government. This trend having achieved a global scale, the United Nations now formally opposes physical discipline and asserts that deciding on discipline is not even the purview of parents. Article 19 of the United Nations Convention on the Rights of the Child says that "States Parties shall take all appropriate legislative, administrative, social and education measures to protect the child from all forms of physical or mental violence . . . while in the care of parent(s)."[43]

Along with the Spock-parenting trend (and maybe partly because of it), the American cultural view of violence changed as well. I'm not smart enough to know why. However, between sometime around the end of World War II and present day, American culture went from seeing violence as a necessary part of life in a fallen world to viewing it as an abhorrent evil. Where boys once "scrapped" on the playground to assert their rights and manhood, they now get immediately suspended for throwing a punch at the bully who is tormenting them. Gone are the days when any self-respecting young man carried a pocket knife, a useful tool; now pocket knives are criminal in schools and government buildings. Farmers are criticized for slaughtering livestock. Kids are suspended from school for pantomiming a gun with their forefinger and thumb. Mothers and fathers tell their children they can't play "cowboys and Indians" because it is violent. And parents aren't supposed to spank children because it teaches them that "might makes right."

The problem with this narrative is that it is hopelessly confused. "Might" might not make right, but it allows the righteous to stop the unrighteous. Nobody wants a military without guns. Nobody wants to eat McDonald's soy-burgers so that cows don't have to die (well, almost nobody). Nobody wants police armed only with loud voices. Nobody wants to watch a football game where the

---

[42] Ibid.
[43] UN Convention on the Rights of the Child, Article 19; as quoted by Religious Tolerance.org; "The anti-spanking position"; accessed Mar 6, 2014; http://www.religioustolerance.org/spankin4.htm

linemen protect the quarterback using clever words. Americans embrace movies where "good guys" use epic violence to stop "bad guys." And so conscientious parents struggle as they hear the voices of fools saying, "All violence is bad" while they see every day that "good" violence is necessary in this fallen world.

These two historical trends—parenting without discipline and aversion to all violence—have resulted in a skewed version of what it means to love your child, and this is the fundamental lie that has to be fought. Satan would have you say, "You never intentionally hurt children you love." God says, "Because they have sin in them, you have to intentionally hurt children you love."

Have you ever taken your young child to get a shot? They hated getting stuck with a needle because it truly hurt them. Yet you knew that the brief but real pain was not going to have any long consequences, and you also knew that the vaccine that is delivered by that pain will protect your child for a lifetime. This is the same perspective we must have with disciplining our children if we want to combat Satan's lie. We must acknowledge that a little pain now helps our children forever.

This is not my idea—it is all over the Bible. It's actually surprising how many times God says in the Bible that discipline is good:

• Know then in your heart that as a man disciplines his son, so the Lord your God disciplines you. (Deuteronomy 8:5)
• Blessed is the one whom God corrects; so do not despise the discipline of the Almighty. (Job 5:17)
• Blessed is the one you discipline, Lord, the one you teach from your law. (Psalm 94:12)
• My son, do not despise the Lord's discipline, and do not resent his rebuke, because the Lord disciplines those he loves, as a father the son he delights in. (Proverbs 3:11-12)
• For lack of discipline they will die, led astray by their own great folly. (Proverbs 5:23)
• Whoever loves discipline loves knowledge, but whoever hates correction is stupid. (Proverbs 12:1)
• Whoever spares the rod hates their children, but the one who loves their children is careful to discipline them. (Proverbs 13:24)
• Discipline your children, for in that there is hope; do not be a willing party to their death. (Proverbs 19:18)
• Folly is bound up in the heart of a child, but the rod of

discipline will drive it far away. (Proverbs 22:15)

• Do not withhold discipline from a child; if you punish them with the rod, they will not die. (Proverbs 23:13)

• Discipline your children, and they will give you peace; they will bring you the delights you desire. (Proverbs 29:17)

• 'I am with you and will save you,' declares the Lord. 'Though I completely destroy all the nations among which I scatter you, I will not completely destroy you. I will discipline you but only in due measure; I will not let you go entirely unpunished.' (Jeremiah 30:11)

• Nevertheless, when we are judged in this way by the Lord, we are being disciplined so that we will not be finally condemned with the world. (1 Corinthians 11:32)

• . . . the Lord disciplines the one he loves, and he chastens everyone he accepts as his son. (Hebrews 12:6)

• If you are not disciplined—and everyone undergoes discipline—then you are not legitimate, not true sons and daughters at all. (Hebrews 12:8)

• God disciplines us for our good, in order that we may share in his holiness. (Hebrews 12:10)

• No discipline seems pleasant at the time, but painful. Later on, however, it produces a harvest of righteousness and peace for those who have been trained by it. (Hebrews 12:11)

• Those whom I [Christ] love I rebuke and discipline. (Revelation 3:19)

Evil would have us believe that physical discipline is hateful, but God says over and over that physical discipline is an essential part of love. In fact, His instructions are so explicit that a parent who does not discipline his (or her) children is guilty of violating God's commands. In other words, the parent who refuses to physically discipline their child is sinning. This is so contrary to what a lot of us have been taught that I think it's worth saying again: If you refuse to discipline your children, you are going against God and are hating your child.

But does this mean I have to administer physical discipline, a.k.a. spanking, a.k.a. corporal punishment, a.k.a. hitting my kid? Yes. Absolutely. Re-read Proverbs 13:24, 22:15, and 23:13. That's why I said that "God wants you to hit your kid."

Now with that said, with wrong motives or wrong understanding spanking can quickly become abuse—and that is just as bad as not spanking at all. So to avoid falling into Satan's trap on the other side of this issue, keep in mind that there is a right way and a wrong way to administer physical discipline. Here are just a few rules of thumb that will help keep your discipline holy and not hellish, but I'd really recommend getting some more detailed advice if you aren't sure about how to do this right.

• Never physically discipline in anger. Corporal punishment is best delivered when you are cool enough to do it right, so give yourself a cool-down period if you need it before you discipline. It's also very effective in making the child consider his consequences when you say, "Son, go to your room and I'll be up in a few minutes to give you a spanking." (But it is important to give this warning immediately after the infraction and not hours later.)

• Never discipline saying, "I'm going to make this hurt so bad that he'll never do it again." The point of a spanking is to accentuate your corrective words and actions with just enough pain that the child understands that this is really important. The purpose of spanking is not to generate so much pain that the child will never repeat the action. If you are using more force than what you'd be willing to use on your own bare skin as a demonstration, you are using too much force.

• Only physically discipline in cases of *willful* disobedience. If your child makes an honest mistake, use non-corporal punishment. Use corporal punishment only when the child knows the right thing and intentionally chooses not to do it.

• Always reconcile after any kind of discipline, especially physical discipline. This means you physically touch them (usually a hug, maybe a hand on the shoulder) and tell them you love them. Most kids will immediately want a hug after being disciplined. Some may wait a while and then seek reconciliation after a short time. With some children you will have to initiate reconciliation, but I have never seen a child who does not want to be affirmed in love after being disciplined.

• Usually discipline in private. This protects you from legal assault (remember the UN is out to get you) and also saves your child from embarrassment.

• Have mercy. God did not say: "Always discipline!" There are times when mercy should triumph over judgment. There will be a point when your child is too old for corporal punishment.

Remember that spanking is an expression of love, not an application of law.

Like a doctor causing the painful prick of a needle to give a life saving vaccine, Christian parents must believe God's Truth and be willing to provide some painful discipline to love their children. Those of us who aren't raising children ourselves would do well to encourage those who are, and to silence the foolish talk of those who would say that good parents never pain their children.

Christian warriors understand that lies about parenting—prioritizing children over spouses, prioritizing income over parenting, or believing that "discipline is bad"—must be fought at every turn.

The more of His people we have speaking this truth, the quicker this battle will be won. Yet even if we win the battle of parenting, Satan will not just walk away. As our children get old enough, he'll try to take them down as well. That's why we need to talk about one last battle line on the Battleground at Home.

## The Battle Line of Youth

In 1942, a young man named Audie Murphy enlisted in the United States Army when he was only 17 years old. (He actually tried to enlist when he was 16 but was deemed too young.) Murphy went on to become one of the most decorated American soldiers in World War II. In 2009, a Texas teacher began choking on an apple, and 10-year-old Kyle Forbes began administering the Heimlich maneuver—saving the teachers life.[44] Just last week, a 3 year old girl named Elisha Powers saved her father's life by dialing 911 when he was bleeding to death after receiving a severe cut from a machete he was using.[45] All three of these heroes were of young age, but all three made incredible differences in the world around them despite age, education, size, and/or capacity.

When we talk about the Battleground at Home, it is not just fought by adults. If you are under the age of 18 and reading this, you too are in battle, and we need your help to win this war. The world tries to tell young people that they aren't old enough to fight,

---

[44] Lindsay Goldenberg; "Surprising Kid Heroes"; accessed Mar 7, 2014; http://mom.me/parenting/2377-surprising-child-heroes/

[45] "Pint Sized Hero Saves Injured Father"; Fox News video; accessed Mar 7, 2014 http://video.foxnews.com/v/3280906106001/pint-sized-hero-saves-injured-father/#sp=show-clips

but in spiritual battle, they most certainly are. In the Bible, the apostle Paul tells young Timothy, "Don't let anyone look down on you because you are young, but set an example for the believers in speech, in conduct, in love, in faith, and in purity."[clx] I think young Christians need to be aware of two big lies that Satan uses to try to take them out of the fight.

The first big lie is that youth are a separate species from adults. While there are obvious physical, mental, and emotional differences between youth and adults, these differences are minor variations amidst a world of commonality. So much in our world today encourages youth to see themselves as part of an independent culture, and so much in our world encourages us old farts to see youth as somehow separate from us. This view is encouraged by visual media, print media, school, and even many in the church.

Television and movies have always shown youth doing youth things and adults doing adult things. However, while in the past these differences tended to be shown in the context of a larger unified picture (e.g. youth adventures in the context of a functional family on "The Brady Bunch"), now these differences are more often shown in stark and near-continual opposition (e.g. a young hero trying to work around his out-of-touch parents in "Transformers").

Many books and magazines cater to specific youth needs, desires, or story lines that are independent of (rather than integrated with) adult needs, desires, and story lines. Advertisers directly target youth audiences and specifically try to create the impression that youth have different consumer needs than adults.

Schools, often with the best of intentions, specifically exclude or limit the interaction of parents and children. At lunch or break times, teachers and students for the most part go their separate ways – creating an additional dynamic of separation between young and adult. With school attendance taking a majority of a young person's waking hours, the net effect is an automatic creation of a youth subculture.

Churches often unwittingly contribute to the creation of this subculture. In an effort to be "relevant," many churches offer separate youth activities with the net affect that a family drives together to church and immediately splits into separate youth and adult activities. The subtle message is that "youth are not like adults."

The Bible speaks of youth as a transitional time period between childhood and adulthood. The NIV translation of the Bible uses the term "youth" 59 times, sometimes as a description of age (e.g. "I have been your leader from my youth")[clxi] and sometimes as a description of a person or group of people of young age (e.g. "I noticed among the young men, a youth who had no sense.")[clxii] Youthfulness is often associated with vigor, health, foolishness, and less discipline. However, the needs of youth – wisdom, knowledge, discipline, and responsibility—are substantially the same as the needs of adults, albeit in different degree. Likewise the capacities for youth to do good or evil are the same as for adults. While the Bible does have specific instructions for children, sons, daughters, young men, young women, older men, and older women,[clxiii] it does not have any specific instructions for a category of people known as youth. The implication is that you are either a child, or you are a man or woman (i.e. an adult).

Satan wants youth to believe that they are fundamentally different than adults. He wants youth to believe that they don't have to do adult-stuff until they are 18 or maybe done with college. He wants them to believe that they can't really do a whole lot until they are "grown up." At an age where, 100 years ago, many of our youth would have been married and working full time, our youth are considering whether they should get up before noon on a Saturday. Satan would have our youth believe that they have to figure out their religious beliefs sometime before they are adults, but not just yet. God wants youth to know that they can have a real and vibrant relationship and life with Christ *right now*.

Here's how we counteract this lie of youth as a separate species:

**Young people:** Believe that God wants you to know that you can make a difference in the world and even show adults how to believe and act (remember Paul's words to Timothy and young David's actions against Goliath).[clxiv] Know that God wants you to be thinking like young men and young women—not like tweens, teens, high school students, college students, or anything else. Is there ignorance in youth? Yes. Lack of self-discipline? Yes. Foolishness? Yes. But you will find all of these in adulthood in varying degrees as well. God may very well want you to be the defining difference in your friends' lives, in your siblings' lives, in your parents' lives, and in your teachers' lives. You can save them from deception and can introduce them to the one who can save them from hell.

**Old people:** While acknowledging the very real shortfalls of youth, we need to quit looking down on young people. We need to quit perpetuating the lie that they are "just kids." We need to fight against those things in our culture that say that youth are supposed to be irresponsible and start setting the bar high for them to be young men and young women. Unless he has a history of proven irresponsibility, if your son is old enough to drive and you are asking him to check-in on the cell phone all the time, you are perpetuating the myth that he's still just a kid. If your daughter comes home and spends the whole evening watching TV and surfing the internet and talking on the phone, tell her to make dinner or do the wash or pay the bills for you (or all of the above)—expect her to be a young adult, not a big child.

The lie is that our youth are their own species. We need to make sure that they know the truth: that they are just younger versions of adults and fully capable of being God's warriors. But there's another lie that we must fight as well, and it can be illustrated by this story:

I once heard a story about a woman who was making a roast as her mother had taught her. "Mom," she asked, "I know why we season the roast and how long we cook it, but why do we always cut the end off?" Her mother looked at her and said, "I'm not sure. I'll have to ask your grandma." So the mom called the woman who had taught her how to cook a roast. "Mother," she asked, "Why did you teach me to cut the end of the roast off before we put it in the oven?" The old woman replied, "Why? Well because we only had a small roasting pan, and it wouldn't fit otherwise."

As this story shows us, sometimes we do things for the wrong reason. Similarly, if we don't know the real reason for a command or instruction, it makes it really hard to be obedient. This is the crux of the second lie that confronts youth on the Battleground at Home. Everyone knows that kids should obey their mom and dad. But why? Why are they supposed to be obedient? Is it because their parents know better? Is it because their parents are smarter and more experienced?

The lie is this: "You should obey your parents, because they know best." The truth is "you should honor your parents because that pleases God."

Note the two big differences between the lie and the truth.

First, we don't do this because of our parents, we do this because of God. Second, we aren't just to obey, we are to honor. These might seem like subtle differences, but they have profound implications.

Let's talk first about our motivation to honor our parents, because our motivation is the foundation of the matter. Here are a few of the things that the Bible says about our relationship with our parents:

• Honor your father and your mother, as the LORD your God has commanded you, so that you may live long and that it may go well with you in the land the LORD your God is giving you. (Deuteronomy 5:16)

• Children, obey your parents in the Lord, for this is right. "Honor your father and mother"—which is the first commandment with a promise— "so that it may go well with you and that you may enjoy long life on the earth." (Ephesians 6:1-3)

• Children, obey your parents in everything, for this pleases the Lord. (Colossians 3:20)

Note that God gives us over and over a reason for honoring parents: "that it may go well with you," "that you may live long," "for this pleases the Lord." Obedience to and honoring of our parents is not "just because." Likewise obedience is not commanded because our parents are smarter or more competent than we are. God tells us to honor our parents out of respect for Him.

I know a teenage Christian lady, who I'll call Kendra, who has a contentious relationship with her mom. Her mom is super nice but has a history of making some poor choices. Kendra's mom also has a habit of using "white lies" to control situations or to avoid conflict. So when Kendra has conflict with her mom, it's hard to make a strong case for obedience based on the "mother knows best" argument. It's also sometimes hard to stand on the "your mom deserves honor" argument because Kendra has a lot of evidence to make the case that her mom doesn't deserve it.

However, the truth is that God has placed both Kendra and her mom in their mother-daughter relationship. He knows all of both of their faults, and He still says, "Honor your mother. Not because she's smarter, not because she deserves it, but because doing so pleases Me . . . and so it will go well with you and you will live long."

For the Christian child of any age, if we remember that we honor our parents to please God, it takes away Satan's ability to detour us based on practicalities. Evil wants children to say things like:

- "I'd obey my dad if he wasn't such a jerk."
- "I try to honor my mom, but she keeps wanting me to do stupid things. I can't honor someone who asks me to waste my time."
- "I don't talk to my mom anymore because when I was 15 she left my dad."
- "I always do what my dad says, except when he asks me to do something that I know is jacked up."

My friend Phil had to put his elderly parents in an assisted-living facility because they were both losing their mental faculties. It was a hard decision but the most loving thing to do because his parents could no longer function without full-time care. If Phil had based "honor your father and mother" on his parents' capacity, he would have turned his back on them years before, but he did not. Phil understood that the fifth commandment is about pleasing God, so he stuck with his parents and cared for them and honored them even when they were not capable of doing anything to deserve honor. That's living the Truth and that's different than what the world teaches.

The second big difference between the lie and the truth of honoring parents revolves around the difference between the ideas of "honor" and "obedience." *Honor* is the idea of esteeming or ascribing value to something. *Obedience* means that we comply with a command or instruction. While these two concepts can be related to each other, they aren't necessarily so. Let me explain with an example.

Some years ago, there was a general in charge of my organization who was the proverbial "horse's rear-end." This egotist would publicly denigrate his subordinate leaders and had a "my way or the highway" attitude, but because he was a general, we all did what he said. We did not honor him, but we certainly obeyed him. Contrast him with a different general that I worked under who was a no-nonsense kind of guy, but who treated his subordinates with respect and compassion. We obeyed this general as well, but we also honored him.

It is a truism that if we honor someone, we will obey him, but it is also possible to *not* honor someone, yet still obey him. So honor includes obedience, but obedience does not necessarily connote honor.

So how does this apply to the relationship of a child to parents? God commands us to honor our parents. That means that if we follow His command, we will esteem or value our parents, which naturally includes being obedient to them. Yet evil wants to convince us that obedience is the main thing and that honor is unnecessary or optional.

This is how this plays out in real life: A parent says to her son, "Please be home from the party by 10 PM." He protests, grouses, and complains. At the party, the young man rails on his "over-controlling" parents and talks about how he can't wait to get out on his own. He walks into his house at 10 sharp, offers a terse good night as he passes his parents on the way to his room, and slams the door behind him. Has this young man done what God has asked him to do? Nope. He was 100% obedient, but he was also 99% dishonoring.

It's natural to ask, "Why does this matter? Didn't he do what his parents wanted?" And in this very question is the heart of the problem. We Christians are not living primarily to please those around us (including our parents). We are living to please God. This question presupposes that "doing what we're asked" is the main thing when the Bible clearly teaches that the orientation of our heart toward God is the main thing (and the "doing" is a consequence of that heart orientation and not an end in itself). Honoring our parents matters because pleasing God matters. Honoring our parents matters because in honoring our earthly fathers (and mothers) we are learning how to honor our heavenly Father.

Let's replay the above scenario in terms of "honor" rather than obedience:

A parent says to her son, "Please be home from the party by 10 PM." Sick of his mom's fearful and controlling attitude, the young man wants to spout off, but he holds his tongue and says simply, "You know the Smiths are very responsible, can't I come home at midnight?" His mom will not relent, however. At the party, the young man tells his friends it's time for him to go. "Man, your folks are so tight," a friend remarks. The young man's response is, "Yeah, they can be, but you have to take the bad with the good."

He walks into his house at 10 sharp, still riled up. Although he doesn't feel like it, he stops to talk to his parents for a few minutes before going to bed for the night. Has this young man done what God has asked him to do? Absolutely. He was 100% obedient, and he was also 100% honoring.

If God is not a liar, this young man will have a long life and it will go well with him.

When we dishonor our parents we miss out on some of God's very real blessings. Many young Christians can't seem to figure out what to do with their lives; many are sure that there is something more to their relationship with God, but can't seem to figure out how to get it; many are longing for a soul-mate, but feel so alone; many are trying to make it in the job market, but seem always to be stuck in dead-end jobs. I wonder how many of these folks would see some or all of these problems go away if they really believed God when He says, "*Honor* your parents . . . that it may go well with you."

Here is the bottom line: The devil would have us believe that we only need to obey our parents when they deserve it, and if we say we are going to obey them even when they don't deserve it, Satan whispers in our ear, "Just so long as you are obedient, you are doing good." God wants us to not simply obey but to honor, and He wants us to do so to please Him. God says that if we do this, "it will go well with you."

Christian warriors understand that our youth are spiritual warriors too. We must do all we can to defeat the lie that they are "a different species" and to remind them that honoring parents brings God's blessings.

Stand shoulder to shoulder with your spouse, with your children, and with your friends and neighbors on the Battleground at Home. If we proclaim God's truth about the Marital Battle Line, the Parenting Battle Line, and the Battle Line of Youth, and if we live out the truth in our own lives, there is no telling what our strong families can do to bring God's Kingdom to this world which so desperately needs Him. Fight the good fight in the home so that you have the strength and energy to fight the good fight on the other battlefields of your life.

## 4-3 THE BATTLEGROUND OF THE CHURCH

As part of my military career, I attended a school in Alabama that was designed to help Air Force officers become better leaders. At that school we studied and discussed a lot of key leadership principles like fostering teamwork, being decisive, structuring rewards and punishments, learning by doing, and so on. There was just one big problem. In order to foster excellence, the school had a system of competition through which the different teams of students could compete for honors at the end of the course. However, this competitive system was designed to reward top outcomes, not top leadership. The consequence was that the team that applied the fewest of the leadership principles (and just let its most naturally-gifted students do everything) would always receive the greatest reward. The institution through its actions discouraged effective leadership-learning even as its curriculum attempted to teach the greatest leadership principles. Needless to say, this school was dysfunctional, and it illustrates a famous axiom in organizational theory: "Every system is perfectly designed to produce exactly what it produces."

If a leadership school is producing poor leaders, something in the school is causing that. Likewise, if a factory produces bent nails, you know that something on the assembly line is bending the nails. If your desire is to produce straight nails, you have to change the machine that is doing the bending. So if your product is not what you want, you know you have to change the system.

Does this axiom apply to the church? You betcha.

Why do so many people sit in pews and not do anything significant with their faith? Why are so many Christian churches destroyed by splits and feuds? Why do Christian pastors leave seminary with a less-Biblical view of life than they had when they entered? Why are there so many different denominations in God's church? Why do 80% of youth leave the faith that they learned in church when they leave home?

These are weighty questions, and the answers to them could probably fill several books. However, those answers could all be boiled down into a simple application of the above axiom: Churches that produce hollow faith do so because they are perfectly designed to do so.

Does this mean that churches are completely messed-up?

By way of answer, is a nail factory that produces bent nails completely messed-up? You could say, "Yes, it doesn't produce straight nails" or you could say, "No, it's not all messed-up, we just need to fix the part that's bending the nails." So it goes with the Christian church. The church has many God-loving people that are doing God-honoring things and bringing people to a saving faith in Christ, but all this notwithstanding, the American church is not consistently and widely being "the light of the world" or "the salt of the earth." So what keeps bending our nails?

For obvious reasons, the church is the target of Satan's lies, and when we believe these lies, we produce "bent nails." What do you think are the fundamental lies that derail the church from God's purposes? I think there are four lies that we would do well to battle when we consider our churches. Each one is pervasive and each one, when believed, can damage or destroy a lot of the goodness that God designed His church to do.

## The Battle Line of Consumerism

You have to be an incredible narcissist to walk into a church and say, "This is all about me." None of us would say this, and yet we think along the lines of this lie all the time.

As a military family, we moved quite often, and so we were forced to go "church shopping" every few years as we moved to a new assignment. This gave me a lot of experience with the lie of consumerism – I saw it in myself all the time. It's natural to think like a consumer when you go to a new church:

- Do I like the music?
- Do I like the way the pastor preaches?
- Do they have ministries that I and my family need?
- Were the people friendly?
- Is their doctrine correct?
- Do I have to dress up or can I dress casually?
- Is their church service at a convenient time?

Notice that all of these questions revolve around what I like, what I agree with, or what I need. None of these questions matter in the end. There is only one question that really matters: "God, do you want me here at this church?"

Lie #1 is the lie of consumerism. You don't have to be looking for a new church to get caught in it. Here are real-life things that I have thought myself or have heard people say in churches.

- "I don't like the way he [the pastor] talks."
- "It's too dark in here."
- "They don't know how to play worship music correctly."
- "They are weird."
- "Somebody sat in the seat that I always sit in."
- "This church has gotten too big [small]."

The implication behind all of these statements is "it's all about me"—about what I like, about what I think is good for my spiritual growth, about what I think will bring me closest to God in the quickest way with the least amount of hassle.

The truth is that the church is all about God. The Bible says that the church is like a body with Christ as the head and with all of us as the pieces and parts. God puts us where He wants us and asks us to do what He wants us to do for the mutual benefit of everyone and so that we can follow Christ together. In following Christ we become like him, and we glorify God.[clxv]

One of my best friends is a member of a huge church. A lot of the hugeness drives him nuts, but he's been a committed member of that church for over a decade, and I suspect he will still be on the day that he dies. You see, my buddy knows that's where God wants him. He sees all the good stuff that God has done (and continues to do) at that church despite all the things that bug him. My friend knows that it's not all about him.

My buddy also thinks that maybe one of the reasons God has him there is to help keep the voices for hugeness from being the only voices heard. Maybe God has him there to help the leadership at that church not lose the common touch.

Do you ever think that maybe God wants YOU to be His agent to do His will at your church? Maybe He wants you in the pew every Sunday, happily enduring boring worship music, so that you can take some ministry at that church to a new level. Maybe He wants you to sit through your pastor's bunny-trail-filled, way-too-long sermons so that you can personally impact just one person with the message of hope, four years from now. Maybe He wants you to be in that too-small church to help it grow.

Satan would have you believe that you are in church for your benefit. God's truth is that you are in church to do His good work and to glorify Him. There is nothing wrong with examining our likes and dislikes, and there is nothing wrong with asking God if you are where He really wants you or even asking Him if He might let you change your church home, but don't let yourself fall into the "it's all about me" thinking. Even through the storms of church life, the one question we always have to be asking is "God, where do you want me to be?"

Christian warriors don't go to church as consumers. They go as producers.

## The Battle Line of Over-Education

Lie #2 on the Battleground of the Church is that "church is about learning." Pastor Mark Batterson says, "Christians are educated way beyond the level of their obedience."[46] That is a problem.

What does your church do? Most churches I've been in learn. When they talk about Sunday services, the emphasis is on the sermon. When they talk about serving, they talk about helping people learn more. Most have "Sunday School." There's usually a women's "study" during the week, and sometimes one for men. If there is a mid-week service, it is probably centered around a sermon. Youth groups are usually focused around verbal instruction.

Now to be fair, every church I've seen spends time praying. They spend time worshipping. They all have some active ministries, and so I am not saying that the only thing we do is learn. However, I am saying that academic learning is the emphasis in far too many churches, and things like prayer, worship, missions, and service are second-tier events.

How much time does your church spend on "announcements" during the Sunday service? Announcements is when the pastor or someone says in effect, "This is what is going on this week . . . this is what we are doing." Every time I have been party to discussions about the programming of announcements, the emphasis has been on keeping them short, minimizing the impact on the rest of the service, and "not boring people." Not to malign a fine game fish, but this is a bass-ackwards way of thinking.

Imagine if I came into the morning briefing of an Air Force combat unit and said, "Airmen, I'm going to teach you something about the principles of war, then the intelligence specialists are

---

46 Mark Batterson. "Get a Life." Aug 14, 2012. Accessed Jan 15, 2015 at http://www.markbatterson.com/uncategorized/get-a-life-2/

going to teach you about enemy doctrine, then we'll have a special presentation from Major Whozit on how to keep calm under pressure. Oh, and you have a combat mission to fly today, if we have time we'll discuss that as well." If I approached real combat this way, you'd rightly think that I was a loon.

Churches often do the spiritual equivalent of what I just described. Learning is a central part of our church experience, but church is NOT about learning, and it's a massive deception to think that it is. Think about any job. It always starts out with learning—you must learn the job. It always involves continued learning—you must keep up with changes or be prepared for new challenges. But the job is not about learning—learning is about doing the job.

Have you ever met one of those career students? He's the guy that went to college and took 6 years to get a Bachelors degree, and then continued on for another 3 years and got his Masters degree, and now just signed up for his Doctoral program in Business Administration. He is almost 30 years old, is a credentialed "expert" on business, and has never been in business except for when he was working at Home Depot to pay for college bills. We do the same thing in church. We learn the basics. Then we learn beyond the basics. We might take a class in theology and then do an online study in eschatology. Then we go back and review the basics because we forgot some of them. We learned all of the names of God but have never shared that name with anyone who doesn't know Him, or we use our colloquial name for God with 4 other letters when our favorite ball team loses. We are all too often "educated beyond our level of obedience."

While faith is about believing, church is fundamentally about doing. It's about loving God and loving others. That doesn't negate the gift of grace nor the fact that our salvation is based on Christ's sacrifice for us and not on our own works. Ephesians 2:10 tells us that Christ made that sacrifice so that we could do the good works that God has prepared for us to do. We were not saved so that we could know more; we were saved so that we can love more.

So how do we combat the lie that church is about learning? First, we who are disciples should change our perspective. We need to participate in church with the expectation that we are there to act, not just to learn. We are there to pray. We are there to worship. We are there to encourage and love on those around us. We are there to reach out to the lost world. And finally, we are there to learn how better to do all these things. Second, those of us who are leaders in the church need to ask ourselves if we are fundamentally helping people to "do" or to "know." Are we university professors or shop teachers? We are supposed to be the latter. Finally, we all need to ask a pointed question: "Do people outside our church know us first as people who do or as people who believe?" Christ was very clear that we are his people because we believe but that we are supposed to be known by what we do.[clxvi]

Christian warriors are warriors, not war theorists.

## The Battle Line of Church Duties

Lie # 3 on the Battleground of the Church is "it is the pastor's church." The role of pastor (or preacher or reverend, whichever you prefer) as it is commonly seen in America is largely non-biblical. I'm not saying it's unbiblical or contrary to the Bible, nor am I saying that pastors are bad. I am just saying that the pastoral role we commonly see in America is in many ways not what we see demonstrated in the Bible.

In modern America, most pastors are paid full-time. In the 1st Century church as described in the New Testament, church leaders were largely (perhaps completely) unsalaried—they were working men who also led churches. In modern America, most churches have a single pastor (or a senior pastor) who is generally regarded as THE leader of the congregation and who does most of the preaching and decision-making. Church leadership proscribed in the New Testament was a shared responsibility; it did not apparently revolve around a single leader. In modern America, pastors usually have to go through seminary and pass an ordination process that largely emphasizes academic and theological proficiency. However, the Biblical standards for church leaders emphasize demonstrated Christ-following character more than theological prowess.[clxvii] In modern America, the pastor works at church and the congregation goes to church. In the early church, everybody was expected to participate in church activities.

These differences aren't necessarily bad, but it is vitally important that we realize that the role of pastor in America does not come directly from the Truth of the Bible. So we can't assume that how we do church and what we expect from our pastors are valid or "God's way." In fact, a strong case can be made that the modern role of pastor derives largely from the clearly unbiblical role of priest as it was practiced in the Catholic church at the time of the Reformation. We have to look at everything with a careful eye.

I'm not pastor-bashing. Pastors assume the role of shepherds and teachers. The vast majority rightly interpret and share God's word. They lead people closer to God. They adhere to the leadership standards as set forth by the apostle Paul in his letters to Timothy and Titus. All of these are Biblically consistent. On the whole they are very good men. But they are only men.

So often, we congregants expect our pastors to **be** the church—we expect them to be excellent comforters during hospital visits, amazing speakers during Sunday services, keen administrators throughout the week, and unflappable in personal conversations. The pastor of your church is not the church owner. He is not supposed to be excellent in all things. He is not supposed to be responsible for your church's success. He is simply the man that God has appointed to lead the believers in your church. The lie is that "it's the pastor's church"; the truth is that "it's God's church" and He uses ALL of us to make it whole and effective.

Is there a ministry need at your church? Go fill it. "I'm not equipped to fill it," you might respond. Well, then, what makes you think the pastor is? If God is big enough to use your pastor to fill the void, He is big enough to use you.

Do you feel like your church is off course? Go talk to the pastor about it, but don't go ask him why the church is screwed up and why he let it get off course. First, go find out if your church is off course in your pastor's view. After all, if your pastor is God's appointed leader, don't you think that God would be likely to tell him that it is off course? And is it possible that God wants you to be the implement that will help your pastor get it on course? If you and your pastor agree that the church is off course, ask what you can do to help get it on course.

Did your pastor goof something up? Maybe he made a statement on Sunday that's not exactly in keeping with the Bible. Maybe he started a ministry that didn't need to be started. Maybe he didn't start a ministry that should have been started. Whatever he did wrong, give him some grace. After all, how many things do you mess up on a given day? Remember that your pastor is a fallen man, saved by grace, trying to do his best, and struggling against his worst, just like you and me. Help him, encourage him, rebuke in love if necessary, but don't hold him solely responsible for your church and don't hold him to a standard that only Jesus could meet.

Don't fall for the lie that your church is your pastor's responsibility. Embrace the truth that we attend *God's* church with our pastor as God's appointed leader, and you and I need to do our part, obedient to God and under the authority of our pastor, to help make the church what God wants it to be.

One note before we move on: Don't exchange the lie of "it's my pastor's church" for the lie of "I'm supposed to blindly follow my pastor." Sadly, there are some pastors who are "wolves" that tear up the church.[clxviii] Other pastors misread a passion for God as a call to full-time ministry and so perform poorly at their chosen profession. Still other pastors have fallen into significant and habitual sin. All of these situations should be dealt with in a way that is consistent with the counsel of the whole Bible. Remember that the point is not that we must become a mindless cheering club for the pastor; the point is that we must embrace our own part and responsibility for the health of our home church and that we must choose to love our pastor before we start to criticize him.

Christian warriors don't go to church. They are the church.

## The Battle Line of Uniformity

Lie #4 on the Battleground of the Church is that "Difference is bad and uniformity is good." I had a good friend in college who belonged to a Church of Christ denomination that I was unfamiliar with. In the course of our conversation, I found out that I was going to hell if I was not part of that denomination since they were the only ones that knew the truth. I have another friend that heard the same lines from some Baptists and another that was told the same about Catholicism. Now to the best of my knowledge none of these denominations officially teaches "my way or the highway" doctrine but there are certainly a lot of churches and a lot of Christians who have bought into the lie that "my way is the only way."

Scroll through the phonebook of any city in America, and you'll find a plethora of churches of various Christian denominations. We know intuitively that there is something wrong when Christianity— a "religion of love"—is full of internal conflict, and if we pay attention to the apostle Paul, we'll hear him say that, "there should be no division in the body."[clxix] But notice that Paul does *not* say, "There should be no difference." When talking about division, Paul uses the Greek word *schisma*, which derives from a root that means to cleave or to split—the same root of our English word "schism." We often look at the many differences between churches and say, "Well shouldn't they all be the same?" One of Satan's deceptions is to say that there should be no difference between churches. There are two inescapable logical outworkings of this belief. If I believe that all churches should be essentially the same, then I will naturally believe that churches *that are not like mine* are messed up. I will also believe that we should all come into uniformity as to doctrine and practice. Let's look at the problems with both of these beliefs.

If I believe that other denominations are messed up, I will always be in opposition to other churches. I will be a source of *schisma*. Suppose I like piano music and hymns. If I'm stuck in this lie of uniformity, I will believe that churches that worship with Christian rock-and-roll are of Satan. Why would we think this way? I don't condemn a guy to hell if I like asparagus and he doesn't. Why would I do it based on taste in worship music? Suppose I like coats and ties and the church down the street likes sandals and T-shirts. If I'm stuck in this lie, I'm going to condemn the sandal wearer as a heathen (ironically, though, he's probably dressed more like Jesus than I am). If I walk into a restaurant for lunch dressed in my business suit, and a fellow walks in dressed in shorts, I don't condemn him. Why would I do it at church? Suppose I believe that Christ turned water into wine, and you believe that Christ turned water into an unfermented grape juice.[clxx] Is that something that we should argue or fight over? I'm a Chevy guy. If I meet a guy who likes Fords, I might have a good-natured argument about who's right, but I won't kick him in the face when he tells me that Fords are better. If I can tolerate different opinions about cars, why would I feel a need to foist my opinion about Christ's first miracle on fellow Christians? Christ does not call us to uniformity. He calls us to unity in Him. So the first outworking of the lie of uniformity is that I will be hostile to Christians that are not like me.

Similarly, if I believe that all churches should look and think like each other—that is, if I seek uniformity in the church—then I will push all churches to adopt my doctrines and practices. This will derail the strength of the diversity in the body of Christ. Suppose I think that all churches should essentially be inwardly focused on the discipleship of their congregants. Wouldn't that be a drag on evangelism? Suppose I think that all churches should essentially be outwardly focused on evangelism. Doesn't that make it hard to grow deeply rooted disciples? Suppose I think that all churches should essentially be a 50/50 blend of evangelism and discipleship. What then do I say to the pastor who hears God's call to go hard toward discipleship (or evangelism)? Do I tell him to ignore God's call since "that's not what churches are supposed to look like"? Satan wants us to believe that "differences are bad and uniformity is good." We can combat this lie by carefully differentiating between differences and division. Differences can be very healthy.

It is an awesome gift from God that in most cities in America if you like traditional, liturgical church services, you can go to a church that worships that way, but if God has made you in such a way that you like contemporary services, you can go to one of those instead. The traditional church is not "better than" the contemporary church just because it is liturgical. The full-gospel church is not better than the Pentecostal church just because it has gospel music. God made us wonderfully different in personality and temperament; isn't it logical that we might have different 'druthers about how to worship Him? Such differences can be celebrated, and we can, as Paul says, "have equal concern for each other."[clxxi]

It is a similarly awesome gift from God that we have some churches that cater to young surfers and others that cater to octogenarians. We have churches that are absolutely phenomenal in building up people to be deeply convicted disciples of Christ, and we have other churches that are absolutely phenomenal at reaching out to the lost. I'm sure we have a few churches that are absolutely phenomenal at both.

However, differences become division when they cause a spiritual separation. When I allow real but spiritually-inconsequential differences to diminish my love and respect for a fellow Christian, then I am succumbing to the devil's deception. If I look at the Pentecostals and say, "They ain't right . . . they don't practice self-control as outlined in Galatians,"[clxxii] then I am a divider and am deceived because I allow our differences to be a spiritual wedge. If I look at the surfer Christians and say, "Those gentlemen are messed up because they don't even have the respect to dress up for church," then I am messed up because I'm allowing inconsequential differences to cause spiritual splits between me and God's people.

I have some friends right now who are faced with a challenge. Their pastor has said to his congregation, "God is calling this church to change the world through evangelism, so I don't want to hear your problems, I need you to get on board." This sounds harsh and kind of unloving, and it would be so if that was the only church in town. But what if God really is calling that church to change the world by focusing on evangelism? My friends (who don't as of now feel the call of this pastor's vision) have a choice. They can succumb to the lie and say, "Pox on you, we're out of here. Your church shouldn't be that way," or they can embrace the truth and say, "God, where do you want us? Are we to be part of this church that you have called to evangelism or do you want us in a congregation that is more oriented toward discipleship, as is our desire?" If God answers, "Go," then they can go loving the church that they are leaving, wishing their former pastor well and at the same time loving that God has given them an opportunity to join a church more in line with their gifts and desires. If God answers, "Stay," then they can embrace the fact that they are being stretched and used to support their church's mission. For my friends, their response rests on a question of uniformity (i.e. all churches must look as we want them to) or unity (i.e. my church evangelizes, yours disciples, but together we are building the kingdom as God has uniquely prepared and called us to do).

The truth is that God calls us to unity and not uniformity.

However, there is counter-deception that we must watch out for. Does a celebration of differences and an emphasis on unity mean that all doctrines are equally valid? Not hardly. The Bible warns us over and over to beware of false teachings, false teachers, and false doctrines, and history is replete with examples of times when these rose in God's church. So how do we balance doctrinal purity with a desire for unity?

First, we need to realize that the word "unity" is not physical unity (we can't literally become "one") and so implies that we are together in something—unity of heart or of doctrine or of effort, perhaps. So what unity does the Bible call us to? Christ tells us that our greatest commandments are to love God and to love others,[clxxiii] and Paul tells us that church is meant to "attain to unity of the faith and of the knowledge of the Son of God to mature manhood, to the measure of the stature of the fullness of Christ."[clxxiv] So it would seem that our unity is to come from faith in and knowledge of Christ, and that faith is evidenced by our carrying out these two greatest commandments.

If this is true, then the question becomes, "how to balance doctrinal purity with a desire for unity-in-Christ?" I would submit that the answer to this question is not to "balance" our doctrine but to ensure that our application of doctrine is subordinated to the unity that we are made for. Some things are essential to the faith: Christ was both man and God, God is Triune, Christ died once and for all for our salvation, all humans are fallen, etc. Without holding to these things, the fundamentals of faith are wrecked. Think of it this way: if I ask you to build me a home and you try to build the foundation out of sand, is that something I can agree to? Of course not. A solid foundation is essential to a home, and similarly, there are some doctrinal truths that are essential to Christianity.

But what about truths that are not necessarily "essential?" Think again of a builder's example. Suppose I tell you to build me a home, and I tell you that I need you to cut a board to 10 foot length. Now suppose you cut it to 10 feet and 1 inch in length. Does that matter? In some cases, it won't; we can use the board as is and just make it fit. However, in other places it matters very much and a wrong-length board might undermine the integrity of a whole wall.

So it is with questions of doctrine. Take, for example, the question of "once-saved-always-saved." Theologians have argued for centuries over whether it is possible to "lose" your salvation once you have put your faith in Christ, and there are some pretty convincing Bible verses to support both sides of the argument. I have my own opinion about who is correct. When we get to Heaven, I believe we will find that one side is right, and the other is not. However, by and large being "100% right" on this question is inconsequential. In most of what we do day-to-day, this really doesn't matter, and arguing vehemently over it is wasteful division. However, there are times when our position on such doctrines matter very much. The once-saved-always-saved adherent who then says, "I asked Jesus to save me, and so I don't need to worry about continuing in sin," has missed a fundamental truth. Likewise the I-can-fall-from-grace adherent who then says, "We must work our way into heaven," has also missed a fundamental truth. Some doctrines are worth dividing the church over. However, the number of these division-worthy doctrines is far, far smaller than the number of doctrines that people in the church have decided to divide over.

As in all things, God is the final answer. If you are seeing differences in the church, don't automatically make them divisions. If you feel pressure to come to common ground, ask if this is about uniformity or true unity in the faith. And if you encounter one of those real issues that you might think warrants division, take it to God in prayer and see what He says.

Fight the lie. Some differences are good, and we need to seek unity of faith not uniformity of practice. No matter the style of your worship, the dress you wear, the color of your skin, the method of your service, or the name of your denomination, if you and I are both followers of Christ, we are on the same team fighting the same enemy, and I'm going to pull for you whenever I can. Will you do the same for me?

Christian warriors are all in the same army, even though they aren't all in the same units.

What is your church to you? Is it a social group or a school? Is it your pastor's place? Is it an exclusive members-only club? Perhaps millions of people go to church each week and find something other than God and His love there, and this happens because too many of us don't hold the line at church. We don't engage effectively in the battle against the lies of consumerism or of over-education. Too many of us slide unthinkingly into the convenient belief that "it's my pastor's church," and all too many Christ-followers seek uniformity before unity. If we fail to engage on these battle lines, our churches' actions will continue to contradict the truth of God's word. Let's get into the fight by speaking the Bible, by encouraging truth and destroying the lies that distract the church from being the minister of God's love to the saved and the proclaimer of God's grace to the unsaved.

Combat at church can be ugly. The enemy will try to convince us that we are "un-Christ-like" as we contend for the truth, and in the battle for unity in faith we may find ourselves witness to schisms and division. But we are not Christ's church if we are not following Christ. We Christian warriors must fight for right in our churches so that "speaking the truth in love, we ... grow up every way into Him who is the head, into Christ." When we are solidly in community with others who follow Christ,[clxxv] we can gain the strength and the "base of operations" to fight on other battlegrounds in our life, not least of which is the Battleground of Education.

4-4. THE BATTLEGROUND IN EDUCATION

In 2011, Newsweek published the results of an interesting survey. After giving the standard US citizenship test to 1000 American adults, they found that 38% of them would not qualify to be citizens. 44% were unable to define the Bill of Rights, two-thirds were unaware that the United States has a capitalist economic system, almost three-quarters didn't know why the Cold War was fought, and a staggering 80% didn't know who the president was during World War I.[47] Most, if not all, of these people were products of the compulsory American educational system. That's bad education.

However, what's worse is the state of moral and spiritual learning in our schools. In January 2014, a Kansas father found out that his 13-year-old daughters "health" class talked about vaginal intercourse, anal sex, and genital fondling, including an "x-rated" poster about how people "express their sexual feelings."[48] In Hawaii, the Department of Education refused to show state legislators the controversial sex-ed curriculum that was currently being used in twelve middle schools because it was "sensitive in nature."[49] A school district in California mandated that seventh-graders be taught the tenets of Islam[50], but a high school principal in Florida faced contempt charges for saying a Christian prayer at a school luncheon.[51] Eighteen-year old Jordan Wiser spent 13 days in jail for having a pocketknife in his car at school—but wait, there's

---

[47] Newsweek Polls Americans on Their Knowledge of Being American; 38% Failed," PR Newswire; March 21, 2011; accessed on March 17, 2014 at http://m.prnewswire.com/new-releases/newsweek-polls-americans-on-their-knowledge-of-being-american-38-percent-failed-118366914.html

[48] Todd Starnes; "Parents upset by X-rated sex ed poster in middle school"; Fox News.com; Jan 17, 2014; accessed on March 17, 2014 at http://www.foxnews.com/opinion/2014/01/17/parents-upset-by-x-rated-sex-ed-poster-in-middle-school/

[49] Courney Crandell; "Vital Signs: Hawaii educators hide 'sensitive' sex-ed curriculum from legislators"; World Magazine; Jan 21, 2014; accessed on March 17, 2014 at http://www.worldmag.com/2014/01/vital_signs_hawaii_educators_hide_sensitive_sex_ed_curriculum_from_legislators

[50] "Islam Studies Required in California District"; WorldNetDaily.com; Jan 11, 2002; accessed March 17, 2014 at http://www.wnd.com/2002/01/12325/

[51] "Florida school officials in prayer case could get jail time"; CNN; Sep 17, 2009; accessed March 17, 2014 at http://edition.cnn.com/2009/CRIME/09/17/florida.school.prayer/index.html

more: Jordan had recently completed a law-enforcement course, had FEMA's National Terror Defense certification, was provisionally accepted to the United States Army, and was currently taking Firefighter 2 and Emergency Medical Technician courses. The pocket knife was part of his emergency responder's kit with all of the other things he needs to help people, and he now faces felony charges. [52]

Our schools are a spiritual battleground, and quite frankly, it is a battleground on which we are losing badly. American kids spend, on average, about 32 hours a week in school—that's about 1/3 of their waking hours. So it makes sense that we should place a fair amount of importance on what kind of influences they get at school. When you sit back and really look at the data, both anecdotally and statistically, you have to conclude that kids are spiritually at risk at school.

With that said, let me make a couple of things clear in this discussion. First, when I say "school," I mean the US public educational experience (up to and including colleges and universities), which about 90% of American children experience. [53] This chapter may or may not apply to parochial and home schooling, depending on the educational environment. Second, this battleground has nothing to do with academic performance. From a spiritual perspective, it is only tangentially relative whether schools perform well academically. This idea can perhaps be best summed up this way: I'd rather my child be a saintly janitor than for him to be a dishonest and selfish rocket-scientist. Academic performance is a valid concern, but that's a discussion for a different forum. Third, we have some absolutely awesome public school teachers and administrators out there and this is no condemnation of them or their faith. They simply work in a system that, by law, fights against the precepts of Christianity. The truth is that some of those teachers are our most important fighters, waging war against a system that tries to suppress the Truth at

---

[52] Dave Urbanski; "He's 18 and Spent 13 Days in Jail for a Pocketknife in a School Parking Lot — and The Story Only Gets Crazier From There"; The Blaze.com; Mar 12, 2014; accessed on Mar 17, 2014 at http://www.theblaze.com/stories/2014/03/12/teen-jailed-for-13-days-after-emt-kit-pocketknife-and-found-in-his-car-and-thats-just-scratching-the-surface-of-jordan-wisers-nightmare/

[53] The US Department of Education national Center for Education Statistics reported that, as of 2007, 88.7% of students attended public schools.

every turn.

There are four primary battle lines that we need to recognize on the Battleground in Education: the battle line of "Spirituality in School," the battle line of "Who Knows Best," the battle line of "Just Academics," and the battle line of "The Free Lunch." I'll talk about each one in detail and then point out some ways that we can fight in these battles.

## The Battle Line of Spirituality in School

The first battle line on this battleground centers on the idea that "schooling is spiritually neutral." This is a bald-faced lie. Put another way, we might say that "school is not a place for religion" or "school and religion are separate." This way of thinking is what might be termed "practical atheism," meaning that God (and the pursuit of Him) only belongs in churches and maybe in private areas like your home. However, "practical atheism" is irreconcilable with the Bible. God establishes unequivocally that our religion cannot be separated from any act of our life, so it is unconscionable for a Christian to support an environment that is anti-Christian.

The truth is that the US school system is not neutral to religion but is anti-Christian. This sounds on the surface like an extreme or even radical statement to make, so I'd ask you to let the idea float for a minute and see if it isn't backed up by a few facts.

First, consider that the Bible is a banned book as school curriculum, but books filled with magic, pornography, socialism, Islam, or hedonism are not. The deceptive phrasing goes something like this: "we're not against the Bible, we just don't think it belongs in school." Think about that for a minute. Imagine if I (Caucasian) said to an African-American, "I'm not against you, I just don't want you in my house." You'd look at me like the pig racist that I would be. Or suppose I told my daughter, "I really think that dress looks nice, but you are forbidden to wear it outside this house." She'd look at me like I had two heads. The automatic effect of banning something is to imply that it is at best worthless (and more likely that it is hazardous) in the place that it is banned. The Supreme Court banned Bible reading in public schools in 1962, which in practice conveys the implicit message that either the Bible is without value or that it is hazardous.

In February 2014, The Watauga, North Carolina school board

voted to keep a book called The *House of Spirits* in their curriculum over the complaints of a number of parents. The *House of Spirits* has numerous scenes of graphic rape, violence, homosexuality, and even child molestation.[54] So, The *House of Spirits* is recommended reading, but the *Holy Bible* is banned. That's not neutrality—that's hostility to Christianity.

Second, consider the numerous cases where students, who have a legal right to practice their religion, are told by educators that they may not. A 7th grader passed out Bible verses to her classmates and was subsequently told by her principal that she could not pass out Bible verses or any religious messages at school. Another 7th grader was not allowed to use the Bible as a reference in her assignment on Roman history.[55] A Minnesota school district banned an after school Bible club from meeting even though non-Bible clubs were permitted to do so,[56] and a New York school district ordered a Christian school teacher to remove a prayer-request box from her desk and to remove a quote from President Ronald Reagan that included the phrase "if we ever forget that we are One Nation Under God, then we will be a Nation gone under."[57] All of these situations either were resolved through legal redress in favor of the Christians or most likely will be, but the point is that the educational environment is largely and endemically hostile to Christian belief.

Finally, consider that teachers who choose to teach "intelligent design"—a scientific theory that acknowledges the evidence for a creator (albeit not necessarily the God of Christianity)—are frequently ridiculed, denied tenure or promotion, or even prohibited from teaching facts that support intelligent design (ID)

---

[54] Jesse Wood; "Watauga School Board Votes 3-2 To Keep 'The House of the Spirits' in the WHS Curriculum Thursday"; HCPress.com; Feb 27, 2014; accessed Mar 17, 2014 at http://www.hcpress.com/news/watauga-county-board-of-education-votes-3-2-to-keep-the-house-of-the-spirits-in-the-whs-curriculum-thursday.html

[55] Matthew Clark; "2012 Victories: Schools Cannot Ban the Bible"; ACLJ; Dec 13, 2012; accessed Mar 17, 2014 at http://aclj.org/school-prayer/2012-victories-schools-cannot-ban-bible

[56] Gary Gore; "Good News Club banned from forming at Minnesota School"; Christian Coalition of America; Sep 15, 2008; accessed Mar 17, 2014 at http://www.cc.org/blog/good_news_club_banned_forming_minnesota_school

[57] Todd Starnes; "School Bans Bible Club Prayer Box, Reagan Quote"; Fox News.com; Jan 14, 2013; accessed Mar 17, 2014 at http://radio.foxnews.com/toddstarnes/top-stories/school-bans-bible-club-prayer-box-reagan-quote.html

or blow holes in evolutionary theory. [58,59] Additionally, the Supreme Court and other courts have handed down three major court cases that prohibit the teaching of ID theory and of flaws in evolutionary theory. I'm no legal eagle, so I can't comment on the legal theory or the legal sufficiency of the justices' conclusions in these cases. However, I can tell you that the court decisions affirm teaching of evolution even while acknowledging that evolutionary theory "is imperfect," and at the same time the decisions prohibit the teaching of ID while stating the work of ID scientists is "simply not science" and is not admissible in a classroom as evidence.[60] The net message is this: My children, if you believe the un-provable theory in your science textbook, you are wise, but if you believe the un-provable Genesis story in the Bible, you are a fool. That's not neutral. That is government establishment of secularism.

The lie that Satan repeats over and over is "School is neutral; it's not about religion." The truth is that the US educational system is, by rule of law, anti-Christian and that it constantly, sometimes explicitly and always implicitly, teaches children that their Christian faith is bad or wrong.

## The Battle Line of Who Knows Best

The second battle line on the Battleground in Education revolves around the lie that "when it comes to educating children, schools know best."

When my oldest son was in fifth grade, he came to me very frustrated with homework from a new math curriculum in which he was supposed to answer word problems. I asked him how the teacher had told him to solve such problems and he said, "She doesn't teach us how. She says we are just supposed to figure it out." I was skeptical that he was accurate in saying that, but after about the third time of this, I went to talk to the teacher. "Ma'am," I said, "I'm having a hard time helping my son with this homework

---

[58] If you view ID with skepticism, I highly recommend you watch Focus on the Family's video "Unlocking the Mystery of Life."

[59] The radically anti-ID bent in academia is well (and humorously) displayed in Ben Stein's movie "Expelled."

[60] David Bailey; "What has been the outcome of court cases testing whether creationism and intelligent design constitute suitable material for public school instruction?" ; Jan 1, 2014; accessed Mar 17, 2014 at http://www.sciencemeetsreligion.org/evolution/court-cases.php

because I'm having to use algebra to solve these 5th grade problems. When I ask my son how he was taught to solve these, he says that he wasn't taught how." My son's teacher replied, "Yes that's right. This is a new curriculum and instead of teaching the kids how to solve the problems, we just give them the problem and see if they can figure it out. It teaches critical thinking." This teacher was a kind lady and perhaps she was a good educator, but when she said that, I thought something like, "I've got some critical thinking for you. How about teaching my son to get his multiplication right before asking him to solve algebra problems?" Here's the point: that curriculum was asinine. It was the kind of thing that happens when educators get tired of teaching the same ol' math.

That's just one personal experience, but the recent history of education is replete with examples of "stupid" (or in more neutral terms, "unwise") education.

• I have a friend whose children are in a school system in Colorado that refuses to fail a student, regardless of performance, until they reach the 8th grade.

• In the town that I last lived in, the county policy was to never give a grade of less than 60 out of 100. It also requires teachers to re-grade a failure and then throw out the original lower score.

• Last year a 7 year old boy was suspended from his second grade class because he shaped one of his Pop Tarts into a gun.

• In August of 2013, the state of California passed a law that essentially prohibits educators from acknowledging gender. In other words, if a boy says he is a girl, he can use the girls' bathroom. Likewise if a girl says she identifies herself as a boy, she must be allowed to compete on the boys' football team.[61] The state also enacted a law in 2011 that requires students to be taught about "the role and contributions of . . . lesbian, gay, bisexual, and transgender Americans."[62]

• Here are some of the courses that you can take at universities in the United States: "Arguing with Judge Judy" (UC Berkley), "The Phallus" (Occidental College), "Alien Sex" (University of

[61] See text of Assembly Bill 1266 at
http://leginfo.legislature.ca.gov/faces/billNavClient.xhtml?bill_id=201320140AB1266
[62] Text of California State Bill 48; Accessed Mar 18, 2014 at
http://www.leginfo.ca.gov/pub/11-12/bill/sen/sb_0001-
0050/sb_48_bill_20110714_chaptered.html

Rochester), "Cyberfeminism" (Cornell), "Queer Musicology" (UCLA), "Underwater Basket Weaving" (Reed College), "Whitewater Skills" (West Virginia U), and—this might be a worthwhile one—"Stupidity" (Occidental College).[63]

The problem with such foolishness is not that policies and programs are foolish, but that foolishness is mandated to the exclusion of the parent. We have a nationally adopted school model that says to parents, "I know better than you. Stand back and let me make your kids better." Education is compulsory and even a homeschooling parent in most places must validate that his/her educational process is acceptable to the state. While the Bible says that parents are to train up their children, our national education frequently overrules our parents.

• Parents, do you want to teach your children that both hard work and failure have consequences? Go ahead, but don't be surprised when they learn the opposite from their teacher as their best friend gets to make up the test she didn't study for and ends up with a better grade.

• Dad, do you want to teach your child that firearms are effective and useful tools? That's fine, but if your son makes one out of a pop-tart, he is going to be shamed and suspended.

• Mom, do you want to teach your daughter that she is "fearfully and wonderfully made" with a gender given by the grace of God? That's fine, but when you send her to school in California, they are going to tell her you are wrong (and you cannot just choose not to send her).

• As you struggle financially to send your child to get a college degree, make sure you pat her on the back for the C+ she gets in her "Cyberfeminism" course.

This lie of "schools know best" has recently come into clearer view at the national level because of the Federal "Common Core" standards that went into effect at the start of 2014. Common Core curriculum standards for middle school sex education in Hawaii include a photo of an educator next to an easel that displays "1.

---

[63] "100 Hilarious College Courses that Really Exist"; OnlineUniversities.com; Oct 21, 2009; Accessed on Mar 18, 2014 at
http://www.onlineuniversities.com/blog/2009/10/100-hilarious-college-courses-that-really-exist/

Oral Sex: mouth on genitals; 2. Vaginal Sex: penis enters vagina; 3. Anal Sex: Penis enters anus."[64] Numerous groups, even the American Federation of Teachers, have protested this legal implementation of the "we know better than you" lie,[65] arguing that education should be "in the hands of those closest to the student: local school leaders and parents." [66]

Satan would love Christian parents to say to themselves, "I'm looking after my kids' education because I send them to public school every day, and the school knows best!" The truth is that the pattern in the Bible is for parents to teach their children—that they should be both the primary overseers and the greatest participants in their children's education.[clxxvi]

If you have a solid faith in Christ, you are a hard target for evil to corrupt. If you raise your children on the foundation of that faith, they will be afforded the best chance for success and blessing. That's why the enemy wants to convince you that you should put your children under the care and guidance of an organization that is secularized and largely dominated by those who turn a blind eye to God's Truth. If he convinces you to relinquish your role, your kids are easy prey.

Schools don't know best. God-following parents do.

## The Battle Line of "Just Academics"

The third battle line on the Battleground in Education hinges on the lie that "school is just about academics." This ties very closely to the first lie that "school is spiritually neutral," but it goes even beyond that. Evil would have us believe that our children go to school to learn "reading, writing, and 'rithmetic," and come home to learn the deeper truths of life. Nothing could be further from the truth. God did not create us as compartmentalized beings—we live life holistically. If I come up to you and sneer at you while saying, "I love you," you won't be filled with gladness

[64] Sara Noble; "Common Core Has a Porn-Sex Education Curricula for Middle School"; Jan 20, 2014; Accessed Mar 18, 2014 at http://www.independentsentinel.com/common-core-has-a-porn-sex-education-curricula-for-middle-school/
[65] Brittany Corona; "Union Leader: Put Stakes Associated with Common Core Tests on Hold"; The Foundry; May 12, 2013; Accessed on May 18, 2014 at http://blog.heritage.org/2013/05/12/union-joins-opposition-to-common-core-national-standards-and-tests/
[66] Lindsey Burke as quoted in Ibid.

that you are loved. You will ask yourself why I am lying. You can't compartmentalize my actions from my words.

So it is with education. When your son goes to school, and he is told that it is a fact that he originated from primordial goo, he doesn't just use that to pass his next science test. He also internalizes, at least to some extent, that he is a random happenstance, not an intentionally created being.

When your daughter goes to school and she is taught from a revisionist historical text that the primary reason for American expansion and greatness was economic motivation, she doesn't just learn history. In part, she is also learning two un-truths: a) our patriotism is founded on greed and b) economic motivation is an appropriate orientation for life.

When my oldest son was starting sixth grade, we had the choice to keep him in public education or enroll him in a private school. We knew for a fact that one of the sixth grade public school teachers was an avowed homosexual and that this man made a point to make his orientation (and the validity of it) known to his students. So we chose private school. Did my son get a better academic education? Arguably not. However, my son did go to a place where, every day, he was taught at least to some extent that "what-God-says-is-right is indeed right." The alternative was for him to go to a place where he would have heard a repeated message that "what-God-says-is-wrong is indeed right." School is not just about academics.

The culture at school is of at least equal and arguably greater importance to your child than are the academics. So what is modern American school culture like? It is in many ways at odds with Biblical living, and it gets progressively worse as age increases.

• In many places, oral sex among middle school students has become commonplace. Patricia Hersch, author of a book on American adolescence, notes that oral sex is "done commonly, with a shrug." [67]

• Profanity at schools has become commonplace. One high school teacher notes "The kids swear almost incessantly." [68]

[67] Laura Stepp; "Unsettling New Fad Alarms Parents: Middle School Oral Sex"; Washington Post; Jul 8, 1999; Accessed Mar 18, 2014 at http://www.washingtonpost.com/wp-srv/style/features/students070899.htm
[68] Valerie Strauss; "More and More, Kids Say the Foulest Things"; Washington Post; Apr 12, 2005; Accessed Mar 18, 2014 at http://www.washingtonpost.com/wp-

- By age 16, about 1/3 of teens have had sex and this increases at about 10% per year until, by age 19, almost ¾ of the teens have had sex. [69]
- 19.9% of middle schools and 22.9% of high schools report that students disrespect teachers at least once a week or daily. [70]
- A survey conducted by the Department of Education showed that almost 40% of high school students reported drinking alcohol[71] and over 23% admitted to using marijuana[72] at least once during the previous 30 days.

It is likely that our children will confront this kind of culture at any school, public or private, to some extent, but there is a big difference between seeing bad behavior that is condemned and seeing bad behavior that is condoned.

If your son attends school amid a bunch of sexually-active adolescents and with them goes to a sex-education class that condones all types of sexual activity and passes out contraceptives, he is going to get a very different message than a son who attends school amid a bunch of sexually-active adolescents and with them goes to a health class that presents sex as it is given in the framework of the Bible.

If your daughter finds herself immersed in a youth culture that embraces alcohol at an institution that implicitly condones underage drinking, she will get a very different message than if she experiences that same culture at an institution where she has to flee campus to indulge in drunkenness.

We have all faced temptation and we have all failed, but we must thank God that when we did, we knew we were doing wrong

dyn/articles/A44779-2005Apr11.html
[69] "Facts on American Teens' Sexual and Reproductive Health"; Guttmacher Institute; June 2013; Accessed Mar 18, 2014 at http://www.guttmacher.org/pubs/FB-ATSRH.html
[70] US Department of Education; "Indicators of School Crime and Safety: 2012"; Accessed Mar 18, 2014 at http://nces.ed.gov/programs/crimeindicators/crimeindicators2012/tables/table_07_1.asp
[71] US Department of Education; "Indicators of School Crime and Safety: 2012"; Accessed Mar 18, 2014 at http://nces.ed.gov/programs/crimeindicators/crimeindicators2012/tables/table_15_1.asp
[72] US Department of Education; "Indicators of School Crime and Safety: 2012"; Accessed Mar 18, 2014 at http://nces.ed.gov/programs/crimeindicators/crimeindicators2012/tables/table_16_1.asp

and so both conscience and the institutions around us helped us to set our sights on what was good and right. However, it's a tragedy when we face temptation and there is no one there to tell us, "Don't do that!" It's an even greater tragedy when the people in charge say, "Yes, do that!"

"Woe to those who call evil good and good evil," [clxxvii] God says. The devil would have us believe that school is just about academics. That way we won't realize that our kids are actually being taught that evil is good. The truth is that school is an education in life, not just in academics, and if we send our kids to an institution that doesn't reinforce what is right, we are setting them up for hardship and failure.

## The Battle Line of "The Free Lunch"

The fourth battle line on the Battleground in Education is really simple and entirely pervasive. It is the lie that "education should be free." This lie is so self-evident that not much needs to be said about it other than to bring it into the light.

We take it as axiomatic that "there is no such thing as a free lunch" and "all good things come with a price." We'll pay to get healthcare for our pets. We'll pay to have 357 channels of TV to choose from. We'll pay for a mocha latte coffee or a slice of pie at our favorite restaurant. We'll pay so that we are financially comfortable in retirement. But we don't want to pay to educate our kids.

The root of this lie is easy: evil says, "If I make you think you don't have a choice of where you can educate your children, than I can make you let me educate your children."

Is there anything more important to you parents than raising your children right? If not, are you willing to pay to see that they are raised right? The truth is that a good education, like all good things, should cost something.

Consider it a blessing if God gives you the option to pay for your children's schooling. It is the best investment you can ever have an opportunity to put your money into.

## Fighting Back on the Battleground in Education

As we survey the Battleground of Education, we see these four great lies:

- "Schooling is spiritually neutral"
- "When it comes to educating children, schools know best"
- "School is just about academics"
- "Education should be free"

When I said earlier that we are largely losing on this battleground, I said that because statistically the overwhelming majority of Christian parents have their children planted right in the middle of these lies. So it is imperative for us, if we are to be warriors in this battle, to discuss how we get them out of it and fill them with Truth.

I believe there are three tactics that can help us turn the tide of this battle:

**1. Get the children out of harm's way.** If you are a parent and it is financially possible to take your children out of the public education system, do so. Quit subjecting them to a constant bombardment of anti-Christian influence that undermines the Truth of God's word. For some, this means sending your children to a private school. For others, it means choosing home-schooling. I am not advocating for one of these choices over the other, but I am advocating that parents put their children in an environment where evil is called evil and good is called good.

Don't just confine this to little children either. One of the most anti-Christian environments in America is on the campuses of many of our colleges and universities. Make the spiritual environment a priority in where you choose to send your children to college.

Choosing to pull kids out of public schools or to go to a Christian university will be financially costly. You may not be able to retire at 65 and may have to work until you are unable to do so any longer. You may have to not go on a family vacation for the next 18 years. You may have to shut off your cable TV. You may have to get a second job. You may have to drive the same car for 20 years. Remember, battle is not comfortable, but your kids are worth it!

Fighting on this battleground may be relationally costly. If you pull your kids out of public education, your children may say, "But I'll have to leave my friends!" You may be severing the natural social connection where most of your current friends are. The only available private schools may be ones which only have so-so academic records or which have some non-essential doctrinal differences with your own faith. Remember that our relational "wants" are sometimes casualties in combat and that God will always provide for all of our relational "needs."

One quick note on taking your children out of public schools: I have had good Christian friends who I love and respect and who say, "We want our kids to be God's light in the public schools." I think that idea is a great principle, but poorly executed. We should be the light of the world, but unless God specifically tells you, "Keep your kids in public school," the rational thing based on overwhelming evidence is to get your kids out of harm's way. I'm aware of many verses that would encourage you to keep your children in an environment of spiritual growth and protection—verses like: "Impress them [God's commandments] on your children"[clxxviii] and "Train up a child in the way he should go"[clxxix] and "Let the little children to come to me and do not hinder them"[clxxx] and "Give justice to the weak"[clxxxi] and "Put on the whole armor of God."[clxxxii] However, I'm not aware of any verses that tell us to use our children as inroads to the unbelieving world. I am not saying it can't happen, but I am saying that, without a specific command from God, the idea of using your kids as evangelistic tools runs across the grain of wisdom even if it is not necessarily contrary to scripture.

Those without children can help in the fight on the Battleground in Education as well. If you are financially blessed, ask God if He wants you to help on this battleground. Maybe you can provide a scholarship to a local private school or maybe you can help a local Christian school with their capital needs. Perhaps you have a friend or family member who is a parent that just can't afford to send their child to a non-public institution. Perhaps God has blessed you so that you can bless them.

Whatever our circumstance, the best way to fight this battle is to get our children out of harm's way if it is at all possible!

**2. Arm the children against the enemy.** The truth is that many parents do not have the resources or suitable alternatives to pull their kids out of the public school system. Thank God that He is more powerful than anything in this world and that nothing in creation can separate us from His love![clxxxiii] If you must leave your children in public school, there is still hope, and we can have confidence that God will overcome the schemes of the evil one. However we still need to protect them from sin and its consequences wherever we can. Here are some ways to do that:

• Parents, pastors, Christian adults, and older Christian students must stay actively engaged with children to teach them to see and disbelieve the lies that bombard them in public education.

• We all need to be praying for our children's spiritual safety constantly.

• Be involved to oppose foolish curriculum and policies. Pay attention to what's going on with school and when things come up, talk to administrators and go to school board meetings.

• Moms and dads, if you aren't aggressively talking about school experiences with your children, you need to start. This isn't talking about "what did you learn in history today" (although that's a good conversation to have, too). This is talking about—and countering—all of the secular cultural influences that your son or daughter faces. I wish I had done this much more when my children were young.

• Encourage and support those awesome public school administrators and teachers who are holding to the Truth in the face of lies. We need to thank God for His followers that work every day in the public school system, and we need to do everything we can to help them push back against the ever-increasing pressure to bow to a secular worldview.

These things take time from our already busy-schedules. They require effort from us. They may require us to get in confrontation with school authorities or other parents. They may require us to forcefully draw out words from our kids (you fathers and mothers of teenage sons know what I mean).

War is tough work. Fight for the kids.

**3. Starve the monster.** Here is a tactic that every American adult can employ. It doesn't matter if you have children or not. Public education is not inherently evil, but when it grows in power to a point where it supersedes the common citizen, it is a monster. The public education monster rules on the force of law, but it is fed by money. This money is influenced greatly by two things: Politicians that establish budgets and school enrollment numbers. Influence either one of these things and you will have started to tame the monster.

America still is a democratic republic and we citizens can still, collectively, have enormous impact through our voices and our votes. It is critical that we remain (or get) engaged with those political bodies (from your local school board up to the President of the United States) to influence them for good. Is your State enacting a foolish, secular curriculum? Let your representatives and governor know you're not happy, and fire them in the next election. Is Congress trying to provide a way for parents to use vouchers to get their kids out of the public school system? Tell your Congressman you are all-in-favor and make sure he gets your vote. Did the President just enact some foolish standards system through the Department of Education? Vote him out. Is your county trying to raise taxes to help "improve education?" Say no. Don't feed the beast. Together we can make a difference.

It will also starve the monster if Christians will more frequently exercise their option to choose Christian schooling (whether through home or private school). Can you imagine what would happen if 25% of American Christians chose to take their kids out of public schooling next fall? Public school budgets, which are largely based on enrollment, would be slashed and the system would have to see the message: if we don't change, we're going to starve. Additionally, options and competition would grow in the private-school industry which would almost certainly lower costs and improve quality. Lastly, an en-masse departure from public education would break the mindset that "the current system is the only option" and might open the door to alternative ideas of government-mandated education.

None of this is easy, and we'll never know if we're making a difference until we've made a difference. If I call my Congressman or support my school board or move my child to a private school, I haven't really made a difference in the system. But if I and 5 million like-minded people do these things, then we'll see some change, and that's good for our kids.

It really is a lot like being on a battlefield. When you are involved in your own little movement or skirmish, you don't know if you're actions are winning the war. However, when we all make our moves and engage our enemies in our own little way, then we find that collectively we have done a great deal. We get to see our fellow soldiers wearing smiles of victory, and we get to see the enemy in retreat. And in this case, we get to see our children protected. That's worth fighting for!

The Battleground in Education is a tough one because almost every young person in America is on it. When you start fighting here, you will truly find out what it means to be "countercultural." In many ways, fighting on this battleground will require real sacrifice—of time, of money, of relationships. So we Christian warriors must remember that God has called us to join the fight and to give up everything to follow Him.[clxxxiv]

Fight for the children! They need to be protected on the Battleground of Education, but that's not the only place where they are at risk. Our children—and ourselves—are also threatened on another battleground that is closer to home. Did you know that there is a Battleground of Media? Are you engaging the enemy there?

## 4-5 THE BATTLEGROUND OF MEDIA

The first movies with sound appeared in the 1920s, and then in 1941, the first two commercial television stations were licensed.[73] Twelve years later, in 1953, the first successful color television broadcast began,[74] and cable television started to become popular in the 1970s with satellite television following in the 1990s. The Internet become mainstream in America in the late 1990s,[75] and then mobile data access came into its own with the advent of 3G and then 4G technology in the first decade of the 21$^{st}$ century. Today we Americans spend time in front of our televisions, our computers, our tablets, and our cell phones—and we spend a lot of it. According to a 2012 Nielsen survey, the average American spends 34 hours a week in front of the TV,[76] and a study by eMarketer in 2013 indicated that the average American spends about 35 hours per week on digital devices (like computers and non-voice activities on mobile devices).[77]

Statistically, media activities (watching TV, surfing the internet, watching movies) consume over half of our waking hours, so it should be no surprise that the enemy attacks on this field. Curiously though, in my experience surprisingly little is said in mainstream Christianity about the Battleground of Media. Now there is no doubt that hard-core pornography and gratuitous violence are universally condemned in most of American Christianity, and most of us don't spend a lot of time watching this stuff (or if we do, we at least know that we shouldn't be doing so). But is that all that the Bible says? "Don't watch porn or gratuitous violence?" No, there is far more to it than this.

---

[73] "Telling The Public About What's On the Air"; Accessed Mar 22, 2014 at http://www.tvhistory.tv/tv_forecast.htm
[74] "Color Television History"; Accessed Mar 22, 2014 at http://inventors.about.com/library/inventors/blcolortelevision.htm
[75] Robert Spiegel; "When Did The Internet Become Mainstream?"; ECommerce Times; Nov 22, 1999; Accessed Mar 22, 2014 at http://www.ecommercetimes.com/story/1731.html
[76] David Hinckley; "Americans spend 34 hours a week watching TV, according to Nielsen numbers"; New York Daily News; Sep 19, 2012; Accessed Mar 22, 2014 at http://www.nydailynews.com/entertainment/tv-movies/americans-spend-34-hours-week-watching-tv-nielsen-numbers-article-1.1162285
[77] "Digital Set to Surpass TV in Time Spent with US Media"; eMarketer; Aug 1, 2013; Accessed Mar 22, 2014 at http://www.emarketer.com/Article/Digital-Set-Surpass-TV-Time-Spent-with-US-Media/1010096#smpjmhUfWtYYMKR2.99

Understandably, the Bible doesn't say anything specific about our conduct regarding types of media that would not be invented for almost 2000 years after the last book of the Bible was written. I think that Satan has taken advantage of this lack of specific Biblical guidance to dupe a lot of us into being quiescent on the Battleground of Media. The Bible is not at all silent on this subject, but it takes some application to know how to apply God's Truth to our media habits. In my two decades of being a believer, I've lived under some absolutely phenomenal pastors, but I can't honestly recall hearing a single sermon dedicated to media and its interaction with the Christian life. I've heard lots of short references and admonitions concerning media during sermons about various topics, but I can't recall any pastor of mine taking the media bull by the horns.

I think this is, in part, because the development of modern media, really over about two generations, has been so fast that we don't really have an established cultural tradition about interacting with media. Evil has used this lack of tradition to keep our media habits largely below the radar of our instruction. There are no verses in the Bible about internet usage, none of the great theologians of the distant past have treatises on "television and the Christian," we (meaning us old fogies who tend to do most of the teaching in church) don't have a reference from our childhood home experience to see how our parents taught us to use digital mobile devices. All of this is to say that American Christianity has largely just accepted media without taking a really hard look at how God would have us live with it. And of course, an unexamined spot like that is a ready planting field for the devil's deceit.

Don't misunderstand: The term "media" in the "Battleground of Media" is not the latest Fox News personality or MSNBC host. "Media" refers to the television shows, the magazines, the video games, the radio programs, the movies, the songs, the websites, and the social networking that we expose ourselves to daily as a part of modern American culture.

Our media habits are killing us spiritually. There are casualties all over this battleground. What do they look like? They look like failed marriages caused by the unfair comparison of a real-world spouse to a picture-perfect (literally) spouse, as seen on TV. They look like children who will kill others without batting an eye, after having watched quite literally tens of thousands of killings on their television and computer. They look like young ladies who have lost their innocence because the hundreds of examples they have seen of sex-outside-of-marriage encouraged them to toss their virginity to the first cute guy who smiled at them. They look like teachers who are ravaged day-in and day-out by the disrespect of students who emulate Bart Simpson or characters on "The Family Guy." These casualties don't have to happen, at least not in the numbers at which they are happening to God's people. Let's take a look at three of the main lies on this battleground and then talk about tactics we can use to defeat them.

### The Battle Line of Extremism

Lie #1 on the Battleground of Media goes something like this: "As long as it's not extreme, God doesn't care about what I watch."

One successful technique in warfare is the feint: I give my enemy a real threat to fix on, and then while he is absorbed in that, I take him by surprise from a different direction. On the Battleground of Media, Satan has used the feint tactic to distract us from the main attack. Look at the real threat that Satan has used as a feint to grab our attention: "Focus on gross violence, gross immorality, and pornography." As dutiful Christian soldiers, we have attacked those threats—and we should. The problem is that while we've been dialed-in on the extreme stuff, we've left our flanks unguarded, and Satan has been surreptitiously taking us from both sides.

Here's what this looks like: I'm a Christian, so I have all of those illicit channels on my cable set blocked. However, I sit with my kids every day and watch shows filled with murder, adultery, and dishonesty. Or maybe it looks like this: I'm a sports fan and a follower of Christ, so I don't watch all that soap-opera crap. However, I don't blink an eye when, during my 3 hour football game, I see 47 commercials pushing drunkenness, mostly-naked girls, and personal irresponsibility.

The truth is that God cares very much about what we watch.

God wants us to be holy—that is "set apart"—for His glory, and we cannot be holy if we are constantly filling our minds with unholy things. The apostle Paul tells us that we should "keep our eyes on those who live as we do"[clxxxv] and that we should focus on "whatever is true, whatever is honorable, whatever is just, whatever is pure, whatever is lovely, whatever is commendable."clxxxvi If I am watching a TV series with a worldview where truth is subjective or if I am watching a movie where people are getting their heads lopped off, I am not focusing on good stuff and I am not keeping my eyes on people who live for Christ.

God cares about what we watch because He not only tells us to focus on good, but He also tells us to "hate evil." Yet when we watch and cheer for evil things being done, we are far from hating evil. Are you thinking, "I never cheer for evil"? I'm willing to bet that you do, because I do (as does most everyone else I know).

I'm a conflicted man. There are a few movies that I really like but that I choose not to watch because I know that what I like in them is not in line with God's Truth. "Taken" is a movie about a father rescuing his daughter, and I really like it. But if I'm truthful, I really like it because the father rampages over the bad guys. I like revenge (but God says I shouldn'tclxxxvii). I like judging the bad guys (but God says I shouldn'tclxxxviii). I like seeing the bad guys killed in a number of different ways (but God says I shouldn'tclxxxix).

The cowboy movie *Tombstone* is the same way for me. It's about good guys beating the bad guys, but the good guys are really not being good—at least not by God's standards. To be fair, Wyatt Earp and his gang do some righteous things—they kill evil men and stop various types of injustice. However that "righteousness" floats in a sea of revenge, hate, and violence. Even as many of their actions are justifiable, the content of their heart as they do those actions is not in keeping with God's truth. In both of these movies I cheer for evil: the evil of "the good guys" doing things that are not in keeping with the Gospel. [78]

God does not want us just to steer clear of hardcore evil. He wants us to fill ourselves up with goodness and light. He tells us to "set your minds on things that are above, not on things that are on earth. For you have died, and your life is hidden with Christ in God."cxc He also reminds us that "whatever you do, do all to the glory of God"cxci-- not "most of what you do" or "what you do at church" or "what you do on Sundays" but "whatever you do." Whatever you watch, do it all for the glory of God. Whatever you

---

[78] I think it's important to clarify that I'm not arguing for pacifism. There are times when good men must fight evil men . . . but there is a Gospel way to do that and an evil way to do that. I think the classic movie "Shane" is an excellent example of a good man using violence to thwart evil.

read, do it all for the glory of God. Wherever you surf on the web, do it all for the glory of God.

The devil would have us ask ourselves, "Is what I'm watching too hardcore for a Christian to watch?" God's Truth says that we should instead be asking, "Does watching this honor God or help me to glorify God?" I've heard friends say so many times, "Well, it's not that bad." In fact, I've said that many times myself. The truth is that we should be turning it off or changing the channel if we can't say affirmatively that God would want us to watch what we are watching.

In this discussion of media content, it's important to differentiate between "exposure" and "choice." Exposure is where we find ourselves confronted with unwholesome media. Choice is where we choose to indulge in unwholesome media. I have been in plenty of situations where, due to circumstance, there is crap playing in front of my eyes (sometimes crap that I don't like, sometimes crap that, in my flesh, I do like), and I didn't really have a good opportunity to turn it off. That's okay. I've also had times when I watched a movie or clicked on a website that I thought was going to be good and turned out to be not-so-good (or really bad). That's okay. God is bigger than all of that. We are not under law where we must manically flee from evil images, and we live under the Great Grace of Christ where we have assurance of forgiveness even when we make wrong choices. In fact, as we follow Christ we might be called into places where exposure is unavoidable, so that we can share the Gospel with those who live in that world. The point is that this battle line is not one of our exposure to media, but rather it is a battle line of our choices in media.

Every time I log into Netflix to choose a movie to watch, I am at battle. Will I choose the sensual one with the racy title and cover graphic? I want to. Will I choose the ultraviolent spy movie? I want to. Will I choose the adrenaline-filled horror flick? I want to, or at least my flesh does.

Yet my spirit wants to honor God. I want to watch a movie that encourages me to love my beautiful, precious wife—not wish she was younger, thinner, richer, or racier. I want to watch a movie that makes me look at people as children of God—not potential targets or threats. I want to watch a movie that focuses on the beauty of love and on what God has created, not the horrors of evil. I know that if I honor God through what I watch, I will be blessed and be a blessing, and so the battle rages between my flesh and my spirit. It's easy to just say, "This movie is not that bad," but that's surrendering the high ground, not fighting the battle. God cares very much about what we watch, and He wants us to choose to watch only what is good for us and for Him.

Christian soldiers don't tolerate what's bad; they choose what's good.

## The Battle Line of My Imperviousness

Lie #2 on the Battleground of Media centers on the lie that says, "What I watch doesn't affect me." You've probably heard this a bunch of times: "I don't let my kids watch that, but I'll watch it 'cuz it doesn't affect me" or "I don't like movies with a lot of sex but violence doesn't affect me" or "that's just comedy; it doesn't affect me." The problem is that it does affect us.

Let's start by looking at what the Bible says about the "it doesn't affect me" line. First, consider that God tells us to put off bad stuff in our lives. In Colossians, He says "put to death, therefore, whatever belongs to your earthly nature: sexual immorality, impurity, lust, evil desires and greed, which is idolatry . . . now you must also rid yourselves of *all* such things as these: anger, rage, malice, slander, and filthy language from your lips."[cxcii] Is this instruction arbitrary? Of course not. God tells us to get rid of these things so that we can be holy so that we can do His will. We must consider also that Christ tells us in the Sermon on the Mount that even thinking evil thoughts is sin,[cxciii] and we know that sin has bad consequences—"the wages of sin is death."[cxciv] So let's consider what happens when I watch a movie with some ungodly stuff.

Suppose I'm watching a TV show where a married guy and his unmarried business partner just jumped in bed. What's happening in me? Well first, my "earthly nature" (the one God says in Colossians I'm supposed to "put to death") gets pretty energized— after all, the girl is hot looking and the scene is steamy. So just in the act of seeing this, my mind is immersed in sexual immorality, lust, and evil desires. But it's just in my mind so it's okay, right? Wrong answer. If Jesus was telling the truth during the Sermon on the Mount, I just entered into sin. Second, I'm taking in the subtle message that affairs are normal. Maybe I don't internalize this from watching this movie once, but once I've seen a few hundred or a few thousand men and women jump into the sack outside of a marital bond, I start to definitively internalize that sin is normal and that the truth in the Bible is an aberration. But "it doesn't affect me."

If I say committing sin doesn't affect me, I'm calling God a liar, because He says sin definitely has effect. Sometimes we don't think much about the vicarious sinning we do through media because it's just in our brains. However, the world doesn't work that way. What we see influences how we think, and what we think is part of who we are. The Bible says of mankind, "For as he thinks within himself, so he is."[cxcv] But the Bible isn't the only thing that contradicts this lie that "it doesn't affect me." Research in psychology does too.

Did you know that there are over 1000 studies that have shown a direct link between violence in youth and violent media?[79] Have you ever found yourself thinking about a powerful scene from the movie you saw yesterday? Wouldn't you consider that an effect? If I saw a graphic murder on TV yesterday and I'm still thinking about it today, I'd say that it is crowding out the good, excellent, and wonderful things that God says I'm supposed to be focused on.

However, there are things going on inside of us that we might not even see in ourselves. The *Journal of the American Medical Association* published a definitive study on TV violence and found that, "in every nation, region, or city with television, there is an immediate explosion of violence on the playground, and within 15 years there is a doubling of the murder rate. Why 15 years? . . . That is how long it takes for you to reap what you have sown when you brutalize and desensitize a three-year-old."[80] Another study done at the University of Utah found that young men who were used to watching TV were far less likely to show any emotional response when confronted with a violent image than were young men who didn't watch TV regularly.

Exposure to media causes both habituation and something

---

[79] July 2000 joint statement of the American Medical Association, American Psychological Association, American Academy of Pediatrics, and American Academy of Child and Adolescent Psychiatry as quoted by Dave Grossman. *On Killing.* New York: Bay Back Books, 2009. Pg xx.
[80] Dave Grossman, "Trained to Kill"; Killology Research Group; Accessed Mar 22, 2014 at http://www.killology.com/art_trained_methods.htm

called "narcotizing."[81]    These are both terms used to explain how media exposure can accustom us to have less response to stimuli (or to need more stimuli to get a response). Practically speaking, this means that if I watch 1000 kisses on television, then the kiss I saw tonight would not mean much to me. Similarly, if I used to be offended by a graphic killing, after repeated exposure such images may not even cause me to feel anything. There is even scientific evidence that exposure to media violence can activate your brain's addictive circuits and cause a form of addiction.[82]

The implications of these types of conditioning for the Christian are profound. It may be hard for me to "love others as myself" when I've seen 10,000 murders on TV or online in the past year. It may be hard for me to "cleave to my wife" if I'm watching 105 pound bikini-clad supermodels on halftime commercials every weekend. It may be impossible for me to "turn the other cheek" if I'm addicted to violent stimulation. Of course, I can just tell myself that "it doesn't affect me" and ignore the fact that both the Bible and science emphatically tell me that I'm wrong.

The truth is that media does affect us—it makes it harder for us to follow hard after God. The sooner we embrace that fact, the sooner we'll be able to approach media the way God would have us do so.

Christian warriors know that what they watch **does** affect them.

## The Battle Line of My Own Time

"My time is my own" is a third great lie that we have to fight on the Battleground of Media.

I received an email from a young man the other day who was lamenting that he was having a hard time getting time off for his planned vacation. His response was, "If they don't give me the time off, I'll just quit." Was this a wise or a rash decision? I suspect it is the latter, but I don't have enough background details to know. What I do know is that his approach reveals an underlying perspective that his time is his. That's the lie that Satan wants us to repeat over and over.

[81] James Potter; "Short and Long Term Media Effects"; The New Media Foundation; Accessed Mar 22, 2014 at http://www.thenewmediafoundation.org/media/values.php
[82] "Element 13: Danger! When the Media Becomes the Environment"; Cracking The Learning Code; Accessed Mar 22, 2014 at http://crackingthelearningcode.com/element13.html

You want me to do something at 6:00 AM? Sorry, that's *my* time to sleep. I was going to come over and hang out with you yesterday afternoon, but that was *my* time to work out. I wanted to be part of that group, but Friday evenings are *my* time to rest and recuperate. Boss, you want me to work 12 hours today? Sorry, I give you 10 hours and the rest is *my* time.

How does the "my time" lie impact the Battleground of Media? When we think that our time is our own, we fill it up with things we want to do. Most of us go through life thinking, "Which show should I watch?" or "Which game should I play?" and not "Should I watch a show?" or "Should I play a game?" If you are like me, you almost feel like you have a right to watch TV or movies or play games, at least a little bit. But we don't have that right.

I'm sometimes amazed to consider that, for millennia, mankind survived the stress of life without taking time to kick back a couple of times a week to watch a movie. God doesn't say, "You have been saved so you can enjoy shows and games." He says that we are saved for His purpose.

President Theodore Roosevelt noted in *The Strenuous Life:* "Freedom from effort in the present merely means that there has been some stored up effort in the past. A man can be freed from the necessity of work only by the fact that he or his fathers before him have worked to good purpose. If the freedom thus purchased is used aright, and the man still does actual work, though of a different kind, whether as a writer or as a general, whether in the field of politics or in the field of exploration and adventure, he shows he deserves his good fortune. But if he treats this period of freedom from the need of actual labor as a period, not of preparation, but of mere enjoyment, even though perhaps not of the vicious enjoyment, he shows that he is simply a cumberer of the earth's surface, and he surely unfits himself to hold his own with his fellows if the need to do so should again arise." [83]

Although in this quote President Roosevelt speaks from a physical work context, his thoughts are equally applicable to our spiritual battle. The average American watches 34 hours of TV a

---

[83] Theodore Roosevelt; "The Strenuous Life"; Apr 10, 1899. Accessed on May 1, 2014 at http://www.bartleby.com/58/1.html

week. That's almost a day and a half. Even if you only watch two hours of TV a day, how much could you do for God's kingdom if you spent those 14 hours on something more constructive? Do you have to spend those hours on God's work? No. But if you did, how many more people could you bless? How many more scriptural truths could you know by heart? How many more hours could you spend worshipping God? How many more lies could you crush?

We live in an unprecedented age where more of our time can be devoted to pleasure than has to be devoted to work. There are about 112 waking hours in the week and most of us only work 30-50 of those. The other half of our lives we are free to spend on ourselves—eating, bathing, reading, watching media, playing sports. Yet too many of us are "cumberers of the earth's surface:" focused more on using our time for our purposes than on remembering it's God's time and it is given to us for His purposes.

Much of media is not bad, but too much media is bad.

God tells us to "walk as children of light,"[cxcvi] to "walk in love,"[cxcvii] and to make "the best use of the time."[cxcviii] He tells us not to eat "the bread of idleness,"[cxcix] He warns us not to be lazy,[cc] and He tells us to devote ourselves "to good works."[cci] When we allow media to take us away from fulfilling God's purposes, it derails us from our true purpose. Edmund Burke famously said, "All that is required for evil to triumph is for good men to do nothing."[84] Yet truthfully, nobody does nothing, because doing nothing is incredibly boring. What should really be said is, "all that is required for evil to triumph is for good men to do nothing good." In many ways, media is the bait that Satan puts before us, saying, "Just do this for a while," and then at the end of the week we find that we really haven't done much of anything of worth.

Our time is not our own. God wants us to use it for good. He wants our whole lives to revolve around doing what He wants us to do—not around the next movie, Facebook post, NFL playoff, video game, or television series.

Christian warriors spend most of their time in battle or preparing for battle, not in front of a TV or computer screen.

## Fighting Back On the Battleground of Media

---

[84] As quoted at http://www.quotationspage.com/quotes/Edmund_Burke/

The military is big on acronyms. One of the things I was taught about seeking cover behind enemy lines was to look for "BLISS"—a hideout that Blends with the surroundings, is Low, has an Irregular shape, is Small, and is Secluded. Acronyms can be helpful to focus us on the essentials of the tactics that we need to employ for success in combat. When it comes to the Battleground of Media, there is an acronym that might help us Christian warriors to battle the three big lies:

"As long as it's not extreme, God doesn't care about what I watch."

"What I watch doesn't affect me."

"My time is my own."

That acronym is POPP: Perspective, Only good, Prioritize time, Put money to work. If we want to see success on the Battleground of Media, we must ensure we have God's perspective, we must focus only on what is good, we must prioritize our time to do the things that He has called us to do, and we must put our money to work for good.

Perspective: To get a healthy perspective, turn it all off for 1 week. Video games—off. Internet surfing—off. Social media—off. Television—off. Netflix and Redbox—off. Music—off. Radio—off.

Turn every piece of electronic media off on Saturday night and don't turn it on again until the Sunday after next. Make no exceptions to this rule except what you must to be responsible to others—that means you can get into email to do work, but it means you can't watch the news with the excuse "a responsible Christian knows what's going on." That means you can get onto the internet to check the church calendar, but it means you can't login to Facebook with the excuse "This is one of the ways I love others." Having everything off will give you perspective—hopefully God's perspective.

When you turn everything off, you will first find out how much of your life currently revolves around media. When you have that desire to turn on a show or jump onto Twitter, ask, "God, why do I want to do this? To glorify You or to glorify myself?" When you turn everything off you will also find out how much time you have. When you find yourself wondering what to do at the time you would normally turn on the ballgame, stop and ask, "God, what do you want me to do with this time?" When you turn everything off and you have children in the house, you'll have a good chance to share perspective with them, as well. When your kids ask, "why did we turn off the _____?," ask them if they think God likes it when you do that activity. Ask them if they know what God wants them to do with their lives. Ask them why they want to immerse themselves in media. A week of having it all turned off will give you a much better perspective on what media actually is doing in your life.

**Only good:** While everything is turned off, commit to keep anything less than "good" out of your media habits. Decide to focus on what is true, noble, right, pure, lovely, admirable, excellent, and praiseworthy.[ccii] Realize that everything you watch affects you—for better and for worse. Ask yourself if you love God enough to give up that TV series that glorifies gangsters every week. Ask yourself if you love God enough to walk out of that #1 movie that everyone is raving about. Ask yourself if you love God enough to quit reading that tabloid magazine which is really just institutionalized gossip. Ask yourself if you love God enough to quit killing other human beings in video games.

Before you turn anything back on, ask God to show you where you are focusing on things that are not good. Ask Him what shows are helpful for you to watch. Before you fire up your DVD player, ask God what kinds of movies He wants you to take in. Before you surf the Internet again, ask God where He wants you to go on the computer.

If you are like me, you'll be tempted to do this step wrong. You'll want to ask, "God, what do I have to get rid of?" Realize that that is the **wrong question.** We don't want to go to God asking "What is too bad?," we want to go to Him asking, "What is good?" Don't ask, "What do You want me to get rid of?," but rather ask "What do you want me to hang onto?"

**Prioritize your time:** Ask God to help you see how much time you should be spending in front of media. Remind yourself that watching even good stuff can be bad if it gets in the way of doing the best stuff. You may spend time every day listening to your favorite pastors online, which is not a "bad" thing. Yet God may be saying, "Keep that computer off. Right now, I don't want you learning more, I want you doing what you've already learned." Before you get back into social media, ask Him how much time you should be spending there and where the line is between gossip and discussion. Allow God to set your priorities in terms of time before you ever turn anything back on.

**Put your money to work:** You know, one of the things about the Battleground of Media is that, like the Battleground in Education, our actions on the battleground have impact far beyond ourselves. A few years ago there was a fuss about major movie companies marketing R movies to teens. Moviemakers got some really bad press, and the industry made a major shift toward PG-13 content. That wasn't because we won the war of ideas. It's because the message went out that we would quit paying for lousy content. Money talks. And it talks both ways.

Recently the movie, *Fifty Shades of Grey* came out. If you are not familiar, this is based on a wildly-popular novel and is a story about extramarital sadomasochistic sex. If Hollywood produces an edgy film that glorifies extramarital sex and we go by the thousands to see it, what do you think the next film will look like? Our $10 movie ticket was a vote for more of the same, and we are setting our peers and our children up for failure because we just encouraged the film executives to listen to the atheistic artists who want to push the boundaries of morality even further.

On the other hand, if Hollywood produces an edgy film that glorifies extramarital sex and it's the lowest grossing movie of all time, do you know how many more of those you'll see? Almost none. Our decision to stay home sent an opposite message: "Make movies like this and you will go out of business."

If Hollywood produces a film filled with Christian values and encouraging messages, and it is a box-office smash, get ready for the flood of similar movies. There are certainly a lot of folks in the media industry who would like to see God's Truth trashed, but the industry is controlled by business people that are in business to make money. It is very true that with our wallets we can proclaim the gospel. How weird is that?

Put your money to work. Go to see films that are spiritually good, even if the acting and special effects are just so-so. Don't see films that are full of evil, even if the acting and effects are out-of-this-world. Don't buy that video game that glorifies stealing cars even if it's the most fun game ever made. Pay for those cable channels that have awesome shows that glorify God's values, and unsubscribe to those channels that are full of junk.

If we Christian warriors will get the right perspective, if we will only focus on good stuff, if we will prioritize our time for God's work, and if we will put our money to work influencing our media culture, we can have success on the Battleground of Media. But if we don't, we will continue to watch our friends and our children slide deeper into that darkened world where good is called evil and evil is called good. [85]

I have to confess that sometimes I feel like this battleground is already lost. We, God's people, are so deeply addicted to media that dishonors Him. I believe it's worth fighting, but I wonder if we are hopelessly outnumbered here. Some years ago, my family subscribed to cable TV, but after having it for about a year, I had it cut off. There really wasn't much good on it, and even those programs that were good were frequently filled with commercials that glorified lust, drinking, violence, relativism, and disrespect.

I have this fantasy that maybe millions of God's people would join me and say, "I'm not paying for this garbage. If you guys want me to pay for cable, you'll have to change your programming." Yet when I have this thought, it occurs to me that most of my friends, even most of the pastors I've known, buy this stuff every month, and I say to myself, "There's no way." I'd hazard a guess that even if you read the discussion above and said, "Yeah, I agree," you probably won't turn it all off. You probably won't sacrifice your opportunity to see all the exciting movies that you'll miss if you only focus on good stuff. You probably won't prioritize your time, and you will likely buy your teenagers that new video game that lets them virtually kill other humans for hours on end.

Am I right about you? Is my fantasy foolish? Have we lost this

---

[85] Let me inject a quick but incredibly critical side note here: It's March as I write, and I read that already this year there have been over 530 million searches for internet porn. If you have young people in your house and you do *not* have a reputable pornography filter on your computers and cell phones and mobile devices, you are irresponsible. That's exactly like having a screen door between your house and a porn shop that just got built next door. Protect your kids, even if it's inconvenient. Protect your kids, even if it means it is hard or impossible to go to some of the sites that you like. Whatever opposition you have to putting a filter on your computer, ask yourself if your objection is worth having your little loved one witnessing men and women having group sex. And don't kid yourself about your child's intentions. They don't have to be looking to find it. If he or she does a search for a school project or clicks on a link sent by a friend or just gets curious, porn will come up. Our little ones are just one click away from losing their innocence. Protect them. That should be a first priority.

war or are there still enough people that are willing to fight? Your actions will tell.

This battleground matters for our children's innocence, it matters for the success of our marriages, it matters for our freedom in our culture, and it matters for saving the lost. Let's get in the fight on the Battleground of Media!

## 4-6 THE BATTLEGROUND IN POLITICS

On a Sunday morning in 1776 the Reverend John Peter Muhlenberg preached to his Lutheran congregation in Woodstock, Virginia. His sermon centered on the book of Ecclesiastes, Chapter 3, which says in part, "To everything there is a season." As he came to the end of his sermon, Reverend Muhlenberg said, "There was a time for all things, a time to preach and a time to pray, but those times have passed away . . . There is a time to fight, and that time has now come!" As he said this, Muhlenberg removed his clerical robes, revealing that he was dressed in a patriot's military uniform. He marched to the back of the church and asked, "Who among you is with me?"[86] Some 300 men followed him, forming the 8th Virginia Regiment of the Continental Army.

That's bold! And that kind of action is totally out of character for our modern American clergy. Historians tell us that the religious Great Awakening of the 1700's set the stage for our American Revolution, and in fact religious thought and trends had a heavy impact on both the revolution itself and the adoption of our constitutional republican form of government.

In the 1700's, religious people were active in politics. The Reverend Jonathan Mayhew is said to have coined "No taxation without representation" and was known for preaching political sermons leading up to the start of the Revolution. The Reverend John Witherspoon compared the bondage in colonial America to the bondage of the Hebrews in Exodus. He went on to join the Continental Congress and signed the Declaration of Independence. In England, the American Revolution was so associated with American pastors that it was often called the "Presbyterian Revolution."[87]

But Christian participation in politics didn't stop in the 1700's. Christian groups were very active in the political fight against slavery in the 1800s, and some Protestants were active in the 1920s as they opposed the first Catholic presidential candidate on

[86] Josh Pittman; "Peter Muhlenberg Pastor and Patriot"; Heritage of the Founding Fathers; Accessed Mar 28, 2014 at
http://www.heritageofthefoundingfathers.com/article11.html
[87] Bob Ellis; "A Brief History of Politics From the Pulpit"; Dakota Voice; May 25, 2010; Accessed Mar 28, 2014 at
http://www.faithandleadership.com/features/articles/politics-the-pulpit

religious grounds. Even as late as the 1960s, the Reverend Martin Luther King, Jr., used the pulpit as a place from which to influence politics.

Yet today, the church is largely silent on politics. Pastors will say, "Vote your conscience." If they are "bold," they might cover the Biblical basis behind some hot-button issues, but have you ever heard a pastor say, "Vote for this candidate, but not that one"?

Statistically, the majority of American Christians don't want to hear about politics (or discuss politics) at church.[88] Chances are that you don't want to hear about politics from the pulpit, but there is a problem with that. That viewpoint is not just "not Biblical" it actually runs against the Bible. That's why there is a Battleground in Politics.

We are a nation "of the people, by the people, and for the people." If the enemy can keep God's people from participating in politics (or if he can keep God's people from being obedient to God in politics), he can crush our nation. It's that simple. And so he has made up some lies to try to keep us from fighting on the political field. For the most part, he has been very effective. Have you fallen for one (or more) of those lies? Are you actively trying to defeat those lies? Let's take a look at the biggest ones so that we know how to fight them.

## The Battle Line of Politics in Church

The first battle line on the Battleground in Politics revolves around the lie that "Politics don't belong in church." Like all effective lies, on the surface this sounds kind of sensible; after all, church is for spiritual stuff, and politics is of this world. However, there's a problem with this line of thinking.

First, if it's valid to say that "politics don't belong in church" because politics aren't spiritual, then we should also say that we shouldn't talk about our jobs at church since they aren't spiritual. Come to think of it, we shouldn't talk about school or education either (unless of course it's Sunday school). And if you continue down that line of thinking, we shouldn't probably talk about television shows or movies or restaurants or pets or the latest natural disaster to hit some poor country—because none of those

[88] David Briggs; "Politics in the Pulpit"; Faith and Leadership; Nov 23, 2010; Accessed Mar 28, 2014 at http://www.faithandleadership.com/features/articles/politics-the-pulpit

are "spiritual." It's kind of silly isn't it?

It's silly because "politics" is part of life, and all of our life has a spiritual bent. In fact, in his letter to the church at Rome, Paul tells us that we are to offer our bodies "as a living and holy sacrifice, acceptable to God" because this is our "spiritual service of worship."[cciii] He says later to the church at Corinth, "whatever you do, do all to the glory of God."[cciv] All of it. Our whole life. For the glory of God.

It is a fundamental tenet of the Christian faith that we live our lives as bond-servants of Christ. We have no spiritual and un-spiritual activities—our very existence is tied to our religion. Saying that "politics don't belong in church" is like saying "a Christian isn't supposed to follow God's will in politics." It is antithetical to the Christian faith.

If I am a Christian and I go out and vote for a candidate who actively opposes God's standards of morality, I have done something unwise (at the very least), and if I did so knowingly, I have sinned. If I am a Christian and I refuse to find out which candidates or ballot initiatives are Biblically supportable, I am doing wrong—either from laziness or pride. The truth is that if we don't follow God's ways, people will suffer, because His ways are best. If we cause people to suffer, whether through an act of commission or omission, then we are not loving them, and that is the exact opposite of what God says we are supposed to do in this life.

So why do you suppose we are so quick to embrace the idea that "politics don't belong in church"? I think there are two reasons. First, we Americans tend to have an independent spirit, so we don't like it when people tell us what to do. If my pastor or an elder tells me whom I should vote for, that rubs me wrong. Mind you, it rubs me wrong because of my foolish pride, but it rubs me wrong nonetheless. So if you give me an excuse not to be rubbed wrong, I'm liable to take it. "Don't tell me how to vote, pastor. Politics don't belong in church."

The second reason we like the "politics don't belong in church" lie is because the religion of politics is confusing. We have some pastors that say, "Abortion is okay" and others that say, "Abortion is a sin." Some of our church friends will say, "We need to vote for candidate Whataguy so we can help the poor" while our other church friends will say, "Candidate Whataguy is throwing pearls before swine, vote for candidate Shesawesome so we can avoid the unbiblical concept of debt." Don't be fooled, there are right answers to these political questions, but they are sometimes hard to find. We have to work to figure out what is good and right, and even when we do find the truth, our disagreements might cause conflict. Is that okay? Or should we just be lazy and say "politics don't belong in church" so that we don't have to deal with hard work? Should we just be peace-fakers so we don't have to deal with contentious issues?

The truth is that our political activity (and even a refusal to be politically active) is part of our religious life. We are to follow God in all things—even the sticky political ones. Just like with all spiritual issues, we are generally better equipped to do the right thing if we work together, as the church, to follow God. Politics belongs in church just like work, relationships, family issues, and all the other facets of our lives do. Don't listen to the lie that says it doesn't.

There is a sub-lie that is advocated in the legal realm in America. Some people wrongly teach that politics don't belong in church because talking about politics will invalidate a church's tax-exempt status. Some pastors won't preach about political issues for fear of losing their income. Historically, the whole notion of political speech being tied to tax-exempt status started in the 1950s when then-Senator Lyndon Johnson pushed a change to the tax code in order to silence non-religious nonprofit organizations that were his political opponents. However, due to the language of the code, churches were impacted by this change as well. Many legal experts believe that this impact is an unconstitutional restriction on religious speech, and, starting in 2008, Christian organizations have attempted to formally challenge this by specifically and publicly preaching for or against political candidates.[89] Pastors have even gone as far as to send copies of their sermons and the date that they were preached to the IRS in an attempt to provoke some sort of retaliatory action. However, as of this writing, the IRS has never tried to revoke tax-exempt status for such religious political speech. Many legal experts believe that this is because the IRS knows that this provision will be overturned if it ever goes to court. Once that happens every church in America will know that they can speak

---

[89] Bob Ellis; "A Brief History of Politics From the Pulpit"; Dakota Voice; May 25, 2010; Accessed Mar 28, 2014 at
http://www.faithandleadership.com/features/articles/politics-the-pulpit

freely, and the tax-status muzzle that is currently on churches will be pulled off.

So how do we fight the "no politics in church" lie? I'd encourage you to engage this lie from a few different angles.

First, be willing to talk about politics. Talk after church. Post your thoughts and questions on Facebook. Bring up some of the political things that have been troubling you at the next church potluck. Cultures are established by the actions of individuals, and through simple conversation you can start to change the culture. But be careful. We don't go to church to talk about politics, we talk about politics at church because that is part of our life following Christ. So if you go to church to try to convince everyone that they should vote Republican or Democrat, you are not helping the problem—you are probably aggravating it. However, if you go to church and discuss the moral implications of current political issues or candidates, you are helping to encourage fellow believers to see their political life as a part of their Christian duty.

Second, make sure that your political views are consistent with the Bible and are not just your own. We'll talk about this more in the next section, but for now suffice it to say that it is destructive to come into a fellowship of believers and say that our own opinion is God's will. Truthfully, the Bible is clear on most of the big political questions, but when it comes to candidates or bills, there are frequently competing and debatable viewpoints. "My way or the highway" is not an appropriate attitude for a follower of Christ, but "God's way or the highway" is. Make sure you know the difference between "your way" and "His way."

Third, speak the truth in love.[ccv] Legalism is bad, and I can be legalistic about anything, including politics. As soon as I make agreement with my political views criteria for being a "good Christian," I have fallen into sin. Suppose I share with my Christian brother a passage of scripture that tells me that abortion is wrong, and he disagrees with my interpretation. Do I ignore him? Hate him? Bring him before the elders? Excommunicate him? Of course not. I explain my belief and if he doesn't get it, I continue to love him as I continue to pray for him to see the truth. As in all things, mercy triumphs over judgment.[ccvi] Remember that without love, our words are just "noisy gongs"[ccvii] that amount to nothing.

Finally, consider whether you should have a talk about this subject with your pastor. I hesitate to make such a recommendation out of the fear that some well-intentioned but immature Christian will run to his pastor and say, "You need to get your act together on this!" The Bible says that those who teach well are worthy of "double honor,"<sup>ccviii</sup> and it also says that those who are in positions of authority have been placed there by God.<sup>ccix</sup> So pray hard before you discuss this with your pastor, and make up your mind to encourage (not rebuke) and to listen (not demand). It may be that your pastor needs your encouragement to open up to political discourse, it may be that he doesn't know about the unconstitutionality of the tax code that prohibits political speech, or it may be that he doesn't talk politics much because he believes that's what God wants him to do. Honor his authority even if you believe that some change is warranted.

Christian warriors bring God into every aspect of their life and so Christian warriors know that discussions about politics **should** be part of our church life.

## The Battle Line of Biblical Clarity

The second battle line on the Battleground in Politics centers on the lie that "the Bible isn't clear on political issues." My daughter goes to a Christian university, and I was talking with her a short while ago about her experiences there. In the course of the conversation the subject of "homosexual marriage" came up and she told me that most of her friends disagreed with the concept of homosexual marriage but didn't believe it was something that should be enforced by law. "Are your friends Christians?" I asked. She assured me they were. I found that very interesting. These are some good young men and women, some of who are trying to follow hard after God. Why then would they be indifferent on a subject that God is not indifferent about? Unless, of course, they don't know that God is not indifferent.

And there lies the challenge. The Bible talks about homosexuality, but doesn't say anything about homosexual marriage. The Bible talks about poverty, but doesn't say anything about federal welfare programs. The Bible talks about peace and war, but doesn't say anything about the "Global War On Terror." The Bible talks about life and birth, but doesn't say anything about abortion. The Bible talks about the kings of Israel and a bit about the Roman government, but doesn't say anything about constitutional government.

So the pertinent question for a Christian asking about political issues is, "Does God tell me what to do in this political context?" The answer that Satan always gives is a loud and emphatic, "NO!" But of course he's not telling the truth.

I'm not going to offer you tactics and strategies to combat this lie because the lie itself disappears if I just talk about the truth. So let me take a minute to go down a list of key political issues and what God says about them. However, before I do that I need to say two things:

First, I write this list as a *man* looking at Truth (the words of the Bible) and applying that Truth to the current situations. In application, there is always the chance that the Truth will get distorted by the man. I don't think I've done that here, but I'll admit to the real possibility. So if you find that you disagree with my conclusions, you might be right to do so, but I will caution the reader to be careful to interpret Truth with Truth and not with a lie. As an example, take the issue of abortion. Maybe you've always believed that abortion is a woman's choice. Maybe that's what every authority in your life has affirmed. When I say, "Abortion is wrong," you will immediately disagree on the basis of those authorities. However, you must ask if those authorities are reliable. Were they speaking God's Truth? The Bible is the only reliable, arguable truth standard.[90] If I can show you from God's word that abortion is wrong, then you either have to find a logical failure in my argument, or you need to find something in God's word that disproves my argument. If God weighs in on an issue, none of the other authorities in our lives matter.

Second, lots of Christians disagree with some of the things I've written below. Some of them do so because they really are "likers of Christ" rather than "followers of Christ." Some of them do so out of ignorance or a hidden agenda, and I'm sure some of them do so because they genuinely disagree with my interpretation. Don't let me or anyone else be your authority. I've written the list below to help guide you to see what God says (that's why I

---

[90] For the sake of theological integrity, let me say that both creation and the Holy Spirit are also Truth sources. However, the physical world is not usually directly relevant as evidence in moral discussions, and personal revelations of the Holy Spirit are not demonstrable (i.e. you can't really argue with someone who says, "I'm right because God told me I am . . . ")

included end notes with Biblical references), but ultimately it's up to you to decide if what I've written is correct. **Read what the Bible says, ask God to help you interpret that, and then do not doubt.** There is a great passage in the Bible where the apostle Paul chastises some of the Corinthian believers for being divided by following Apollos or Paul or Peter. Ultimately Paul says, "All things belong to you, and you belong to Christ, and Christ belongs to God."[ccx] So it is with you. Consider, but don't be swayed by human teachers, famous or not, no matter how many degrees they have. God is with you; use His word as the standard and see what He has to say about each of these issues.

With all that said, here is a rundown on what God says about some of the most key and contentious political issues.

**Poverty and Welfare.** *We have a responsibility to help people that are impoverished by circumstances and not their own choices; Government can be the means of combating poverty but isn't necessarily that means.* It is a Biblical principle that we should take care of the poor,[ccxi] and the Bible often mentions specifically taking care of orphans and widows.[ccxii] Frequently in the political arena, barbs are thrown that certain groups or candidates "don't care about the poor." However, the almost universal reality is that everyone cares about the poor, but people disagree over whether the poor should be cared for by the local community or by the state or federal government. The Bible says nothing proscriptive about whether a government (as opposed to individuals or churches) is supposed to fulfill the role of taking care of the poor. There were a number of times where Christ appears to turn an indifferent eye toward poverty (e.g. John 12:1-8, Luke 21:1-4) when he obviously had the potential capacity to do something about it (c.f. the coin in the fish's mouth, Matthew 17:24-26); however, this may not be normative since his particular reason for coming to the earth was to die for our sins, not to abolish poverty. It is probably unrealistic for us to think that we might eradicate poverty; Christ said, "the poor you always have with you."[ccxiii] The Bible is very clear that we do not have a responsibility to help those poor who are needy because of their own laziness,[ccxiv] and it also says that widows should be taken care of first by their children or grandchildren,[ccxv] implying that families are to take care of their own needy ones.

**Wealth and Capitalism.** *Wealth and capitalism can honor God or can dishonor God.* The Bible teaches that wealth (or material blessing) comes from God,[ccxvi] is often awarded for righteousness[ccxvii], and is to be used for good. Great wealth is often used to bless God (e.g. Solomon's Temple[ccxviii] and Martha's perfume[ccxix]) or to bless people. The Bible also teaches us that we should not hoard money,[ccxx] nor store up excessively for the future.[ccxxi] God tells us not to love money.[ccxxii] Diligent work is rewarded with wealth,[ccxxiii] but businesses that take advantage of the poor are condemned.[ccxxiv]

**Communism and Socialism.** *Both communism and socialism are unbiblical because they fail to acknowledge man's fallen nature.* The Bible teaches that everyone is sinful and has a fallen nature.[ccxxv] In discussing communism or socialism, there are two key consequences of this fallen nature. First, when given power over others without a structure to check his natural tendency toward sin, fallen man will oppress his fellow man. Second, when given a chance to loaf or be lazy, fallen man will do so. In the Biblical worldview, neither socialism nor communism can possibly work because they depend on fallen mankind to adopt an un-fallen nature (which is impossible without God's intervention[ccxxvi]).

**Debt.** *Debt should be avoided if possible, should be short term, and must always be paid back.* The Bible says that we are always to pay back our debts.[ccxxvii] The Bible also says that we become a slave to our lender when we enter into debt.[ccxxviii] God approves lending explicitly in Matthew 5:42 and implicitly in Deuteronomy 15:6 and 28:12. Debts are supposed to be short term (7 years in Deuteronomy 15). The Bible does NOT say it is a sin to be in debt, but the general tone of the Bible is that it is not good to be in debt. Romans 13:8 tells us to "owe no one anything, except to love each other." I am not aware of any examples of God providing for His people through a loan. Since debt is frequently caused by "wants" and not "needs," when discussing debt it is important to pay attention to the many verses that tell us not to seek more material goods or wealth[ccxxix] and to be happy with what we have.[ccxxx]

**War and National Defense[91].** *Participation in war can be consistent with the Bible, as is providing for the national defense.* In Ecclesiastes, we read that there "is a time for war and a time for peace." [ccxxxi] God repeatedly uses war and violence to accomplish His purposes in the Old Testament. God's people are told to fight their enemies many

---

[91] For a more complete discussion of the Biblical perspective on war, search for "Just War Theory" or "Jus Ad Bellum" on the internet.

times (e.g. Joshua at Jericho[ccxxxii]). Jesus is sometimes mischaracterized as a pacifist, but this is inconsistent with his behavior in the Bible. Christ is better characterized as a lover of peace. He made a whip and used it to chase people out of the temple,[ccxxxiii] and Christ also said, "Do not think that I have come to bring peace to the earth. I have not come to bring peace, but a sword."[ccxxxiv] Before he died, he told his followers to buy a sword if they did not have one.[ccxxxv] Jesus implicitly acknowledges the morality of military professions: when Roman soldiers ask, "What should we do?," Jesus does not tell them to change professions, but rather instructs them to be moral within their profession.[ccxxxvi] Jesus, as shown in the book of Revelation, is an incredibly violent warrior as he executes final judgment.[ccxxxvii] At the same time, the mandate to pursue peace when possible is undeniable.[ccxxxviii]

**Homosexuality.** *Homosexual conduct is sinful.* In both the Old and New Testament, God says that homosexuality is sinful. It is both specifically prohibited,[ccxxxix] and used as an example of immoral conduct.[ccxl] Often people will argue that this is not a correct interpretation of the Bible because "some people are made this way." However, from a scientific perspective, the validity of the premise that homosexuality is an innate quality is suspect.[92] More importantly, one should note that this line of reasoning would also mean that adultery must not be a sin because most heterosexual men are innately attracted to women other than their wives. Some will argue as well that as an expression of "love," homosexuality complies with the command to "love your neighbor"[ccxli]. However, this is not Biblically consistent. First, the Greek word for love in "love your neighbor" is *agapao*, which refers to non-sexual, self-sacrificial love. As a physical sexual expression, homosexuality would use a different Greek word for love: *eros*, which refers to sexual or romantic love. It is possible for two people to love (*agapao*) each other without engaging in physical love (*eros*). *Agapao* love between members of the same sex would be consistent with the Biblical admonition to "love others" but *eros* love would not. Second, if one claims that "love" makes homosexuality Biblically correct, then one would also have to say that pedophilia, incest, polygamy, and polyamory are also Biblically

---

[92] See *Genetics and Homosexuality: Are People Born Gay? The Biological Basis for Sexual Orientation* at
http://www.godandscience.org/evolution/genetics_of_homosexuality.html

correct.

**Homosexual Marriage.** *Approval of homosexual marriage condones sin.* Christ establishes the basis for marriage in Matthew 19:4-6 on the basis of the pattern of the creation of man and woman as shown in Genesis 1:27 and 2:24. Because the consummation of marriage implies sexual union, the Biblical view of homosexuality (see above paragraph) makes "homosexual marriage" an inherently sinful practice as it both facilitates and condones homosexual acts. It follows that governmental approval or establishment of homosexual marriage is functionally the approval or establishment of sinful conduct.

**Abortion.** *You cannot condone abortion and be in line with the Bible.* There are three key principles to consider. First, a baby in the womb is a created, treasured person. God acknowledges that babies are His intentional creation even before birth, saying that we are "knitted together in [our] mother's womb,"[ccxlii] that we are "fearfully and wonderfully made,"[ccxliii] that we can be "called from the womb,"[ccxliv] and that He knows us and sets us apart before we are "formed . . . in the womb."[ccxlv] As further affirmation that the unborn are created and valuable, Exodus 21:22-24 specifically mandates protection for the unborn from intentional injury. Second, intentionally killing a person without just cause is murder. The Bible prohibits murder[ccxlvi] and specifically condemns the sacrifice of children.[ccxlvii] Lastly, the Bible tells us that we are to make right choices and let God determine final outcomes. This is clearly illustrated in the stories of Joseph and Daniel and is explained through the truths that God has plans for our lives[ccxlviii], that He "causes all things to work together for good to those who love God"[ccxlix], and that He disciplines those that He loves.[ccl] Accordingly, advocating for abortion because the baby will be "unloved" or "uncared for" or because the mother doesn't think she can handle the inconvenience of a child denies the fundamental truth that God can work *all* things for good.

**The Role of Government.** *Government is appointed by God to provide for the good of people and to restrain evil.* All authorities are instituted by God, and Christians are supposed to show respect and honor for authorities out of respect for God.[ccli] It is legitimate for a government to use its authority to do what is right and to punish wrongdoing.[cclii] It is also legitimate for an authority to collect taxes.[ccliii] Jesus' instruction in Matthew 22 to "give to Caesar what is Caesar's and to God what is God's" implies that government can legitimately have a purpose that is not religious (albeit not anti-Christian). In a government-by-the-people, there is a moral responsibility for Christian citizens to be "salt and light" through participation in the political process.[ccliv]

**Personal Character.** *From a Biblical perspective, a candidate's personal character is of fundamental importance.* In politics a person's "character"—that is, their integrity and personal value set—is sometimes raised as an issue. In other cases, people will say that "what someone does in private" is irrelevant to their performance in political office. While the Bible does not provide a checklist for the qualifications of government officials, in 1 Timothy 3 and Titus 1, God does provide clear guidance on what should be expected from a religious leader, and it is reasonable to extend many of these qualifications to a non-religious leader. A leader should be "above reproach, the husband of one wife, sober-minded, self-controlled, respectable . . . not a drunkard, not violent but gentle, not quarrelsome, not a lover of money."[cclv] It is interesting that the requirement to be respectable is repeated multiple times for all types of leaders.[cclvi] There are also many proverbs that stress the importance of character: righteous actions bring blessing, wicked actions bring curses;[cclvii] God "detests" anyone (including political leaders) whose heart is not right;[cclviii] a man or woman who lacks self-control is "like a city whose walls are broken through."[cclix] Finally, dishonesty is clearly condemned by God, both as one of the Ten Commandments[cclx] and repeatedly in other places in the Bible including Proverbs 17:7: "Eloquent lips are unsuited to a godless fool— how much worse lying lips to a ruler!"

**A Candidate's Christian Belief.** *God's way is always best, so it logically follows that a Christian voter should desire to elect a follower of Christ if possible.* There are three primary reasons why this is so. First, one who is a *genuine* Christian will normally seek to follow God's will. Proverbs 19:21 says that, "Many are the plans in a person's heart, but it is the Lord's purpose that prevails."(NASB) Following God's will is always best,[cclxi] and a political representative who keeps his or her eye on God will be able to lead in a way that follows God's will rather than opposes Him. Second, one who is a genuine Christian will have the Holy Spirit to guide him to make good decisions and to keep him or herself from sin. Jesus promised that those of us who follow him would receive a "Counselor"—the

"Spirit of Truth"—to guide us "into all truth."[cclxii] With the Holy Spirit we have wisdom from God. It is a very real truth that a believing politician can make the right choice, under the influence of the Holy Spirit, even if he lacks the actual knowledge or life-experience to make that decision on his own basis. Third, one who is a genuine Christian is more likely to depend on God to effect good government and not rely on force, deception, or worldly powers. Because the Christian knows that the final outcome in this world is guaranteed, she can choose to do the right thing without resorting to the pragmatism which may require using a wrong means to attempt to reach a desired end. A Christian who has truly given up her life for Christ can readily accept political defeat, financial loss, and ridicule as consequence for a right decision. That Christian also has the power of the Holy Spirit to protect her from the temptations of worldly power and fame. Overall, the principle that we should elect followers of Christ would best be illustrated by Joshua at Jericho: Would you rather elect someone who can take a city with no losses by assaulting it God's way, or would you rather elect someone who is a tactical genius that would attempt to breach the walls by a violent assault?

As the paragraphs above show, the Bible is not silent on most of the big issues that we confront on the political battleground. However, even when we know what the Bible says, we can sometimes still be perplexed. This is because the Bible has no established set of priorities to follow if we encounter a situation with competing Biblical principles. For example, how does a Christian vote if Candidate Mellonhead is against abortion but has a history of cheating on his wife, while Candidate Knuckledragger appears to have a sterling character but thinks abortion is okay? As another example, should a Christian vote for a ballot initiative that provides money for the poor but causes a sizeable increase to an already significant debt? I could tell you what I think in each of these cases, but I can't tell you authoritatively what the Bible says. In such cases we need to pray, and having done that we are left to use what we know is true (the principles in the Bible), with the rational way we've been taught to think (logic and the wisdom of the Bible), under the influence of the Holy Spirit (God with us), to come up with our answer as to what we think God wants us to do.

But here is the important thing to remember: while there are some tough calls to make, **most of our choices aren't like the**

**above examples.** It's been my experience that the vast majority of political choices are straightforward. Usually the candidates who are against Biblical principle have sketchy lives as well (at least as sketchy or more so than the candidate they are opposing). Similarly, after you've done your research, usually ballot initiatives are pretty straightforward as to what they are trying to do—they are either in-line with the Bible or against it.

The Bible does have something to say about the political issues and candidates that we are called to vote about. We have to avoid listening to the lie that says that the Bible is silent on politics. The truth is that in the vast majority of situations, with prayer and a little bit of research and work and discussion with our fellow Christians, we can find what way God would want us to vote if we truly want to honor Him.

Christian warriors understand that God's word is relevant to all facets of our lives, including politics. Participation in the political process is one of the ways God calls us to be salt and light.

## The Battle Line of Sin's Impact

The final battle line on the Battleground in Politics confronts the lie that "sin is an individual thing."

A prominent Christian leader in Texas recently had in "inappropriate" relationship with a young woman in his congregation. Satan would have us believe that this just caused him to lose his position of ministry, but when his sin came to light, it didn't just affect this leader. It hurt the young woman he had an affair with. It hurt his wife. It hurt his church. It put him at odds (and in fact, in litigation against) his former friends. It destroyed a multi-million dollar ministry.

I have a friend who is in jail for violating his probation terms. His wife has struggled for over five months to raise their three children alone. Their friends and family have had to do things to reach out and assist his wife. My friend has no current income and may have a hard time getting one when he gets out of jail. His children cry that they want their daddy. His sin was an individual choice, but it was not an individual thing. Sin's consequence is far-reaching.

God is unmistakably clear that sin has consequences far beyond the sinner alone. There are both physical and spiritual impacts of sin. Consider first those physical impacts: sin has real practical consequences that have broad results—the examples above show this. The Bible tells us this too. It tells us that the "wages of sin is death."cclxiii We see that Adam and Eve's bad choice impacts all mankind. We see that Jephthah's rash pledge results in the death of his innocent daughter, Mizpah.cclxiv We see that the wickedness of Er, Judah's son, leads to family strife, more wickedness, lying, and incest.cclxv King David's affair with Bathsheba results in the murder of a good man, the death of one son, and the uprising and death of another.cclxvi Sin has direct impact far beyond the sinner. The boss at work may end up destroying the whole business by the simple act of cheating on his taxes. The wife at home may end up alienating her husband and her kids by becoming too intimate with the neighbor next door. The student at school may destroy friendships well beyond his own by starting a spiteful rumor in an attempt to look "cool." Your coworker may make everyone in your office miss out on an epic bonus this year when she makes a pass at the married CEO of your company's biggest customer and scuttles the "deal-of-the-century." These are all real, physical, practical consequences of sin: anger, crushed relationships, lost trust, addiction, financial loss, physical harm, destroyed ministry, shame, suicide—and they extend well beyond just the sinner.

The Bible says, "Righteousness exalts a nation, but sin is a reproach to any people."cclxvii There is an undeniable *corporate* consequence of unchecked sin. This means that even if you and I do everything right, we are still liable to fall under the miserable consequences of sin. Consider Korah's rebellion in the Bible. Out of pride and against God's will, Korah led 250 others in opposing Moses. In response, God destroyed Korah, the other 250 men, *and their whole households.* Then as the Israelites grumbled about this whole event, God sent a plague that killed almost 15,000 people.cclxviii We see this pattern of corporate consequence repeated over and over in the Bible. Perhaps the best example is when, after years of denying God and following idols, the whole nation of Israel (both those following God and those who weren't) is taken into captivity by the Babylonians. Awareness of the corporate, spiritual consequence for sin is partly why the Jewish leaders were so eager to crucify Jesus (who they believed to be a heretic) and is also why so many of the books of the New Testament adamantly warn against the presence of evil amidst God's people.

Satan would have you believe that sin is like a bullet that pierces the life of the sinner, but the truth is that sin is a bomb that blows up the sinner and hurls fragments and death at everyone around him. That's why our engagement in the political arena is so very important. I get fired up about politics partly because it's my Christian duty to do good, but I also get fired up about politics because I'm scared.

I'm scared because I know that, even though I live an essentially debt-free life, the debt that my nation is accruing will put my children and grandchildren in bondage that I wouldn't wish on my worst enemies. I'm scared because I know that if we as a nation embrace homosexuality as a good thing, we will have called evil "good," and so we will suffer, maybe economically, maybe in war, maybe in health, maybe all of the above. I'm scared because I know that the Bible says that sin has consequence, and even though I wholeheartedly oppose abortion, God will not stay His hand forever while our nation collectively kills over 1 million babies each year.

In the big picture of experiencing blessing in this life, it might not matter how good you and I try to be. It might not matter if most of the time we are personally successful at overcoming our temptations. It might not matter because if we are immersed in a society that has earned God's judgment; we will be caught in the frag pattern. Sin is a bomb.

People fuss on the news all the time about the threat of "climate change" and all the chaos it will produce. But "climate change" is a questionable theory based on arguable science. The corporate consequence of sinful action is not arguable—the Bible warns us clearly about it and history reminds us over and over that when a nation strays from God's principles, that nation will be destroyed. Drought? Maybe. Foreign invasion? Maybe. Economic collapse? Maybe. Civil war? Maybe. Plague? Maybe. I don't know what it will look like, but I do know that the nation that doesn't follow God will most certainly fall.

We're all in this together. When I look at the Bible, I see lots of people that suffered because of God's response to the corporate sins of others. I don't want to go through that, I don't want you to go through that, and I don't want my kids or grandkids to go through that. But the truth is that God says, "The wages of sin is death,"[cclxix] that it is His to avenge and that He will repay,[cclxx] that "woe" comes to those who call good evil and evil good.[cclxxi]

Participation in the political arena is one of the key ways that we in America can curb wrongdoing and maintain a culture that honors God.

Christian warriors know that sin is a bomb that affects everyone, not just the sinner. Through political involvement, we can help defuse the bomb of sin. We can, for both ourselves and more importantly for our future generations, take hold of the blessings which God has promised for those who follow Him.

In a democratic republic like ours, failure to engage in the political process as Christians is a failure to be the salt and light that God has called us to be. We must fight the lie that politics doesn't belong at church. We must fight the lie that the Bible really doesn't tell us how to vote. We must fight the lie that says that sin does not affect all of us. In this life, we - both those that follow Christ and those that do not - will sink or swim as "one nation under God." We will be one nation under His blessing, or we will be one nation under His judgment. And so perhaps we should listen to Moses.

At the end of his life, Moses says to the nation of Israel:

"See, I set before you today life and prosperity, death and destruction. For I command you today to love the Lord your God, to walk in obedience to him, and to keep his commands, decrees and laws; then you will live and increase, and the Lord your God will bless you in the land you are entering to possess. But if your heart turns away and you are not obedient, and if you are drawn away to bow down to other gods and worship them, I declare to you this day that you will certainly be destroyed . . . I have set before you life and death, blessings and curses. Now choose life, so that you and your children may live . . ."cclxxii

There are many ways that we can 'choose life', but it is undeniable that our Christian influence in the American political process is a primary way that we can choose life and blessings and not death and curses.

Christian warriors, vote your faith. Influence the political process. Let's "choose life" in the political arena, so that we and our children may live.

# PART 5: FINAL VICTORY

In 2010, I was deployed with a rescue helicopter unit in Iraq. I was taking care of some business when an airman came up and said, "Sir, you better come to the TOC [Tactical Operations Center]!" I sensed from the words and the tone of voice that something was up—something not good. As I came into the operations center, men and women were gathered around our satellite radio and our intelligence specialists were monitoring our classified Internet chat programs. The mood in the TOC was heavy. I was filled in on what had happened so far and slowly the pieces came together. One of the helicopters from our sister unit in Afghanistan was down. It appeared to have been shot down. These were our friends we were hearing about. Many of us were sure to know some or all of those in the unfortunate helicopter. Words came in: It was definitely one of our helicopters; "expectant"—that meant someone was dying, and the helicopter was on fire at the crash site. Over the next hours and days we learned the painful truth: one of our helicopters had been shot down on a rescue mission, and most of the crew was dead. I watched some of our Air Force's best men and women, seasoned combat veterans, as they cried.

Sometimes combat sucks. There are losses and defeats. Sometimes the casualty is us. Sometimes we don't ever come home. But for all its horrors, a life of combat is better than a life of ease. Those brave men who died on that day in Afghanistan we call "heroes," but they aren't heroes because of that mission they died on. They are heroes because they chose to leave a life of safety. They chose to get up every day and risk everything to oppose the enemy and save people's lives. They are heroes because they chose to live a life of significance and not just exist. I wonder if we will be worthy of them.

Like those brave men, God calls all of His people to be heroes: to die to ourselves, to fight the good fight, to make a difference in the world, to engage in combat against the enemy. That's Christian combat.

As I draw this book to a close, I'd be wrong if I didn't depart from the analogy of war and look at those specific realities of Christian Combat that differ from the realities of physical combat on the modern battlefield. Our fight is not of this world[cclxxiii] and so sometimes our fight looks a bit different than the fights of this world.

**1. Christian Combat effectiveness is measured in obedience, not outcome.** The measure of success in physical combat most often centers on outcome: whether we took control of a hill, sank the enemy's ships, captured our opponent's headquarters, or had a lower casualty count. In spiritual combat, however, we don't measure success the same way. Christ called us to a life of obedience and said that we are to depend on God to determine the outcomes. Think of the apostle Paul: it doesn't seem like success when you are lowered from a window to escape persecution or when you get arrested and flogged or when you get shipwrecked. Yet God called Paul to all of these situations because they were steps in God's perfect plan. If Paul had been focused on the tangible outcomes of what he did, I suspect he never would have preached much.

You don't have to live in the first century to see how this truth plays out. Consider the case of a couple in Oregon, Aaron and Melissa Klein, who refused to comply when they were called to compromise their Christian beliefs by baking a cake for a homosexual marriage ceremony. Their names were all over the national news, and they subsequently lost their business. [93]It would

[93] Todd Starnes; "TODD'S AMERICAN DISPATCH: Christian bakery closes after LGBT threats, protests"; Fox News.com; Sep3, 2013; Accessed Apr 5, 2014 at http://www.foxnews.com/opinion/2013/09/03/todd-american-dispatch-christian-

seem on the surface that the best outcome would have come from a willingness on their part to compromise on what they believe is right. However, they realized that we are called to obedience and so chose to do what they felt God wanted them to do, regardless of the outcome. That's what success looks like in the arena of Christian combat.

When we think of being in spiritual combat, it is easy to fall into the trap that we should measure our effectiveness through things like "number of salvations," "number of baptisms," or even just accolades from other people. However, we must remember that the only accolade that matters is the one from our Father in Heaven, and He showers us with His blessing because we are obedient, not because we are impressive.

**2. In Christian Combat not all defeats are failures.** When we are obedient to God's instruction, sometimes an event will look like a defeat when it is actually part of God's victory plan. Since God is in charge and His plans are so far above our understanding, it is foolishness to set our own standards for what amounts to victory or defeat on any of the battlegrounds in our lives. Let me give you a concrete example.

I once met a couple who related a story from earlier in their lives when they had been in youth ministry. The couple served at a church in the southeast where there was a young girl, let's call her Judy, who always seemed wayward and far from God. They tried to reach her with the gospel but saw no result. As they prepared to move to follow a new job, they said to each other, "Well, I guess we failed Judy." That was their defeat, or so they thought. But the story didn't end there. Years later, the couple received a letter from Judy that said something to the effect of, "I have given my life to Christ, and I wanted you to know that the love you showed me while you were with me was instrumental in making me turn to Christ."

If you have done what God called you to do and the results are not what you would expect, don't give up on yourself or on God. In fact, see if you can't rejoice in the fact that you were able to be obedient even when the outcome looks like a defeat. Joseph was "defeated" by being put in jail for a crime he did not commit.[cclxxiv]

bakery-closes-after-lgbt-threats-protests/

Moses was "defeated" nine times by Pharaoh before his people were finally let go.[cclxxv] David was "defeated" when Absalom took over his kingdom.[cclxxvi] John the Baptist was "defeated" when he was put in jail.[cclxxvii] All the disciples were "defeated" when Christ was arrested.[cclxxviii] Christ was "defeated" when he was put to death.[cclxxix] But of course, none of these seeming "defeats" actually were losses and that last example was the ultimate victory. During tough times, we do well to remind ourselves that God is in control and that His victory is certain.

**3. Victory is certain.** That's the third big difference between the spiritual battlefield and the physical battlefield: when you are serving an all-powerful, all-knowing God, you can be absolutely certain that His side will win the war. *His victory is a sure thing.* However, sometimes we have a hard time believing this truth because, in the midst of life's storms, it sure doesn't feel like we're winning anything.

We need to remember that, here on earth, God more commonly saves us *through* difficulty and not *from* difficulty. Put another way, God usually gives us what it takes to get through the hard times rather than giving us a supernatural deliverance from hard times.

I recently read a news story about a fisherman from Mexico whose boat motor quit, setting him adrift for almost 14 months. He finally made landfall in the South Pacific. Did God deliver that fisherman? Yes, but probably not in the way or the timing that the man expected. Suppose you and I are on a ship that sinks and find ourselves floating on a life raft in the middle of the ocean. The sun beats down on us, we are out of fresh water, and there is no help in sight. God might send a boat or a rescue helicopter. He might send an angel to whisk us to land. He might teleport us to the nearest city in the blink of an eye. Then again, He might just give us the strength and provision we need to make it until we slowly drift to shore. That's how God works in this world. We know heaven is coming, but He is here with us even now, and our victory begins now with His enabling us to overcome the things of this world.

I've always been fascinated by the account of Jesus and Peter before Christ's death. Christ tells Peter that, "Satan demanded to have you . . . but I have prayed for you that your faith may not fail."[cclxxx] This fascinates me because Christ did not say, "But I have bound Satan" or " But I have put a hedge of protection around you." Instead Jesus effectively says, "Pete, you are going to go through it, but I've made sure you are going to come through just fine."

This truth is echoed by the apostle Paul when he says, "We are afflicted in every way, but not crushed; perplexed, but not driven to despair; persecuted, but not forsaken; struck down, but not destroyed."[cclxxxi] Our victory in this world is not delivery *from* challenges, but rather living victoriously *through* challenges. Paul goes on to say, "So we do not lose heart. Though our outer self is wasting away, our inner self is being renewed day by day. For this light and momentary affliction is preparing for us an eternal weight of glory beyond all comparison."[cclxxxii] I was once told a profound truth that I've found to be very helpful: we don't get to choose whether we go through the hardships of life, but we do get to choose whether we go through them with God or without God.

Victory *is* certain—both victory now through the challenges of this world and victory later as we join God in Heaven. However, knowing that "victory is certain" has implications that are both enormously wonderful and extremely dangerous.

Let's consider the positive implications first. If victory is certain, we can focus on obedience rather than outcome because we serve a God who will make sure that all final outcomes are excellent. If victory is certain, we don't have to worry about events that appear to be defeats because we know that things will come out to success in the end. If victory is certain, when it feels like we are getting our clocks cleaned on the Battleground in Education or the Battleground at Home or the Battleground in Politics, we can say with confidence that we know the final outcome. We know that we will not fail, we will not be crushed, we will prevail—all through the power of our Almighty Father. God will make all things good for all of us that are following Him.

Now let's consider the other side of the coin: the dangerous implications of knowing that "victory is certain." If we know that victory is certain, we can be tempted to ignore the plight of those around us because we know God's going to work it all out for the top three: me, myself, and I. If we know that victory is certain, we'll be tempted to sit on our butts and do nothing. We might say to ourselves, "God's going to take care of it all anyway, so why should I fight evil and go through relational chaos or physical strife or hard, hard work? I'll just wait on Him to do it all." You'll notice this response centers around "me" rather than "He." So it's important for us to remember that when we pass from death into life it is as God's slaves[cclxxxiii] —to live for Him and His purposes in order that He might be glorified. It's also important to remember that, for reasons I don't understand, God chose to use us to bring victory to the world. So we must be careful not to listen to the whispers of the devil when he tries to convince us that "victory is certain" means we should just pull up an easy chair, pop open a Coke, and grab a big tub of popcorn to watch and wait for God to do His thing.

**4. Life on the field of Christian Combat is good.** This is the last huge difference between Christian Combat and physical combat. Soldiers often leave the field of physical battle scarred by combat and struggling with PTSD, but in Christian Combat, we leave the field of battle strengthened. While war truly can be Hell on Earth, life on the field of Christian Combat is good. It's very good. So often we Christians foolishly focus on Heaven and life-after-death to the exclusion of the abundant life that God gives us here and now on this earth. In Philippians, Paul doesn't write, "I've learned the secret of enduring all things in this crappy world until God calls me home." Instead, he writes, "I have learned the secret of being content in any and every situation, whether well fed or hungry, whether living in plenty or in want."[cclxxxiv] That secret is life in Jesus Christ.

When God calls us to join the spiritual battle, He's not calling us to misery, but to abundance. Look around at your own experience (and no, I don't mean the fantasies on TV and movies). Who are the happiest folks? Are they the rich people? Are they the privileged folks? Are they the super healthy or super athletic? My experience is that the folks I know who are truly close to God are the happiest. There's my severely disabled aunt who has battled multiple-sclerosis for over 30 years and still embraces life with a smile. There's my pastor and his wife who just celebrated their 50th anniversary – drawn ever closer together by their mutual love of God. There is my buddy Roger who lives every day of his life pursuing God and who seems to always have a smile on his face.

It seems sometimes that giving up on ourselves and the things of this world is sacrifice—that somehow when we enter the field of

Christian Combat we become solemn-faced toilers, going about the drudgery of waiting for our own deaths and the glory promised thereafter. Yet this is so far from the truth. When we are fully committed to following Christ, our relationships are deeper. Our challenges seem smaller. Our losses hurt less. Our gains are more extravagant to us. Our weaknesses become inconsequential. Our strengths are magnified by the lens of goodness. We have an answer to the problem of our own inadequacies.

If you haven't fought on one of the fields of Christian combat, you probably think what I'm writing here is a bunch of malarkey. You haven't experienced that when you sacrifice yourself, you really do experience abundance. There is only so much that I can write. To truly understand this truth, you need to join the fight. If you do, you'll find that your life is amazing, and all because of God.

Christian Combat is not easy, but it is certainly good. Missionary Jim Elliot said, "He is no fool who gives what he cannot keep to gain what he cannot lose."[94] True words!

---

[94] Quoted at http://www.goodreads.com/author/quotes/2125255.Jim_Elliot

# FINAL WORDS

I read the news this morning. Somebody stabbed 20 people at a Pennsylvania school. A major US university revoked its honorary degree from a woman because she criticized Islam. Young men and women on spring break last week on both sides of the nation were rioting, having sex, drinking, doing drugs. A pro-life teen was called a "domestic terrorist" for advocating for the unborn. One of the currently most-watched television series employs six porn stars. The CEO of a major US technology company was just ousted because he made a personal donation to an effort to define marriage as a man-and-woman institution. A federal appeals court ruled that public schools can ban renting school facilities to churches.

It looks bad. Sometimes it makes me want to give up.

I look at my own life and wonder. I've made some bad choices. I still make some bad choices. I'm not that good at sharing the gospel. I'm certainly nobody of influence. Who am I to encourage others to contend for God? I'm not great at contending myself.

It looks bad. Sometimes it makes me want to give up.

Yet I have a hope. I have this hope that God will use me to make a difference. I have this hope that if I and a few million of my closest friends will do our best, we can turn around the news stories. I have a hope that we will remain One Nation Under God and not a nation gone under. You might call my hope a fantasy. Except for one little significant piece of history.

Imagine yourself in a small Mediterranean town in 30 AD. Rome is the great power. Nobody can oppose them financially or on strength of arms. To oppose Rome's Caesar is to invite certain death. Greek culture dominates, and pantheistic religions are everywhere. You walk by local shrine prostitutes every day on your way to the market. Deception and dishonesty are a way of life both in the local marketplace and in politics. In your view, nothing short of an invasion could change the power structures, the moral structures, the cultural structures. Yet if you could fast forward a few hundred years, you would find that these structures were changing at an incredible pace. You would find that governments were changing, morals were changing, culture was changing. Why? Because 12 men did what their teacher asked them to do. They were inconsequential men, largely uneducated, without influence and without authority, but they did what God asked.

And the people they shared with did what God asked.

And the people that those people shared with did what God asked.

And soon, the entire western world changed. And slowly they impacted the entire world. It happened not on the basis of the great power of one man or woman, but on the actions of thousands upon thousands of weak, inconsequential, meaningless men and women who had Great Power and chose to do something with it.

Hope. Do. *Live* your faith.

By God's grace and power, we are the ones who can make a difference. Get into the fight. Let God use you to save our world.

"Now choose life, so that you and your children may live . . . "
- Deuteronomy 30:19 (NIV)

Join me in the discussion at ChristianCombat.com

# ABOUT THE AUTHOR

Dan Maruyama was born in Santa Clara, California, to Joseph and Joyce Maruyama and grew up in and around Los Gatos, California. He attended the United States Air Force Academy, graduating with a Bachelor of Engineering Science degree in 1991.

In the fall of 1992, he earned his Air Force pilot wings at Sheppard Air Force Base in Wichita Falls, Texas. While stationed in Wichita Falls, he fell in love with Monica Walker and her two sons, Jordan and Jake. Monica and Dan were married in 1993, and Dan adopted his sons shortly thereafter. During this time, Dan was assigned as a T-37 instructor pilot at the 35th Flying Training Squadron and then the 64th Operations Support Squadron at Reese Air Force Base in Lubbock, Texas. While in Lubbock, God blessed Monica and Dan with the birth of their third child, Megan.

In 1996, Dan started helicopter pilot training at Fort Rucker, Alabama, and attended mission qualification training in the HH-60G Pave Hawk helicopter at Kirtland Air Force Base, New Mexico. Upon completion of that training in 1997, Dan was officially a combat rescue helicopter pilot and took his family to Kadena Air Base in Okinawa, Japan, where he was assigned to the 33rd Rescue Squadron as the Chief of Mobility and then the Combat Readiness Flight Commander. In 2000, the Maruyamas returned to the United States where Dan was reassigned to a classified location, and they then transferred in 2004 to the 66th Rescue Squadron in Las Vegas, Nevada. While in Las Vegas, Dan and Monica led a middle-school student ministry, and Dan served on the Board of Elders at the Crossing Christian Church.

Following his tour in Las Vegas, Dan became the Operational Test Director for a new Air Force rescue helicopter program, and in 2007 his family moved to Hurlburt Field on the gulf coast of Florida. Two years later, they were reassigned to Moody Air Force Base in Valdosta, Georgia, where Dan became the Director of Operations for the 347th Operations Support Squadron. Dan then commanded that squadron from July 2010 to November 2012. After he completed his tour as a squadron commander, he became the 347th Rescue Group Deputy Commander. While in Georgia, Dan led the student ministry at Christ's Fellowship Church. In 2013, Dan retired from active duty as a Lieutenant Colonel with

Sharing God's Grace through Henry's Place

over 3900 flying hours in the HH-60G, T-37B, UH-1, F-16, and T-34 aircraft. During his tours of duty, Dan twice commanded rescue squadrons while deployed to Afghanistan and Iraq and also commanded a deployed rescue group. His decorations include the Meritorious Service Medal with three oak leaf clusters and the Air Medal.

In 2013, Dan and Monica moved to Utah to help start Henry's Place Camp and Retreat Center – a Christian camp being developed just outside of Cedar City, Utah, that will bring life-changing experiences to at-risk youth (**www.HenrysPlace.org**). Dan currently is the Henry's Place Camp Director, serves as an elder at his local church, teaches high school Bible curriculum periodically at the Cedar Bible Institute, and substitute teaches at local schools.

The Board of Directors of Henry's Place are always open to donors and volunteers who are also called to this service. Please visit the website for more information. www.HenrysPlace.org

i Matthew 12:30
ii John 12:31, 14:30, 16:11
iii Luke 12:51
iv E.g. see 1 Chronicles 21:1, Job 1:6, Mark 1:13
v 1 Peter 5:8
vi Luke 4:1-10
vii 2 Timothy 2:26
viii 2 Corinthians 11:14
ix Genesis 22:18
x Jonah 3:5-10
xi Genesis 45:4-11
xii Genesis 19:24-25
xiii Numbers 25:1-9
xiv Jeremiah 25:8-9
xv Deuteronomy 30:15-20
xvi John 15:5
xvii Ephesians 4:1-16
xviii Mark 1:16-20
xix Ephesians 4:22-23
xx Luke 14:33 (NIV)
xxi Matthew 5:22
xxii 2 Corinthians 5:17
xxiii 1 Peter 1:23
xxiv Matthew 28:19-20
xxv Romans 7:24-25 (NIV)
xxvi Psalm 103:12
xxvii John 14:15
xxviii 1 John 5:3 (NIV)
xxix 1 John 2:4-5 (NIV)
xxx John 8:11
xxxi 1 Corinthians 9:24 (NIV)
xxxii Philippians 3:16 (NASB)
xxxiii 1 John 2:6 (NIV)
xxxiv Matthew 13:20-21
xxxv John 16:33
xxxvi Romans 5:3-5; James 1:2-4; 1 Peter 1:6-7
xxxvii 2 Corinthians 4:8-9
xxxviii John 10:28
xxxix Matthew 7:1 (NASB)
xl 1 Corinthians 2:15
xli Philippians 2:12
xlii Romans 10:9
xliii E.g. 2 Corinthians 12:7-9, Galatians 6:1, James 5:16-20, 1 John 2:1-2
xliv Matthew 21:28-31, John 14:21, John 15:10, James 2:17, 1 John 2:4,
xlv 1 Corinthians 5:1-13
xlvi 1 John 4:8
xlvii e.g., Exodus 12:29
xlviii e.g., Revelation 19:21

xlix 2 Corinthians 10:4 (NIV)
l Ephesians 6:17
li Hebrews 4:12
lii 2Timothy 3:16
liii John 3:16
liv 2 Corinthians 5:21
lv Philippians 4:11
lvi 1 Corinthians 2:10-13
lvii Mark 13:11
lviii Romans 8:31
lix Ephesians 4:1-16
lx For example, Exodus 23:17, Numbers 23
lxi Proverbs 19:20, 20:18
lxii Ecclesiastes 4:9-12
lxiii 1 Corinthians 11; 1 Timothy 2
lxiv Ephesians 4:1-16
lxv Hebrews 10:24-25
lxvi James 5:14-16, 19-20
lxvii 1 Timothy 2:12
lxviii Judges 11:30-39
lxix 1 Corinthians 13:8
lxx John 16:13
lxxi Acts 5:31
lxxii Romans 3:23
lxxiii John 2:15
lxxiv Mark 8:33
lxxv Matthew 23:27, 33
lxxvi Revelation 19:21
lxxvii John 16:7, 13-15
lxxviii John 3:8
lxxix John 16:13
lxxx John 16:7
lxxxi Galatians 5:22-23
lxxxii Ephesians 4:11-13
lxxxiii Ephesians 4:11
lxxxiv Galatians 5:22
lxxxv Philippians 4:13
lxxxvi Mark 13:11
lxxxvii John 16:13
lxxxviii John 14:26-27; 1 Corinthians 13; Galatians 5:22
lxxxix Isaiah 59:2
xc E.g. See Christ's prayer in the Garden of Gethsemane, Matthew 26:36-46
xci Matthew 13:57
xcii 1 Timothy 1:16, 2 Corinthians 12:8-9
xciii Galatians 2:11-12
xciv Acts 15:39
xcv Philippians 2:14
xcvi 1 Thessalonians 5:11
xcvii Matthew 7:15
xcviii Matthew 24:24

xcix Acts 20:29-31
c Galatians 2:4 (NIV)
ci 2 Peter 2:1
cii Jude 4
ciii Matthew 14:23; Matthew 26:36; Luke 6:12; Luke 9:28; Luke 11:1
civ Matthew 6:6; Matthew 26:41; Luke 18:1-8
cv Leviticus 23:23-25
cvi Leviticus 23:26-32
cvii Leviticus 23:33-39
cviii Numbers 25:1-7
cix Matthew 11:28
cx See Matthew 12:1-8 and Mark 3:1-6 for some of Jesus' teaching about the Sabbath
cxi E.g. Proverbs 6:6-11, 12:24
cxii Genesis 45:7
cxiii Exodus 20:14
cxiv Genesis 12:1
cxv Proverbs 23:13-14 (NIV)
cxvi James 2:13
cxvii Deuteronomy 32-34
cxviii James 1:6-7
cxix Matthew 7:11
cxx Philippians 4:11 (NASB)
cxxi 2 Corinthians 10:3-6 (NIV)
cxxii Acts 3-4
cxxiii James 2:18
cxxiv John 13:35
cxxv Ephesians 2:10 (NIV)
cxxvi Genesis 1:27
cxxvii Romans 3:23
cxxviii Ecclesiastes 7:20 (NIV)
cxxix 2 Corinthians 12:9
cxxx 1 John 4:19
cxxxi Romans 5:8
cxxxii Isaiah 1:18
cxxxiii Philippians 1:6
cxxxiv Romans 3:23
cxxxv Ecclesiastes 7:20 (NIV)
cxxxvi Ephesians 5:22-24, Colossians 3:18, 1 Peter 3:1
cxxxvii Leviticus 18:22, Leviticus 20:13, Romans 1:26-17, 1 Corinthians 6:9, 1 Timothy 1:10
cxxxviii E.g. Deuteronomy 4:36
cxxxix E.g. Job 5:17, Proverbs 3:12
cxl E.g. Proverbs 5:23, 13:24, 19:18
cxli Genesis 3:4
cxlii Luke 12:16-20
cxliii Matthew 6:34
cxliv Hebrews 3:7
cxlv Matthew 19:5-6
cxlvi Matthew 19:9
cxlvii Matthew 5:37
cxlviii Matthew 6:33

cxlix Ephesians 6:4, Colossians 3:21
cl Matthew 19:14, Leviticus 20:2, Psalm 127
cli Deuteronomy 6:7, Ephesians 6:4
clii Proverbs 22:6, Proverbs 29:15
cliii Proverbs 13:24
cliv 2 Corinthians 12:1, Luke 11:13
clv Matthew 6:19
clvi Luke 12:15
clvii Exodus 20:17
clviii Luke 8:14
clix Matthew 6:25
clx 1 Timothy 4:12 (NIV)
clxi 1 Samuel 12:2
clxii Proverbs 7:7 (NIV)
clxiii E.g. Ephesians 6:1, Proverbs 1:8, Deuteronomy 12:12, Titus 2:6, Titus 2:4, Titus 2:3, Titus 2:2
clxiv 1 Samuel 17
clxv 1 Corinthians 12:12-27; Ephesians 4:1-16. Colossians 1:18;
clxvi John 13:35
clxvii E.g. 1 Timothy 3; Titus 1
clxviii Acts 20:29
clxix 1 Corinthians 12:25. See also, 1 Corinthians 1:10, 11:18, and Romans 16:17
clxx John 2:1-11
clxxi 1 Corinthians 12:25 (NIV)
clxxii Galatians 5:23
clxxiii Mark 12:29-31
clxxiv Ephesians 4:13
clxxv Ephesians 4:15
clxxvi Deuteronomy 4:9-10, 11:19; Ephesians 6:4; See also the pattern of a father teaching his son throughout Proverbs
clxxvii Isaiah 5:20
clxxviii Deuteronomy 6:7 (NIV)
clxxix Proverbs 22:6
clxxx Matthew 19:14
clxxxi Psalm 82:3
clxxxii Ephesians 6:11
clxxxiii Romans 8:39
clxxxiv Matthew 16:24
clxxxv Philippians 3:17 (NIV)
clxxxvi Philippians 4:8
clxxxvii Deuteronomy 32:35
clxxxviii Matthew 7:1
clxxxix 1 Peter 3:9
cxc Colossians 3:2-3
cxci 1 Corinthians 10:31
cxcii Colossians 3:5,8 (NIV) [Emphasis mine]
cxciii Matthew 5:21-28
cxciv Romans 6:23
cxcv Proverbs 23:7 (NASB)
cxcvi Ephesians 5:8

[cxcvii] Ephesians 5:2
[cxcviii] Ephesians 5:16
[cxcix] Proverbs 31:27
[cc] Hebrews 6:12
[cci] Titus 3:8
[ccii] Philippians 4:8
[cciii] Romans 12:1 (NASB)
[cciv] 1 Corinthians 10:31
[ccv] Ephesians 4:15
[ccvi] James 2:13
[ccvii] 1 Corinthians 13:1
[ccviii] 1 Timothy 5:17
[ccix] Romans 13:1
[ccx] 1 Corinthians 3:22-23 (NASB)
[ccxi] Exodus 23:11, Leviticus 19:10, Leviticus 25:35, Deuteronomy 15:11, Luke 11:41 and many others
[ccxii] Deuteronomy 26:12, Acts 6:1, 1 Timothy 5:3, James 1:27
[ccxiii] John 12:8
[ccxiv] 2 Thessalonians 3:10; See also Proverbs 19:15
[ccxv] 1 Timothy 5:3-4
[ccxvi] Deuteronomy 8:17-18
[ccxvii] Psalm 112: 1-3; Genesis 24:35; 1 Kings 3:5-13
[ccxviii] 1 Kings 6
[ccxix] John 12:1-8
[ccxx] Ecclesiastes 5:13
[ccxxi] Psalm 73:12
[ccxxii] 1 Timothy 6:10
[ccxxiii] Proverbs 10:4
[ccxxiv] Proverbs 28:8
[ccxxv] Romans 3:10, 23; Psalm 14:1-3
[ccxxvi] John 6:44, 14:6
[ccxxvii] Psalm 37:21; Ecclesiastes 5:4; Romans 13:7
[ccxxviii] Proverbs 22:7
[ccxxix] Matthew 6:19; Matthew 6:24; Matthew 6:31; Luke 8:14
[ccxxx] Philippians 4:12; Hebrews 13:5
[ccxxxi] Ecclesiastes 3:8
[ccxxxii] Joshua 6
[ccxxxiii] John 2:15
[ccxxxiv] Matthew 10:34
[ccxxxv] Luke 22:36
[ccxxxvi] Luke 3:14
[ccxxxvii] Revelation 19:11-22
[ccxxxviii] Matthew 5:9, 38-40; Romans 12:18-19; Hebrews 12:14
[ccxxxix] Leviticus 18:22, Leviticus 20:13
[ccxl] Genesis 19:1-13; Romans 1:26-27, 1 Corinthians 6:9; 1 Timothy 1:10
[ccxli] Matthew 22:39
[ccxlii] Psalm 139:13; See also Job 31:15
[ccxliii] Psalm 139:14
[ccxliv] Isaiah 49:1
[ccxlv] Jeremiah 1:5

ccxlvi Exodus 20:13
ccxlvii Psalm 106:38
ccxlviii Jeremiah 29:11
ccxlix Romans 8:28 (NASB)
ccl Hebrews 12:6
ccli Romans 13:1-2; 1 Peter 2:13
cclii Romans 13:3-4; 1 Peter 2:14
ccliii Matthew 22:15-22; Romans 13:7
ccliv Proverbs 24:11-12; Matthew 5:13-14
cclv 1 Timothy 3:2-3; See also Titus 1:6-7
cclvi 1 Timothy 3:2, 8, 11
cclvii Proverbs 10:6, 8,9,11, 25; 12:2; 21:21
cclviii Proverbs 11:20
cclix Proverbs 25:28 (NIV)
cclx Exodus 20:16
cclxi Proverbs 3:5-6, Matthew 6:33
cclxii John 14:16-17, 16:13
cclxiii Romans 6:23
cclxiv Judges 11
cclxv Genesis 38
cclxvi 2 Samuel 12:9-14
cclxvii Proverbs 14:34
cclxviii Numbers 16
cclxix Romans 6:23
cclxx Deuteronomy 32:35
cclxxi Isaiah 5:20
cclxxii Deuteronomy 30:15-19 (NIV)
cclxxiii 2 Corinthians 10:3
cclxxiv Genesis 39
cclxxv Exodus 5-10
cclxxvi 2 Samuel 15
cclxxvii Matthew 14:3
cclxxviii Luke 22
cclxxix John 19
cclxxx Luke 22:31-32
cclxxxi 2 Corinthians 4:8-9
cclxxxii 2 Corinthians 4:16-17
cclxxxiii Romans 6:19, Ephesians 6:6-7
cclxxxiv Philippians 4:12

All scripture quotations are from the English Standard Version unless otherwise noted.

41047178R00139

Made in the USA
Lexington, KY
29 April 2015